As the men continued their cackling and drinking, I couldn't help but take a good, long look at each of them. They were all fine, strong men, I thought. Sure, they were a bit rowdy and coarse, but the heat, the harsh living conditions, and the hell of a swamp war were not conducive to the milksop and the mollycoddle. War was, in fact, a bitch, and these men did not refrain from calling it a bitch and treating it as such. And neither did I as I mentally prepared to depart from my friends the next day. I knew I would soon be stepping smack in the middle of the shit hitting the fan, once again meeting the enemy right on his front doorstep.

With these thoughts, I suddenly raised a can of beer and bellowed, "If I die at Nam Canh, men, put this verse on my tombstone: 'And when he goes to Heaven, to Saint Peter he will tell: Another Navy SEAL reporting, sir; I've spent my time in hell!' "

"Hoo-yah!" a couple of men chorused, then we all drank the night away. . . .

By Gary R. Smith and Alan Maki
Published by Ivy Books:

DEATH IN THE JUNGLE: DIARY OF A NAVY SEAL
DEATH IN THE DELTA: DIARY OF A NAVY SEAL

DEATH IN THE DELTA

Diary of a Navy SEAL

Gary R. Smith
and
Alan Maki

IVY BOOKS • NEW YORK

Ivy Books
Published by Ballantine Books
Copyright © 1995 by Gary R. Smith and Alan Maki

http://www.randomhouse.com

Library of Congress Catalog Card Number: 95-95306

ISBN 0-8041-0943-5

Manufactured in the United States of America

First Ballantine Books Edition: May 1996

10 9 8 7 6 5 4 3 2

ACKNOWLEDGMENTS

The authors wish to thank their families for their support and encouragement; Owen Lock, Editor, Ivy Books; and Ethan Ellenberg, Literary Agent, for their patience.

For my UDT/SEAL/EOD teammates I offer my thanks to Alan Todd and John Odusch for their introductions. I especially appreciate Alan Todd's detailed recollections of Hotel Platoon's Brightlight mission, platoon roster and photo, and roster of their MST/BSU personnel; and John Odusch's recollections on the Aqua Dart. A special thanks goes to Lou DiCroce for X-Ray platoon's total KIA and WIA list. I am very grateful to Al Betters (curator for the West Coast UDT/SEAL Museum in Redwood, CA), Mike Rush, and Paul "Lee" Pittman for their timely assistance in locating the rare Echo, Foxtrot, and Golf Platoon rosters and pictures for this book. Lastly, I thank Doc Holmes for giving me the names of UDT-11's Golf Platoon and their SEAL Float detachment picture.

Certainly not least, I wish to thank Alan Maki for editing a good portion of this book for me and Dennis Cummings for his historical assistance and insights.

And most of all, a special thanks and salute to all of Gary's UDT/SEAL/EOD mates, those still alive and those who have passed over the bar.

Introduction

The room was very formal and carefully arranged to be as intimidating as possible. There was a series of windows which overlooked the railroad yard that led into the old Studebaker plant, but the blinds were closed and the only light was of the sterile overhead fluorescent variety. I had been waiting for some time, so I got up, parted the blinds, and looked out at a typical cold, gray day common in northern Indiana in late November. I remember thinking about how my mother would take me with her when she visited her sister and I would look down on the same tracks from my aunt's apartment window. The difference was that back then the yard seemed almost alive, the activity reminding me of ants swarming over a decaying animal carcass. Jeeps and amphibious vehicles were produced in the plant, and they were rushed from here to there for loading and transportation to some far-off battlefield. Now it looked like the ants had finished their task and gone on to whatever else ants do, leaving only the skeleton of a factory that had produced one of the finest cars ever made in this country.

My nostalgic journey ended abruptly when I was jerked back to reality by the less than friendly voice of the South Bend, Indiana, Superintendent of Schools.

"If you persist in this foolishness, you will never work in this school district again," he said pointedly. I was somewhat, but not completely, taken aback by the frontal assault because I had long suspected that the superintendent was not the avuncular gentleman he would have everyone believe he was.

"Look," I replied, "my country is at war and I feel strongly that it is my duty to do my share. I find it very difficult to hide behind a schoolteacher's deferment when there's a war going on." My position was somewhat preposterous by today's standards, but it was 1964 and my early childhood had been spent exploring Rumvillage Woods, Bullfrog Pond, and Pinhook Lagoon. On Saturdays, for fourteen cents, my cousins and I had watched John Wayne win World War II at the Indiana Theater. Actually, we started out with twenty-five cents earned by collecting and selling old newspapers and scrap to the junkyard. The movie consisted of a double feature, a cartoon, and a serial, usually Lash Larue or Flash Gordon. We would spend ten cents on gedunk, which left us with a penny. The sporting goods store was next to the theater, and they sold BBs in penny packs—guess what we spent our last cent on? In any case, the superintendent was not impressed with my explanation of why I wanted to break my teaching contract, but he was true to his word—I never worked in that school district again.

What I didn't tell the superintendent was that I had already been accepted into the U.S. Naval Officers' Candidate School at Newport, Rhode Island. My plan was to breeze through the required four-month course and follow Richard Widmark's webbed footprints (I had been very impressed by the movie *Naked Warriors*) into UDT/SEAL training. After all, how long could it take to get my commission, complete the required training, and win the war in Vietnam? There is very little I care to remember about OCS at Newport, but UDT/SEAL training is where I, and everyone else in the class, grew up!

Our class was number thirty-six, and it was unique in many ways. We were about the last class to graduate before the powers that be realized what SEALs were capable of and decided that they wanted more. Well, the making of a SEAL is a long, difficult, delicate, complex art which requires the correct chemistry to get the desired results. SEALs cannot be mass-produced simply because there is a need for them, but that's another long and controversial story. In our case, a total of one hundred sixteen officers and men began the program—thirty graduated, and of the thirty, the general consensus among us was that six did not fully measure up to what we felt a SEAL should be.

In SEAL training there is no differentiation between enlisted men and commissioned officers. Stripped naked, everyone shares the same hell. You get to know the real person, who is cleansed of all the protective insulation we wrap around ourselves to get by in society. It doesn't matter who your father is; if you are a doctor, an Olympic champion, a Ph.D., or graduated at the bottom of your high school class—what matters is that you actually do that which is required of you. Talk is of no value; performance is everything!

Our class was a microcosm of society. We had the great-grandson of a president of the United States, a U.S. senator's son, a lieutenant who went on to become the admiral in charge of all unconventional warfare for the navy, two guys from Hell's Kitchen, and just about everything in between. They were twenty-nine of the best men I have ever known, and if I were forced to choose the most outstanding of the bunch, I would have to go with the man in the middle of the front row of our class picture—Gary Smith!

Of course, you can't really single out one individual and say he was the best, because each man was gifted in his own way. However, there was something about Smitty that set him apart from the rest of us, and it wasn't his tattoos. The best tattoo, hands down, belonged to Barney House.

Smitty's rate was radioman, but he was no more a radio-man than I am a star of the Bolshoi Ballet. He was, and is, a born gunners' mate. He breezed through Explosive Ordnance Disposal School and ended up in charge of the ordnance locker for the teams. He has an almost sixth sense for weapons and weapon systems, proven by his recent return from Kuwait, where he helped clean up unexploded ordnance left over from the Gulf War. The key word here is *return*—not everyone did! I could go on about how he was one of the best runners in the teams, how he set the record for penetrating the simulated border-crossing obstacle course at Stead's Air Force Global Survival School, what a great operator and leader he was in the field in Vietnam, but what really set Smitty apart, in my opinion, is the fact that, at the cost of considerable ridicule, he kept a diary. Not only did he keep a diary, but he kept it with almost religious fervor. I have seen him write notes on toilet paper so as not to lose certain facts he wanted to remember, but all of his scribbling was done after the operation was completed and the gear stowed.

If there was a discrepancy between an official navy report of an operation and Smitty's version of the same encounter, I would float my stick with Smitty every time!

Probably the most entertaining and prolific western author of our time was Louis L'Amour. He once said that if he wrote about a stream, that stream was where he said it was, and furthermore the water was good to drink. If Smitty tells you about a stream somewhere in Vietnam, you can go to the bank with the fact that that stream is where he says it is. However, I doubt that the water would be good to drink!

John M. Odusch, Lt. USNR
Houston, Texas
October 1993

FOREWORD

In the late summer of 1993, I received a call from someone who wanted information about a joint POW rescue operation (code named Brightlight) that my platoon—SEAL
Team One Hotel Platoon—had participated in more than
twenty-three years before in the Thanh Phu Secret Zone in
South Vietnam. To be honest, I hadn't given the operation
much, if any, thought in the intervening years—I stored it
away in my memory as just another operation of the fifty
or so Hotel Platoon had conducted, with varying degrees of
success, during our tour of duty there. That tour of duty had
been sandwiched between an earlier tour as an Underwater
Demolition Team Twelve Platoon commander conducting
hydrographic reconnaissance of selected Vietnamese coastal
areas (in addition to other classified special operations assigned to us from time to time) and a subsequent tour of
duty as the commander of all SEAL Team One assets in
Vietnam. I left that assignment with the "distinction" of being the last U.S. Navy SEAL to leave Vietnam.

After a couple of minutes it finally dawned on me that I
was talking to Smitty. (That's Master Chief Gary Smith,
USN [Retired] to most of you.) Smitty and I had crossed
paths many times during the Vietnam conflict—first in
Underwater Demolition Team Twelve and later in SEAL
Team One. Even in those early days, Smitty had gained a
reputation as a consummate professional, a superbly trained
technician who epitomized everything a Navy SEAL was
supposed to be. In addition to his expertise in Special Warfare, Smitty became certified in Explosive Ordnance

Disposal—something only a select few Navy SEALs ever attained. It was, then, with great anticipation that I awaited the manuscript for *Death in the Delta*. I expected to find an honest, detailed, action-oriented account of events that took place in 1969 and 1970 during one of Smitty's many tours in Vietnam—and I wasn't disappointed.

Some of the events, especially the Brightlight operation mentioned above, I can confirm because I personally, along with my platoon, took part in the operation. Most of the other events were known not only by me but by several other SEAL Team One members through after-action reports and eyewitnesses. The perceptive reader will come away from *Death in the Delta* with a much greater appreciation for the day-to-day life of a Navy SEAL during this period of the Vietnam conflict. Although some of the combat operations are the stuff action-adventure movies are made of, most of the time combat operations are just plain, hard, gritty work with little to write about at the end of the day—80 percent boredom interrupted by 20 percent stark terror. Smitty pulls no punches here. He writes about both the sucessess and the failures—and with a grasp of detail that is astounding. Again, the careful reader will gain a lot more knowledge about the conduct of SEAL Team operations, the weapons used, and the tactics employed than from several military handbooks.

But I want to warn you ahead of time, some of this book is not for the faint of heart. It is here that Smitty is willing to expose his inner feelings about the Vietnamese he fought alongside of and those he fought against. the book will be found to be coarse, rowdy, and earthy—even atavistic—to some readers but such was the nature of combat in that part of the Third World. Smitty may very well be accused of having "pulled the pin on the sensitivity grenade."

Smitty learned, like most of us who lived through that experience, that in combat, more than any other situation, Murphy was alive and well and accompanied us on most of our operations. Throw in that we were operating in a foreign country with comrades whose culture we could only begin to appreciate and most of us ended up believing that, indeed, Murphy was an optimist! Nevertheless, we carried on, believing that, as Admiral Arleigh Burke so eloquently put it, "[r]eality is a very demanding mistress. And if you ignore something, and hope that it will go away, or don't want to tackle it because it is difficult and because it makes you unpopular, then you lose."

I get asked all the time about the "defining quality" of a Navy SEAL. I tell most people that the Teams train most of us to have absolute confidence in our abilities—physical and mental. We are also taught that taking calculated risks is a necessary part of the vast majority of successful Special Warfare operations. And the reader will learn that Smitty trained his Vietnamese counterparts the same way. In fact, the chapters Smitty devotes to this subject are some of the best in the book. Some of Smitty's stories about the period he spent as an adviser to the Vietnamese SEALs seem to indicate that the Vietnamese SEALs were early disciples of Terrance Deal, who explained that the "worse the screw up, the better the story. If you flame out on your pathway to the future, please do it in a way that someone will remember you were once here on this earth."

Finally, I want to commend Smitty for relating, at the close of the book, the importance some of us placed, and still place, on our personal religious beliefs to help us overcome what appeared to be impossible obstacles. For although we were trained to be self-reliant, most of us knew then and continue to believe now that without God's help we could not have achieved our numerous successes nor survived our many failures.

Al Todd, Capt. USNR
Santa Barbara, California
December 14, 1993

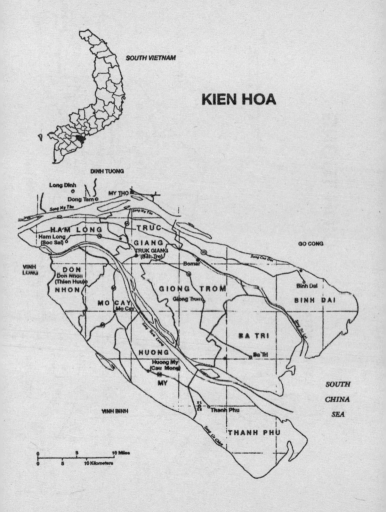

SOUTH VIETNAM

KIEN HOA

DINH TUONG

Long Dinh
Dong Tam
MY THO
Song Ng Tre

HAM LONG
TRUC

Ham Long
(Soc Sat)
GIANG
GO CONG

TRUC GIANG
(Ben Tre)

Bomar
Song Cai Die

DON
VINH
LONG
Don Nhon
(Thien Huu)
GIONG TROM

NHON
Binh Dai

MO CAY
Giong Trom
BINH DAI

Mo Cay

BA TRI

HUONG
Ba Tri

Huong My
(Cau Mong)
SOUTH

MY
CHINA

VINH BINH
SEA

Thanh Phu

THANH PHU

0   5   10 Miles
0   5   10 Kilometers

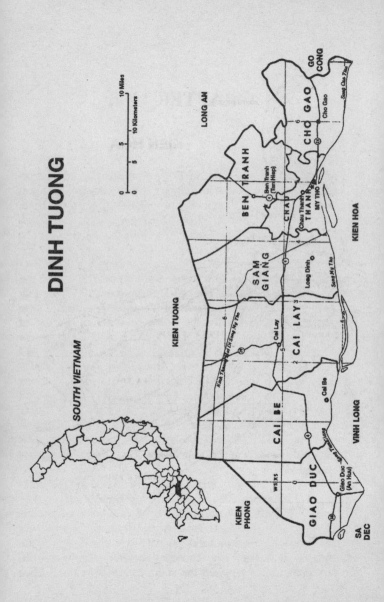

DINH TUONG

CHAPTER ONE

I walked into the ComNavForV (Commander, Naval Forces Vietnam) building in Saigon on February 11, 1970, at 1200 hours. I was beginning my fourth tour in Vietnam, this time as an LDNN (Lien Doi Nguoi Nhia, i.e., South Vietnamese SEALs) adviser. My third tour had been a tough one in which I'd seen a lot of action and death, having led and advised a PRU (Vietnamese Provincial Reconnaissance Unit) in a then-secret operation called the PHOENIX PROGRAM. The PRU consisted of hardened, indigenous mercenaries, some of whom were criminals who had elected to fight for the South in order to get out of Vietnamese jail. Most had had their wives and children or relatives killed by the VC/NVA, and they thirsted for and often got revenge. Still others were ex-VC/NVA, Cambodian, or of Chinese Nung descent. I had initially been an adviser of a 185–man team in Kien Giang Province and later was transferred to a 135–man team in Dinh Tuong Province, both of which were in the delta, or MR IV (Military Region IV). I came close to death several times at their hands while attempting to manage their fierce tempers in combat.

NavForV was the headquarters for Naval Forces Vietnam. The three-story building contained offices for SpecWar (Special Warfare) staff officers who supported the SEAL platoons, SEAL Boat Support Units (BSUs), and other Special Warfare folks concerned with administration and logistics. They also coordinated with other U.S. military personnel. I climbed the stairs to a second-floor office where Lieutenant (jg) Kuhn, the senior LDNN adviser, was awaiting my arrival.

When my eyes fell on the lieutenant as I approached his desk, I judged him to be about twenty-six years old, which was a couple of years younger than myself, and a bit heavier than my 175 pounds. After I introduced myself, he asked me to sit down in one of the chairs before his desk. He had a friendly way about him that immediately put me at ease. There seemed to be an instant rapport between us.

"I've heard a lot about you, Gary, and the good work you do," he began. I was impressed by the fact that he called me by my first name. "I understand you work well with the Vietnamese?"

"Yes, sir," I answered, relaxing in the chair. "I enjoyed working with Petty Officer Ty, an LDNN, when I was with Foxtrot Platoon in Nha Be in '67 and '68. I also have a special friend in the PRUs named Sao Lam who's still the assistant PRU chief in My Tho, Dinh Tuong Province. He's a good friend, and I hope to serve with him again some day."

Lieutenant Kuhn nodded his head approvingly, then sat slightly forward in his chair. His cheerful blue eyes focused squarely on my face. "Gary," he said, then he paused thoughtfully for a moment before continuing, "as you may have heard when Captain Schaible asked you to come over here so soon again, we're having a hard time finding anyone within SEAL Team One or Two who's had more than a tour or two over here that are available. About ninety-five percent of the guys don't re-enlist."

I nodded my head, knowing the statistics all too well.

Maintaining solid eye contact, softened by a slight smile, Kuhn explained, "I need men who are good instructors, who know their job and have the ability and desire not only to work with the Vietnamese but who will maintain a good rapport with them through thick and thin." Pausing, the lieutenant looked to me for a response.

"I understand," I replied, "and I believe I'm one who can meet this need."

Lieutenant Kuhn's grin grew a little bigger. "Fine," he blurted, looking down at a pen on his desktop. "We've got a lot of work ahead of us. Next week we'll start building an LDNN training camp at the Naval Support Detachment at Cam Ranh Bay. President Nixon's policy of Vietnamization must be put in force ASAP." The lieutenant's eyes rediscovered my face. "Our goal is to train enough LDNN platoons to replace all of the SEAL platoons in-country. As an adviser, Gary, you'll be responsible to insure we observe protocol and establish rapport with all allied and Vietnamese agencies and military units within your area of operation. You'll be invaluable in coordinating with U.S. agencies for any cumshaw needs."

As I nodded, the lieutenant paused a moment to draw a deeper breath. Reaching for the pen, he toyed with it as he continued, "You'll be working with SH1 Claude Willis, Doc Marshall, and myself. Willis is currently taking his chief petty officer's test down south. I'm not sure when he'll return."

Sliding his chair back from his desk, the lieutenant started to stand up. I rose as he did and discovered him to be the same height as I, six-feet-two.

"I suggest you enjoy the next couple of days visiting your old haunts at Nha Be or My Tho while you can, Gary," he said, smiling kindly. "Just check in with me before you head out of town." He reached across the desk with his right hand. As we shook hands, Lieutenant Kuhn gave more advice.

"Check with QM1 Hardegrew when you need a vehicle. Oh, yes, and check with Chief Corpsman Riojas at the Le Lai Hotel for your berthing. He's from SEAL Team Two." I let go of his hand and thanked him. He dismissed me, then called to me as I went out the door, "Hopefully, you'll be back in the field advising an LDNN platoon in Dinh Tuong Province within a few weeks!"

After I met with Lieutenant Kuhn, QM1 Hardegrew and I drove a jeep seven miles south of Saigon to the Navy Support Detachment at Nha Be, where I had been with

Foxtrot Platoon in 1967–68. Hootches built on stilts lined both sides of the hard-packed gravel road for approximately a half mile before the base gate.

Nha Be had grown! One of the hootches on the left and near the base gate had a sign on its front saying "NGA'S." I stopped the jeep, told Hardegrew to wait a minute, and hurried inside the hootch.

The almond-shaped eyes of three old Vietnamese men, who were sitting at a small table near the door, followed me as I walked past them toward the middle-aged woman working behind the laundry counter. The mamma-san raised her face toward me when I lightly tapped my knuckles on the countertop. Breaking into a wide smile, which revealed three gaps in her betelnut-stained teeth, Nga addressed me the same way she always had when I was stationed in Nha Be more than two years earlier.

"How you, Smit-ty?"

"Toi manh gioi," I responded, telling her I was fine. With outstretched arms, Nga leaned over the counter to give me a hug. It felt good to see this kind woman again.

Still grinning, Nga released me and said, "I do clothes for you, Smit-ty. Be ready, two day." As was her habit, she held up two slightly crooked fingers to emphasize her words. I nodded my head, confident that I would frequent her little store whenever possible throughout my seven-month tour, though I knew my patronage would be sporadic.

After a couple more minutes of pleasantries, I told Nga good-bye and headed for the jeep.

"Chao," Nga called after me, waving a hand.

I climbed into the driver's seat of the jeep and drove Hardegrew and myself onto the naval base. I drove right to the enlisted men's club near the old Quonset hut that had been our first EM club in 1967–68. Hardegrew and I walked inside, where plenty of beer and members of SEAL Team Two met us. We drank several Pabst Blue Ribbon beers apiece until curfew, which was 2000 hours, at which time we left and drove back to Saigon.

After we arrived at the Le Lai Hotel, we couldn't find CPO Riojas at the bar or in his room. Fortunately, Hardegrew had an extra bed in his room and invited me to stay there for the night. My tired head hit the pillow at 2230 hours.

As much as I desired to fall quickly to sleep, I could not. Instead, I lay in bed marveling at the fact that I was back in Vietnam so soon after the completion of my third tour. I had spent only four months in the States at Camp Billy Machen, which was named after the first SEAL to die in combat (the camp was located several miles northwest of a small community near the shores of Lake Cuyamaca in the Southern California mountains), as a camp guard when Captain Schaible called me into his office and asked if I'd go back to 'Nam as a Vietnamese SEAL adviser. The decision was an easy one. With most of the SEAL Team guys failing to re-enlist after their three-year hitches were up, the command had a real need for experienced SEALs in Vietnam to help train.

Tossing and turning in my bed, I pondered my answering "yes" to Captain Schaible so soon after all the killing I'd seen with the PRU in the PHOENIX PROGRAM, through which "the Company" (the Central Intelligence Agency) had us use the paid mercenaries to capture or kill military and political leaders of the Vietcong infrastructure (VCI). Our goal had been to neutralize or weaken the VCI's control and manipulation of the rice farmers, who were their main source of tax money, rice, manpower, and political power (from "the barrel of a gun," à la Mao Zedong). It was dangerous, nasty work and hard to forget.

As a welcome fuzziness finally enveloped my brain and my body seemed ready to give in, a tiny seed of thought planted itself and started to grow. Before I could snip it, I had to open my eyes and stare into a story I'd been unable to shake—the night Randy Sheridan and I went on a mission with eighteen PRU to capture three VC and one VCI in Cho Gao District. Our source of information had been a Hoi Chanh—ex-VC—who went with us. Sao Lam, a fierce warrior and middle-aged man of average stature and looks, led the patrol across mud-hardened rice dikes that criss-crossed a foot above flooded rice paddies like a network of raised sidewalks.

In the black of the night, when every place became a free-fire zone and everyone was restricted to their homes, we slipped past clusters of coconut trees and dozens of hootches, quiet as mice. I carried a Czechoslovakian folding-stock AK-47 automatic rifle. Most of the PRU preferred communist weapons. The rest of the men toted AK-47s, RPD machine guns, and an M-79 grenade launcher. From our point of view, we were the "good guys," and we certainly had the firepower to wreak some major havoc. The only possibility of a "green fly in the soup" would be if the Hoi Chanh was leading us into an ambush. However, he'd be the first to die if he did.

As we patrolled, all was quiet until we approached a small hootch silhouetted beside a row of coconut trees to our left. From inside the thatched hut came the sound of a woman's giggling, then a man's raucous laughter. As our team filed by the hootch just fifteen feet away, I could tell that the man and woman were playfully chasing one another around the house, and they were enjoying themselves immensely. I couldn't believe the contrast between what I was doing and what they were doing. There I was, mentally prepared to shoot and kill human beings—to end life—while that merry couple was seemingly preparing to love and make new life. It almost flipped my brain out.

None of our men made so much as a snicker as we distanced ourselves from the hootch. The hard reality was that on this night we were messengers of death and could not afford a reckless cackle.

We moved another half mile to the hootch where the four VC were supposed to be living. It was 0300 hours and the hootch was dark and quiet. Sao Lam motioned for the men to form a skirmish line about twenty-five meters from the front of the hut, then he signaled for two men to advance toward the door as had been prearranged at his briefing on the mission. I watched the two in the starlight as they took a few steps forward before stopping to whisper to one another. A second later, they raised their weapons at the hootch and suddenly opened fire on it. Instantly, the rest of the PRU joined the assault in a deafening roar of gunfire while Randy and I stood there aghast. Seventeen automatic weapons and one grenade launcher were blowing the hootch to pieces, not to mention my battle-weary eardrums.

After more than one thousand rounds had torn apart the palm frond walls of the hootch, Randy and I began shouting at the top of our lungs, "Cease fire!" The PRU, having gone mad with blood lust and the desire for revenge, ignored our cries. One thousand more rounds ripped into the ruined house, which would surely be unfit for human habitation ever again.

Finally, the shooting ended, and it took several seconds for my mind to work through the initial shock of going from a thousand decibels of blast to zero decibels of complete silence. My whole head reverberated as I fought to adjust. Looking through the dark at Randy, I saw him squeeze his eyes shut and slowly shake his head.

Then a piercing scream of absolute terror rang out from inside the demolished hootch. A woman had survived the staggering wallop and was now horror-struck in the aftermath. As she squelched her shriek to draw a breath of air, a baby's cry sounded and my stomach twisted over inside of me. I could hardly accept the fact that a woman and a baby were inside the hootch, let alone that they were still alive.

Sao Lam quickly ordered a few of the PRU to enter the hut to gather weapons and documents. Randy and I stayed off to the side, disgusted that the "capture" had so rashly turned to killing. It would be hard to get good intelligence information if we killed our best sources. Neither of us desired to look in the hootch at the dead bodies or the female survivor and baby, who continued their screaming and bawling.

The searchers came back with their findings—a certificate of award for capturing an American army captain in Cai Be District in 1965 and other documents, along with a few weapons—and the twenty-one of us moved out as fast as possible, going back a slightly different way than we had come in.

The VCI had been a tax collector, and two of the others had been VC squad leaders. Unfortunately, we had no captives and no information about the army captain, either. The woman's suffering, as her wails diminished to a wheeze that assured me she had taken some bullets and was probably dying, didn't help my attitude any. The baby's cries, however, grew stronger and could be heard behind us for several hundred meters in the dead of the night. I was relieved when the sound finally died away, even though I knew the memory of it would be with me for a lifetime.

As we filed past the hootch in which the man and woman had been playing around, not a peep was heard. For that matter, not a sound came from any hootch. The thunder of grenades and automatic weapons fire in the village had induced an obvious effect: fear. And less than six months later, the bloodbath was causing another problem: sleeplessness.

I sat up in the bed and stared at the sliver of light beneath the door to the hotel hallway, hoping this fourth tour would bring better days and that the Vietnamese SEALs would exercise better control.

CHAPTER TWO

Over the next week, I spent the days killing time, waiting to transfer to Cam Ranh Bay with the LDNN trainees with whom I'd be working for the next six months. Each day consisted of primarily the same routine: making the rounds between the Le Lai, Ky Son, Hung Dao, President, and Metropol hotels for meals and drinking plenty of 33 Beer, dropping by NavForV to check on various things, and sitting around and just talking with other Navy SEALs. I visited the LDNN trainees at the Vietnamese shipyard a few times for some pretraining exercises, which involved an hour or so of PT and running. I also used the slack time for shopping, purchasing a couple of Chinese porcelain vases purported to be 150 years old, as well as for making two trips to Nga's for laundry purposes and enjoyable conversation.

Finally, on Wednesday, February 18, I escorted fourteen LDNN trainees to 8th Aerial at Tan Son Nhut and we flew air force to Cam Ranh Bay. Lieutenant Kuhn took ten men, flew by navy aircraft, and joined us at Cam Ranh, where the Seabees picked us up and drove us to the small naval base at the southern tip of the Cam Ranh peninsula. Two rectangular, framed sea huts to the north of the base and approximately one hundred meters outside and to the right of its main gate, were set up for living quarters until we could build or cumshaw more as time and resources allowed.

Having arrived at Cam Ranh just after 1800 hours, there was time only to assign cots, unpack gear, grab a bite to eat at the base mess deck—chow hall—and hit the rack. Unfortunately, I had no blanket, and the temperature dropped to sixty degrees during the night. I spent more time shivering than sleeping. Adding to my wakefulness was the fact that several rockets blew up about a mile north of the base at around 0100 hours. In response, the base went to General Quarters (GQ). Two 81-mm mortars just fifty feet from our berthing quarters fired a dozen illumination rounds above the hills to our north, and the base personnel lit up the entire base, which seemed quite strange to me. However, the next morning the executive officer (XO), Lieutenant Commander Wayne, explained that the lights were turned on to prevent the base personnel from shooting one another. He might have had a point.

Reveille sounded at 0630 hours, but I was already up and shaving. After breakfast at the chow hall, Lieutenant Kuhn, PO2 Tran Van Qua, PO1 Le Van Manh, PO2 Le Van Tuong, and I had a conference with Lieutenant Commander Wayne, who spelled out some very strict base regulations to us. One surprising rule was that no firearms or knives with blades over six inches in length could be carried on the base. Considering there was no authorized liberty on the peninsula, which meant no women, in principle I had to agree with the policy. The Seabees were working twelve-hour days seven days a week building Vietnamese living quarters, and the "black shoe" navy were working near the same. Under such difficult conditions perceived wrongs could be difficult if not impossible to reconcile.

Thirty minutes into our meeting, Lieutenant White, who was in charge of security and base clubs, entered the room. The XO briefed him on our desires concerning the construction of the LDNN camp. Lieutenant White decided to go with us to the site outside the north gate. Once there, we stood by the SEAL adviser sea hut and discussed further plans with the lieutenant and Boatswain's Mate Senior Chief Lightening.

At 1130 hours we ate lunch, then I grabbed a welcome nap until 1300. Upon waking, I borrowed a five-ton truck from Security for us to use to cart sandbags to our compound area. The twenty-four LDNN trainees, Lieutenant Kuhn, and I worked at building a bunker by digging a pit approximately eight feet wide by ten feet long and three feet deep, then placing a steel conex box that was six and one half feet wide by eight and one half feet long by six and one half feet high within it and covering it with sandbags. We worked until 1600 hours. We then went to our huts, put on our swim gear, and jogged to the picturesque tropical cove with its sandy beach and crystal-clear water that ran along the southern edge of the base. I led the group in a half hour PT workout, then a two-mile run along the beach and through the shallow surf, then directed everyone to plunge into the ocean and swim out a hundred meters and back. The water felt very refreshing. After the swim, Lieutenant Kuhn and I walked to the officers' club, and each of us drank a beer while discussing our troops.

"I think the guys look pretty good," I said. "I especially like Tu Uy [Ensign] Son's attitude. He's motivated and responds well to my suggestions. All he would need is a good chief or LPO (Leading Petty Officer) to keep the men in tow. I think PO2 Tran Van Qua would be a great LPO. And just maybe I'd be lucky enough to be assigned to Tu Uy Son's platoon and introduce them to the province of Dinh Tuong, huh?"

Lieutenant Kuhn didn't take long to respond to my last comment. "I'm afraid the LDNNs are in much the same condition SEAL Team One is. They simply don't have enough experienced senior enlisted personnel available. In other words, your chances of getting someone of PO2 Qua's qualifications are slim to none."

"Well, if Ensign Son doesn't have an experienced chief or LPO, he won't have the time or energy to coordinate with the Vietnamese and U.S. military and civilian agencies at sector and subsector, much less plan missions and fulfill

Tu Ta Hiep's [Hiep was the LDNN commanding officer] policies and quirks."

Grinning, Lieutenant Kuhn looked me square in the face and said, "Well, I guess we'll have to be creative and invent what Mr. Son will need for his new platoon, hey?"

I grinned, raised my beer in a toast, and replied, "Yes, sir! I volunteer to be his LPO until 'we' can create one."

"Yeah, or we'll forget the Tu Uy and I'll take his place, then we'll all have some fun," he said, laughing.

"My bags are packed! I'm ready to go! Hoo-yah!" I exclaimed.

After leaving the club, I returned to our camp outside the main gate. PO2 Tran Van Qua and Chief Petty Officer (CPO) "Doc" Riojas were free-sparring with each other in a sandy area near the sea huts. About a dozen VN (Vietnamese) students were standing around watching them. I knew that Qua had a black belt in karate—most of the VN SEAL instructors did. However, Doc seemed to be holding his own. Considering his 185 pounds and height of five feet ten inches, he could remain defensive and continue to use only basic punches, blocks, and kicks if his endurance held out.

"When did you get here, Doc?" I yelled.

Distracted, Doc turned his head toward me. Taking advantage of the situation, Qua gave Doc a roundhouse kick to his left shoulder with a loud "Yeauh!" Doc gave me a look that would have frozen vodka.

Doc looked at Qua, saying, "Time out, Qua! I need a rest. How are you, Smitty?"

I started laughing. "Doc, you're getting too old for karate. Besides, your belly is beginning to hang over your belt buckle and your right index finger is permanently crooked to carry only a coffee cup. Yessir, you're beginning to look like a real navy chief."

"Okay, hotshot, you get in there for a couple rounds with this buzzsaw," Doc quickly responded.

I was beginning to wish I hadn't been so lighthearted.

It must have been those last two beers that did it. Qua was looking at me. He was grinning. Well, I thought, when a man's image is at stake, it's time to put up or shut up. Besides, in my blue-and-gold T-shirt, UDT khaki swim trunks, and gray coral booties, I was already dressed for action.

"Okay, Qua, be easy on me. I've only got a green belt in karate," I said. At that, Qua really grinned. Without a reply he began moving closer to me.

I quickly decided to be defensive throughout the workout and to be careful that I didn't make Qua look bad, assuming I could. I regretted mentioning my green belt because if I made him look bad, he would lose face in the presence of the VN trainees.

I grinned at Qua and gradually circled counterclockwise. Fortunately, I was able to use both of my feet, kicking better with my left foot than my right even though I'm right-handed. I had always shot a bow left-handed and kicked a football left-footed.

Qua's first move was to fake a jumping right-frontal high kick followed by a left jump kick to my stomach. I responded by taking a half step to my right and partly blocking his kick with my right arm. I then countered with a right-side kick to his left knee. The soft sand slowed my movements and my balance was off.

Qua quickly responded with a nice roundhouse kick for my kidneys. I stepped into his spin and lightly punched him in the kidney, letting his leg hit my shoulder. He reversed his spin and caught me in my right ear with his fist. I was hoping his fist hurt worse than my head, as my ear was throbbing and I felt blood running down my neck. I could also feel my anger rising. Once the blood started flowing, it always became a whole 'nother ball game with me.

In the background Doc yelled, "You were a little slow with that block, Smitty. Hang in there. It can't get much worse!"

I remember thinking, "Who needs enemies when I've got friends like Doc!"

Qua and I were circling each other, first counterclockwise, then clockwise, looking for an opening. Suddenly, Qua noticed the blood flowing down my neck. He straightened up and said, "Smitty, you ear not so good. Maybe Doc fix."

"Thank goodness!" I thought. An escape route. I knew that I shouldn't get into a knock-down-drag-out fight with our number-one VN SEAL instructor, even though I wanted to get revenge and nail him a good one. My better judgment overruled my anger, though, so I waved Qua away, pointing at my ear, and I moved toward Doc.

Frowning, I looked at Doc and said, "This is all your fault. You set me up, didn't you?" He broke into a grin. "Don't bother answering me 'cause I won't listen. There is only one way we can settle this and that must be over a few beers at the CPO club."

Doc looked me in the eyes, put his arm around my shoulders, and said softly, *"Vamanos por la casa de cervesa, mi amigo."*

"I thought you would never ask," I said. "All's well that ends well, huh? I'm glad you're here, Doc. Now maybe you fix ear, huh?"

We stayed at the CPO club till 1830 hours, then lightheartedly headed for the sea huts for another cold night without a blanket or a mosquito net. As a matter of fact, we weren't in much of a mood to worry about such trivial matters. As long as we had a rack to lie down in, we were happy.

However, giving some thought to the night before, we decided to try to procure a couple of blankets and mosquito nets. Maybe it was our breath. Whatever the reason, we couldn't beg, borrow, or buy 'em. We could've stolen some, and the thought certainly crossed our minds, but then someone else would have had to shiver all night long, which is what we ended up doing. And with no blanket and no protective mosquito netting around our cots, the mosquitos had free access to our bodies. Having already given blood to

Qua, I didn't appreciate serving up some more to the Culicidae family, but serve it up we did, as hundreds of the little bastards bloated themselves at our expense.

CHAPTER THREE

As I lay on my cot alternately swatting or attempting to ignore the biting beasts of the evening, I drifted again to the place where my thoughts always went lately when I had too much time to think: my third tour of Vietnam. I closed my eyes and saw myself talking to an army first lieutenant who was assigned to the Ranger company of the 9th Infantry Division at Dong Tam. Since I was under civilian cover, all that this young but seasoned officer knew about me was that I was working for the CIA with the PRU mercenaries. He didn't know I was a navy SEAL, much less just an E-5 and not an officer. But what he didn't know wouldn't hurt him, and what he didn't know was that I was just an enlisted puke.

Because SEAL Team ONE's Golf platoon at Ben Luc wasn't available, I contacted the First Lieutenant and asked him and his chosen men to accompany the PRU's and me on a mission in the center of the VC/NVA controlled Cai Be district. My primary motive for asking the Rangers to come along was that they had access to Huey slicks, gunships, OV-10s, reliable communications equipment, artillery support and Army snipers who had match-grade, scoped M-14s and match ammunition. In other words, they had all of the support and resources that I needed to penetrate that particular enemy stronghold to capture a few specific VCI that were judiciously listed on Dinh Tuong Province's Phung Hoang committee's blacklist of VCI. The Ranger notified me the following day that they were ready and anxious to engage and destroy a bunch of Communist pigs. I couldn't have been happier.

Two days later on a hot and humid afternoon in July 1969, I directed the helo operation's blocking- and sweeping-unit insertions in the midst of a village that had a known VC/NVA battalion-size unit located in a nearby tree line. The mission was complicated in that it required timely and reliable intelligence information and, initially, the simultaneous insertion of three blocking elements of troops on enemy escape routes outside a hamlet where the targeted VC infrastructure lived. After the blocking elements were in place, the sweeping element of troops would be inserted and start to move toward the three blocking elements and the target, squeezing the enemy into a small area where they could be captured or killed. This was known as the hammer-and-anvil tactic.

I stayed in the command and control (C & C) ship, coordinating the insertions, until the initial movement of the sweeping element toward the enemy hootches. The army sniper shot two VC, body count, but I didn't get one of the blocking elements into position quickly enough so most of the VCI slipped to safety through well-established escape routes. Just one slight delay inserting one blocking element blew everything.

I had the C & C insert me with the sweeping element, where my VN counterpart, Sao Lam, was, as it advanced on the numerous targeted hootches in the hamlet. I had my old M-16/XM-148 standby—a basic M-16 rifle with a 40-mm grenade launcher tube below the barrel. The grenade launcher had a maximum range of about 350 meters.

Knowing the PRUs' tendency to forget their perimeter security when they got angry—and I knew they'd be irate after learning that most of the VCI had escaped—I asked the Ranger captain to position his men as perimeter security. When the PRU members fully realized that the district Communist party secretary—the man we had primarily wanted to capture—had escaped, their anger quickly escalated. Many of the PRU had had relatives killed in that area by the communists, who had used terror to take control of the hamlet and to set up their political and military infrastructure. And now the PRU were looking for revenge. I almost immediately lost control of the men as five of the PRU entered the hootch of the party secretary. They dragged outside an old, gray-bearded Vietnamese man and a pretty woman holding a two- or three-month-old baby.

A PRU named Hoang shouted at the old man, who was dressed in white pajamas, and demanded to know where the party secretary and other VCI had gone. When the old man didn't respond, Hoang forcefully jammed the barrel of his M-16 into the old man's left rib cage, causing the old man to double over in pain.

"Where is the party secretary?" Hoang yelled, then he cursed and beat the old man. When the old man didn't answer, Hoang punched him in the face with his right fist. The old man's head snapped back from the blow, but he quickly recovered and remained quiet, staring at the ground, visibly shaken and silently crying.

I intervened at this time and told Sao Lam through the interpreter that I didn't want any torture and that we must gather up the VCI that we did have and start patrolling out of there. I said that PIC (the Provincial Interrogation Center) could take care of the interrogation. Sao Lam tried to get Hoang and other PRU under control, but he couldn't.

I then threw a temper tantrum and cursed a blue streak in Vietnamese, but to no avail. I got between Hoang and the old man, all the while yelling and saying, "That's enough! He's just an old man!" But Hoang would not acknowledge my presence. Neither did any of the others. Even Sao Lam could do nothing.

Hoang threatened the old man with blindness if he didn't reveal the locations of the VCI and specifically the party secretary. As before, when the old man refused to speak, Hoang beat his face. Then he kicked him hard in the shins, then slapped the gun barrel across the top of his head. Instantly, a stream of blood ran down his forehead and off his nose.

The old man's brown eyes lifted momentarily and settled

on my face. The look they gave me was one of great sorrow and grief, yet there was also finality, strength, and determination. I knew the old man would die before he would reveal the location of his son, the party secretary. When his eyes shifted back toward the ground, Hoang slugged the old man in the jaw with his rifle stock, knocking him over onto his side. The old man was openly weeping and sobbing as he tried to raise himself when Hoang whacked him across the back with the rifle, then kicked him under the chin and laid him flat. I turned away as Hoang swore and kicked the old man several more times.

Suddenly aware of a slight pause in the beating, I looked back to see Hoang moving away from the old man and toward the woman with the small baby. Hoang grabbed the baby out of the woman's arms and handed it quickly to another of the PRU. To my surprise, the woman, who appeared to be in her mid-twenties, did not wail or beg, much less utter a sound. Knowing she was next, she stood stoically before Hoang.

"Where did your husband go?" Hoang demanded. He waited all of three seconds for a reply, and when none was forthcoming, he slapped the woman's face with great force. Her head spun, but the rest of her body stayed put. Hoang quickly rammed his fist into the woman's stomach, which doubled her over. Then he violently jerked her upright again.

"Dammit!" I barked, getting involved again. "Son of a bitch, Hoang, that's enough! What in the hell are you doin'?" I threw a temper tantrum again and cussed up a storm, using both English and Vietnamese, trying to gain control of the situation, which was headed in a ghastly direction. Hoang did not look at me, but I felt the eyes of a couple of the other PRU members. I knew that I was on the edge. My own life would be in jeopardy if I pushed much further. These men had a hard-core blood lust and were resolute on getting revenge; right then, I was the only object in their way.

Hoang persisted, the woman stood silent, so he grabbed a handful of her hair at the back of her head with his left hand, which still clutched his M-16, and steadied her face as he slapped her twice and backhanded her once.

I couldn't help myself. "Shit!" I cried, knowing that I'd either have to start mowing down my own men or back off and let Hoang finish what he had started. My heart directed me to start shooting, but my head told me that that would be suicidal, dangerous not only for me but possibly for the captain and his men.

While I debated with myself, Hoang fired a shot, which focused my attention back on him and his antics. He had raised the end of the barrel of his rifle to within a couple inches of the woman's left ear and squeezed the trigger. The muzzle blast must have surely burst her eardrum. She winced but never made a cry or sound.

Hoang grabbed her by an arm and jerked her past me, forcing her toward a small canal about ten feet wide. The rest of the PRU followed, leaving the old man lying on the ground in the hot sun. The rest of the PRU, about fifty all told, approached us, having heard the commotion and the gunshots and wondering what was happening. Fortunately, the captain and his dozen men were maintaining security perimeter. At least we couldn't be surprised by the enemy.

In full view of everyone—including the old man, who was still sobbing and lying in the hot sun—Hoang muscled the young woman a few yards to the edge of the rather deep irrigation canal that ran near her hootch. He made her stand on the bank, facing the canal, with her toes just inches from the drop-off to the water.

Again, Hoang demanded to know where her husband had gone. In the ensuing silence, he lifted the muzzle of his rifle next to the woman's right ear. With the barrel pointing toward a cluster of palm trees beyond the canal, Hoang pulled the trigger. The explosion shook me, but the woman only winced and said nothing.

Wanting desperately to save the woman from further torture, I took a chance and stepped up to Hoang's right side. "We must move out of this area if we are to get out of here at all. There are large VC and NVA units near here. We must leave here now!"

Hoang's fierce-looking eyes were focused on the woman's back. I stared at his eyes for a moment, then shifted my stare to where he was looking. I was but three feet from the pretty, petite, yet unbelievably courageous woman. Hoang's rifle was pointed at the center of her back, which was covered by a white pajama top. My eyes traced the inches between the muzzle and the white cloth.

Pow! Pow! Pow! The reports came so quickly that they almost sounded like one big blast. My body shuddered at the wallop, but my eyes soaked in the three hits. Three little holes, just an inch apart, were torn through the white cloth. The woman tumbled forward, face first into the canal, and disappeared under the water.

Several seconds passed as I just stood there in shock. While I was still staring at the ripples in the water where the woman's body had splashed, my mouth somehow managed to blurt the necessary order. "Okay, let's move out!"

As I turned away from the canal, my eyes fell on the old Vietnamese man, who was still sitting hunched over on the ground in the hot sun, sobbing. There was blood on his swollen face, and the tears from his closed eyes streamed down his cheeks and mixed with the blood. I wonder whether Hoang's beating or the awful sight of the young woman's murder had shut his eyes.

Realizing that the old man was still in danger of being shot, I attempted to distract everyone from paying attention to him by shouting out further directives. The ruse worked, and we hurried away from that little hamlet in Cai Be District, leaving the old man with his life. And with his god-awful memories.

A mosquito stabbed me on the back of my left hand, reminding me that I was being eaten alive in the middle of the night, and reminding me also that I was reminiscing again. Only *reminiscing* was too nice a word for what I had been doing. More realistically, I had been having a nightmare.

CHAPTER FOUR

After that second terrible night of cold and bloodsucking mosquitoes, I made up my mind that there would be no third. I was out of the hut before reveille and shaking down the base for a couple of blankets and mosquito nets. I had no luck, but since GMG1 Deal had been assigned to help us procure the things we needed, I went to him and told him that Doc Riojas and I desperately needed blankets and mosquito nets and that we might as well get a few extras on hand for emergencies.

An hour later, a blanket was spread out on my cot and a new net shrouded my sleeping area. Extra blankets and mosquito nets were neatly stacked on the bar for Doc and others in need. Deal had come through for us. Certainly, he had saved me from the torture; I had no doubt that the word had spread among the skeeter colonies that a somewhat abused piece of red meat lay unprotected and available in Sea Hut #1. It's a good thing I had been taking my weekly malaria pills. I'd always hated those things because they occasionally upset my digestive tract, which created a true problem with a sense of urgency—severe diarrhea.

At 0830 hours, after a hearty breakfast of steak and eggs, the twenty-four LDNN trainees and our advisory staff ran in formation to the new camp that we were working to finish near the north bunker. By 1500 hours, we had completed it.

I got a quick burr haircut at the base barbershop so I'd have less trouble with the dry scalp that I got from so much

salt water, then joined the others again at the beach for PT
and a one-mile run. As always, I enjoyed the exercise, as I
liked staying in shape.

I ate supper at 1730 hours, then went to the club and
drank a Coke while talking with some of the LDNN
trainees. Afterward, I went to the outdoor movie, which
was showing *The Wild Bunch*. It sure was a bloody movie,
too bloody for me, so I left early. I'd seen enough blood in
real life to want to watch it flow all over a movie screen.

The next morning, February 21, 1970, the trainees started
work on the southeast corner of the bunker. I told PO1 Le
Van Manh that if the men finished before noon, we would
do PT and our run at 1300 hours and take the rest of the
day off. That was all the incentive the men needed; the
bunker was completed by 1130 hours.

After PT and the run, Deal and I, clad in our swim
trunks, walked down the beach to an old French bunker.
There were two, actually, one at each end of the long beach
and adjacent to the thick underbrush and small trees. Of reinforced cement with flat roofs and circular, they would
have made outstanding Coke stands. The walls were approximately one foot thick and had small slits eighteen
inches in length and four inches in height to allow covering
fire at any potential enemy approaches from the beach or
the sea. The bunkers were half full of sand and concertina
wire.

We hunted the beach for shells, finding a small subspe-
cies of the tridacna and several types of cowries, snails with
glossy, brightly colored shells. We decided to walk to the
far western end of the beach, where the jungle began, then
swim out about a quarter of a mile to a reef of coral formations with narrow crevices. We knew that all types of tropical fish, large and small, and lobsters up to ten pounds
shared the coral shelves with the occasional moray eel and
sea snake.

What a pleasure it was to swim and free-dive in beautiful
water that was so plentiful with sea life. The visibility
underwater was about fifty feet; the water temperature was

comfortable. We saw squid eighteen to twenty-four inches long move rapidly through the area as if late for an appointment. Since we had no Hawaii sling—a type of gig with a five-foot fiberglass shaft powered by a surgical-rubber loop at one end and three steel barbs at the other end—we couldn't spear the squid for dinner.

In several dives, I found small tridacnas and saw a beautiful dark green six-foot-long moray eel with yellow spots. The eel was swimming along slowly, but without a Hawaiian sling, I decided to leave the eel alone; I was not in the mood for a savage bite.

Later, I dove down about thirty-five feet and spotted two needlefish, which were very slender and about three feet long. With long and narrow jaws and elongated bodies like pike, they closely resemble garfish. I decided to see how close I could get to them. I swam slowly toward them, watching them intently. When I got to within ten feet, they started moving slowly away from me. When I put on a burst of speed toward them, they zoomed away into the depths of the South China Sea.

After an hour of diving, Deal and I began swimming back toward the beach. I chose to dive down about thirty-five feet, cruising about twenty feet above the sandy bottom to take one last look for a large tridacna. Luckily, I found one, but my lungs were screaming for oxygen. After going up for air, I dove again, grabbed the tridacna as his valves closed, and pulled with all my strength to break his hold on the coral and the sand. When he finally broke loose, I kicked with a sense of urgency to get back to the surface. I thought I would have to drop it because of its weight, but I kept my eyes on the surface and just barely made it in time for a much-needed breath of air. I swam slowly toward the beach with my prize and there I admired him and his size. He was about twenty inches long and twelve wide with his valves closed. He was the largest I had found up to that time. He was a beauty and a keeper.

Deal and I gathered up all our booty and walked back to

our hut, laughing all the way. Our afternoon of diving had been wonderful fun.

Back at the sea hut, we were greeted by SH1 Claude Willis, two LDNN instructors, and seven new trainees who had flown in that afternoon. Willis was a black man with black eyes who stood five feet ten inches tall and weighed about two hundred pounds. He had a reputation as a winner at gambling, and I was determined to check it out when the opportunity arose.

"Hey, what's happening, Bro? What it is?" I yelled.

"Smitty, long time no see," Bro responded with a blazing grin that showed a gold star imbedded in his right front tooth.

I dropped my tridacna as we hugged each other, grinning and laughing as only teammates can.

"Looks like you been diving. You see any bugs?" Bro asked.

I became serious, saying, "Yeah, I saw several in the five-pound class, but there's a nine-foot eel that seems to guard this crevice, kind of like a sheriff protectin' his prisoners from the lynch mob. Every time I'd grab a lobster, he'd put his ugly face into my face mask and show me a set of plentiful inch-long teeth." Willis and I laughed, then I continued. "The second time he got in my face mask, I began to feel like a thief in the night and finally decided that those huge bugs weren't mine to take. The fear of the consequences was just too much for me. And, besides, I didn't have a swim partner."

Bro laughed again, put his arm around my sunburned shoulders, and said, "You gots ah swim pardner now!"

As we started toward the instructors' sea hut, we began singing an old team ditty.

We're off to see the Wild West Show;
the elephants and the kangaroos.
As long as we're together we'll never fear the weather.
We're off to see the Wild West Show.

Ladies and Gentlemen; in this corner is the incredible
   O-rang-u-tang!

When we got inside our sea hut and were standing next
to our new, unvarnished bar top, I introduced Bro Willis to
Doc Riojas. "Bro, meet Doc Riojas from SEAL Team Two.
He ain't all bad. He serves a wicked Cuba Libre with a
twist of lime, and while you guys get acquainted I'll set up
the beer."

It wasn't long before Lieutenant Kuhn and Deal came in.
That's when the party really began. By taps (2200 hours),
we were all boasting how we would wring that fifteen-foot
moray eel's neck with only our hands. Then we would slit
him from orifice to orifice and feed him to the Vietnamese
trainees. There was much merriment and camaraderie in
that little sea hut that night.

Over the next few days we continued to work on the new
compound. By then we had three sea huts, and all were furnished with bunks, footlockers, blankets, and mosquito nets.
One was for the trainees, one for the Vietnamese instructors, and one for animals with their unvarnished bar top.
The trainees dug a barbecue pit, and the Seabees gener-
ously completed it and also furnished a large, reinforced
grill to cover it. In order to maintain our image, the trainees
kept the grounds around the sea huts clean and raked daily.

On February 26, the camp was in good enough shape for
everyone to move in even though there were still many
tasks to be completed. We also went deep into the business
of cumshawing the things we needed by trading communist
weapons to the Seabees for pipe for our flagpole, nails, a
faucet, a large cooking pan, two-by-four lumber, and four-
by-eight-foot plywood sheets, along with chairs, a couple of
lockers, and a fan from the army. The smile on my face
grew bigger and bigger as the camp became more and more
comfortable and ready to train Vietnamese SEALs.

On March 5, HM1 Doc Marshall arrived on the scene.
He was a five-foot-nine, 220-pound man of average looks
and a bad case of "Dunlap's disease," which meant he had

a belly that "done lapped over his belt buckle." He had an easygoing attitude and a tendency to walk like a duck. His sister had married the famed (well, in the teams) "Doc" Churchill of SEAL Team One. Churchill had served in World War II, Korea, and Vietnam, and had eight purple hearts. It didn't take Doc Marshall but a few minutes to locate an empty bunk on which to lie down and open up a book about the Old West.

Throughout the month of March, several more trainees arrived, and Lieutenant Kuhn, Willis, Riojas, and I, in cooperation with the VN instructors, accompanied the trainees on ocean swims, PT and running, and combat hydrographic reconnaissance; teaching them tactics that included night patrolling, stealth and concealment, helicopter insertions and extractions, immediate action drills, weapons and demolition, ambushing techniques, etc.

In the middle of the month, we staged a four-thousand-meter race with seven-man crews in IBS (inflatable boat, small) boats. These small, black-rubber, inflatable boats were powered by paddles and hard work. Six trainees paddled each, three to port and three to starboard. The seventh man, usually an officer, was the coxswain. His primary responsibility was to lead the boat crew and to insure that the boat stayed on course by steering it with his paddle or by having port or starboard paddlers hold water in order to quickly change the direction of the boat. Occasionally, the coxswain might even have to lay a little wood on top of a paddler's head for emphasis. The number-one starboard position was for the stroke man, who sets the pace as directed by the coxswain. He also sang out a cadence when needed for motivation and/or coordination.

My crew was fairly fast but was not paddling in unison; still, we managed to take the lead on the other five boats. After a while, though, another boat began gaining on us. When it got to within a few meters of us, I couldn't stand just watching any longer and I moved quickly to replace the stroke man. I immediately started a cadence and used a longer, stronger stroke. Soon the trainees began to paddle in unison, putting their backs into it instead of just their arms. The race was on! Our image, our manhood, the fast-growing pride of our boat crew, our competitiveness, and yes, even some tears were now at stake. Motivation was the foundation for power, especially "team power." The other boats didn't have a chance. We rapidly pulled away from them, thereby proving the old adage, "You show me a good loser and I'll show you a loser." We beat them by two hundred meters.

When the rest of the Vietnamese instructors and trainees got in to shore, I saw by their facial expressions that they were not well pleased with the margin of our victory. My judgments were confirmed when the other instructors ordered my boat crew, minus myself, to do dozens and dozens of push-ups with the IBS on their backs. Since we had made the VN instructors lose face, they had decided to work the trainees over a bit. At first, as I watched my crew struggle through the punishment, I was angry, but while I thought about it, I started laughing. With VN Hell Week coming soon, I figured the trainees might as well get used to the abuse. Everyone ignored me as I stood back and covered my mouth with my hand.

The next day, the instructors and trainees didn't even try to stifle their hee-haws concerning me. After Lieutenant Kuhn, Deal, and I had gone to the beach, where we swam some and threw sand at one another, Kuhn playfully shoved me while we were washing off the dirt at our camp and I fell backwards into some concertina wire, razor-sharp, coiled barbed wire. It suddenly occurred to me that I should enliven Doc Marshall a little. Seizing the opportunity, I screamed like a gutshot panther, which, I am told, caused Doc Marshall to spit his cigarette onto his protruding belly. Then, with a sense of urgency, he fell out of his rack cursing, spilling his ashtray, and kicking his butts and beer across the deck.

Suddenly Doc appeared from the hut, waddling toward me with a look of revenge on his puffy face. By then another cigarette was hanging from his thin lips, but his hands were shaking too badly to light it. I realized that my best tactic should be one of humility and pain. I looked at him with a face that clearly begged for sympathy, saying, "Doc, I'm cut bad. I think I need a tourniquet." Apparently he saw through my ruse. If Lieutenant Kuhn hadn't started laughing, I might have gotten away with it.

"The only tourniquet you're gonna get is one around your scrawny neck!" Doc responded. "If I had a large enough needle and syringe and some tetanus vaccine, I'd take great joy in shoving the whole works where the sun don't shine!"

I hung my head and said, "Doc, I thought we were buddies."

I could tell by his expression that he was suddenly feeling guilty. "Yeah, we're buddies all right. Get in the jeep. I'll drive you over to the dispensary and watch them sew you up and poke a few needles in you," he said gruffly. "Actually, your cuts need medical attention at sick bay and the compulsory tetanus shot in the ass."

Later on that afternoon, when we returned to the sea hut, everyone was delighted and amazed that Doc had actually stayed out of his bunk for such a long period of time.

On an evening near the end of March, Deal, both Docs, Bro, and I went to the army PX and bought ten bottles of liquor, ten cases of beer, and two cases of soda pop. After supper at the mess hall we all gathered around our new bar with the unvarnished top, for which I had been elected treasurer, and we drank to our bladders' discontent.

At 2130 hours, Commander Jones and Lieutenant Commander Wayne joined us for a few beers. Pretty soon Wayne revealed a knife with a six-inch blade and challenged us to throw it and make it stick in our plywood door. Deal was the first to toss the knife, but it smacked handle-first against the door and fell to the floor. He tried again with the same results.

In the back of the sea hut, Doc Marshall yelled from his bunk, "Gimme a try, sir?"

I barked back, "Doc, you couldn't shave a guy's crotch without cutting him, much less throw a knife!" Doc Marshall gave me the worst "stink eye" I'd ever received up to that time. Then Doc Riojas attempted the feat twice, and after failing both times, Commander Jones gave it two tries.

Picking the knife up off the floor after the second miss, Lieutenant Commander Wayne chuckled. "I shoulda brought my Arkansas toothpick so you guys could throw a real knife," he said with a grin. He backed away from the door, getting ready to throw his knife at it. "But I figured I'd let you guys try this here little ol' weapon first to see how you'd do." He raised the knife to his ear, paused a second, then flung it at the door. The knife flipped over once in the air, then flipped a quarter turn more before striking its full length against the wood and dropping it to the floor with a clatter.

"Almost!" Wayne chirped, sounding as if he had come closer than anyone else, which he hadn't. He quickly grabbed the knife, looked at me, and sang out, "Your turn, Smitty!"

I didn't really care to throw the knife, but Mr. Wayne stuck it right under my nose and I took it.

"Drill the damn door, Gary," Deal encouraged me as I faced the door from a spot about twenty feet away. Because the blade was sharpened on both sides and the pommel was flush with the grip, I decided to throw it by its handle. I lay the handle in the palm of my right hand, gripping it lightly, palm facing upwards. My feet were spaced evenly and about sixteen inches apart. I held the knife out before me, feeling for its weight and balance as my good friend Mario Martinez in Abilene, Texas, taught me when we were in grade school and junior high school together.

"Oh, look at this, will ya!" bellowed Wayne, chuckling. "This guy thinks he's a pro!"

Ignoring the barb, I took aim and slowly lowered my right arm, continuing to move it behind me until it was at about a forty-five-degree angle to the floor. My left foot moved forward as I swiftly raised the knife until my arm was parallel to the floor. When my left foot and my right hand reached their destinations simultaneously, I released the knife with power. The knife made one clockwise turn and struck the plywood door soundly and decisively, buried there, five feet above the floor.

"Hoo-yah!" I shouted, using the cry adopted by all SEAL teams.

Wayne's mouth dropped open in disbelief, then he exclaimed with great enthusiasm, "Smitty, you must see my Arkansas toothpick!"

I just grinned and went back to tending my beer.

"Hot damn! Herr von Schmidt!" piped up Doc Riojas, clapping his hands together once.

"Damn you, Smitty, you asshole," yelled Doc Marshall with a pleased grin on his face.

I looked at Marshall grinning and said, "I love you, too, Doc."

A couple of nights later, after a night combat surface swimmer reconnaissance with the trainees, all of us met at the club for a USO show. I started drinking double vodkas and orange. Everyone else was drinking heavily, too, and it wasn't long before we were really raising hell.

An Aussie showgirl got Willis up on the stage, and all of us SEALs stood up and yelled hoo-yah every chance we got. I had a fun time, I think. All of the booze flooding through my veins made it a bit difficult to recall exactly how much fun I actually had.

I did remember, however, that later on that night I decided to judo-chop the club's bar. I didn't remember the reason for it. Then later I tried to ram my elbow right through the bar. When I brought my elbow down, I hit a glass ashtray and smashed it to bits. The glass exploded with such force that it cut me below my right wrist and gave me a big gash above my right eye. The glass also sliced into my elbow, but I felt no pain. I should have felt embarrassed, but the liquor saved me from feeling anything negative at all. Of course, it was the liquor that got me messed up both mentally and physically in the first place.

The next morning, as I cleaned up the hut and dealt with

a head-pounding hangover, one of the LDNN instructors walked in and told me some terrible news. One of our trainees had gone to Dung Island and somehow ended up in hand-to-hand combat with a VC. The VC ended up pulling out a pistol and shooting the trainee in the back of the head.

I sat down on my bed, shook the cobwebs from my head, and decided it was time for me to get my act together and set a better example of how a seasoned warrior should act, to show the trainees how to become real warriors and some of the toughest men alive. It was time to do so, for Hell Week was about to begin.

CHAPTER FIVE

Hell Week was a five-and-a-half-day physical marathon during which the trainees were directed by their instructors through a rigorous and unsparing test of their ability, endurance, and motivation. While getting perhaps only six to eight hours of sleep throughout the whole week, the trainees were pushed to run about seventy miles, carry an IBS for twenty miles, swim ten miles, and paddle a hundred miles, always in seven-man boat crews and in competition with all other boat crews. Designated sleeping periods lasted just twenty to thirty minutes, and only winning crews that made no mistakes were allotted the full time to doze. The idea behind Hell Week was to separate the men from the boys, the strong from the weak, and to drive the human body to such a degree that individualism perished in that no one person could survive without the help of the rest of the boat crew. To "graduate," every ounce of strength was required, along with teamwork. Navy SEALs are unique in that they understand that their strength as a team is based on togetherness—nonconformity is not tolerated. A standard maxim applied directly to us: "You're only as strong as the weakest man and only as fast as the slowest man."

My own personal experience with Hell Week took place in UDT Training Class 36 at the Naval Amphibious Base in Coronado, California, in September 1965. There I was introduced to the infamous mudflats in the Silver Strand in San Diego, where the Coronado Cays are now located. The mudflats was an old sewage area where the watery muck was two to four feet deep. On two days during Hell Week,

instructors Chief McNally, SM3 Barney House (affection-
ately known as "The Ripper"), GMG1 Enoch, PO1
"Friendly" Frederickson, BMC A1 "I'm your friend" Huey,
and BM2 "Whop-a-Hoh" (that is, half Indian and half
Whop) Olivera temporarily cleansed themselves of all
anger, wrath, bitterness, unforgiveness, vindictiveness, spite-
fulness, revenge, and other unmentionable forms of depravity at the flats on Class 36.

There are few things worse than being a "sacrificial
lamb." There was no doubt our demonic instructors were
trying to separate the sheep from the goats. It didn't take us
long to learn we had better start "baa'ing" in unison like
scapegoats if we were to survive. There was no room for
sheep in the outfit. We had volunteered for the ordeal, so
we knew we had better pretend to enjoy it with smiles on
our mud-covered faces and a joyful "baa" of content on our
lips.

The instructors were masters of harassment, deceit, and
intimidation while directing IBS boat crew competitions in
the mud. For the better part of two days, I was forced to
swim and crawl and race in the foul-smelling flats. We
even had a diving competition into the muck. Naturally,
two student lifeguards were always stationed nearby. Some
trainee divers were stuck upside down with legs flailing the
air. Whop-a-Hoh refused to let the lifeguards rescue any
trainee until the diver's legs stopped flailing. He said it
wouldn't be safe to rescue the "white-eyes" till then.

Our second day at the mudflats brought our morale to its
lowest ebb during Hell Week. Unfortunately, "The Ripper"
had sensed our weakness and delighted in casting rocks,
driftwood, clods, and sand at our faces and into our mouths.
As we sat in muck up to our chests, Chief "I'm your
friend" Huey directed Friendly Frederickson to cast our box
lunches into our midst. What a friend we had in "good ole
Al"! As we scrambled for our rapidly disappearing box
lunches, "The Ripper" continued his bombardment with
amazing accuracy.

The mudflats was no place for a weak heart or a weak

stomach. There was nothing more appetizing than a ham
sandwich covered with mud and human dung. It was a terrible meal. Our favorite, Whop-a-Hoh, danced with delight
up and down the beach, screaming threats of scalpings and
cannibalism.

One hundred sixteen men started Class 36 and only thirty
graduated. No wonder they called that Hell Week! Memories to warm the heart.

At 2200 hours on March 29, 1970—the evening of
Easter Sunday—Hell Week began for the LDNN trainees. I
wasn't there for the start, as the instructors and advisers
were on shifts and the first shift called for me to get a good
night's sleep. While I slept, the trainees were busy paddling
around all night and into the next morning in their IBS
boats. Then, from 0400 to 0500 hours, they spent their time
running.

Reveille was at 0600 hours, and after breakfast I shaved,
made coffee, and cleaned some of my gear while the trainees had PT and finally chow.

At 0800 hours, I joined the trainees as they hoisted the
IBS boats and carried them one and a half miles to the
northeastern beach. They put the boats in the water and
paddled down around the south point of the peninsula and
into the little cove of the base's southern beach. After paddling around a while, they paddled out of the cove to the
west and around the point of entrance into Cam Ranh Bay,
finishing at the Navy EOD detachment shop, which was located about a mile from our camp. During the lunch that
followed, I was relieved by my good buddy Doc "Dunlap"
Marshall.

I slept a couple of hours, lifted weights, and took a
shower. After chow and a couple more hours of sleep, I
walked to an abandoned village where the trainees were
practicing inserting by IBS. The VN instructors had the
men practice hiding their rubber boats, then had them re-
connoiter different areas of responsibility. Each boat crew
was being graded as to its attention to security, detail, team-

work, command and control, etc. The winning boat crew—
if there was one—would get an extra ten minutes of rest at
the appointed time.

At 2315 hours, under the light of a full moon, we paddled the IBS boats to Repair, just inside Cam Ranh Bay and
on the west side of the naval base, where we ate mid-rats
and allowed the trainees to doze for twenty minutes. Then
we returned to our camp, left the boats on shore, and
started running. I ran with the trainees, content to stay with
the middle of the pack until PO1 Manh eased up to me,
saying, "Let's go!" Then he sped up his pace and rapidly
pulled away from me. He knew I was a good runner but he
didn't know how good.

Manh reminded me of how the NVA/VC were always
probing our military base defenses, their objective being to
test our strength and covertly uncover our weaknesses, that
is, response time, determination, preparedness, morale, etc.
But Manh didn't know that in March 1966, during the
UDT-12 Team Olympics, I won the twelve-and-a-half-mile
run down the Silver Strand to a former naval auxiliary
communication unit near the Mexican border. I was a fast
runner, and I had no doubt as to the outcome of this race
with Manh.

As I decided to step it up and catch Manh, my body felt
strong and responded well to the up-tempo pace. Manh had
been positioned five yards ahead of me in the night when
I dashed into a higher gear, and ten seconds later I was
moving past him and kicking sand back at him. Manh re-
acted to my sudden surge by increasing his speed, which I
counteracted with my own burst.

I ran hard for half a minute before looking back to note
Manh's position, but in the darkness I didn't see him. A
grin of contentment swept across my face as I looked forward again and cranked up my speed one more notch just
to make things final and to bury Manh in defeat.

Manh was the best swimmer and I was the best runner.
I thought maybe I could convince him that we should have

a combination run, swim, and obstacle course race to see who was the best overall.

After another fast quarter of a mile, I backed off and just cruised for a half mile before stopping and turning around to wait for Manh. About two minutes passed before someone showed up, and it wasn't Manh. Manh wasn't the second to appear, either; he was the seventh. He had pressed too hard and his legs had given out enough that the trainees had caught and passed him in the last few hundred meters.

I was proud of the trainees for their motivation and endurance. They had had no more than two hours of sleep in forty-three activity-filled hours.

Next, the boat crews started patrolling to the park at the foot of the mountain northwest of the base. The walk was only about two miles. When we arrived at the park, the men were allowed to sleep for a grand twenty minutes. The mosquitoes were terrible, but none of the trainees let the bloodsuckers bother them. So, while the men crashed, the skeeters had lunch. Since I had little need of sleep, I killed every mosquito that showed interest in me.

After I had a hundred KIAs credited to my account, I helped the VN instructors wake the trainees. We patrolled to the road back to the base and one of the instructors ordered a footrace to the beach behind the Officers' Club. This time I jogged in the middle of the pack without any challenges from the VN instructors.

Once at the beach, most of the trainees were allowed to sit in the sand and sing. But the slowest five had to stand waist-deep in the surf for half an hour. When they came out of the water, all five had chattering teeth.

At 0400 hours, I walked to our sea hut and woke Doc Marshall, who relieved me. I hit the rack as Doc waddled out to support the harassment of the trainees.

Hell Week moved along rather softly, actually, as only three trainees had quit after two and a half days. Back on the Strand, where Hell Week was run strictly by concerned instructors of House, Frederickson, Al Huey, and Olivera's repute, these VN trainees would have tossed in the towel by the end of the first day.

At 0800 hours on Wednesday, April 1, the instructors decided to toughen the testing by directing the trainees to climb a two-hundred-meter-high hill that was overgrown with thick brush, thorns, wait-a-minute bushes, and cacti. The foliage was so dense and prickly that it would've been tough for a rabbit to make its way to the top, let alone a human being. Before we departed, I reminded the trainees to keep a sharp watch for cobras, mambas, bamboo vipers, and VC booby traps.

"When we reach our destination [a large boulder near the top] we'll paint SEAL on it," I told the men, trying to encourage them. Gradually, as we hiked upward, the men's tired eyes began to show some concern. I smiled and told them, "I'll lead the way."

Two of the boat crews didn't make it to the large boulder fast enough to suit the instructors so they were sent off to scale another formidable hill. The rest of the trainees and I painted the large boulder, then patrolled to a little park area north of the base and were allowed to relax beneath a large old mango tree.

While PO1 Manh, PO2 Qua, and I waited for the others to join us, I got into a conversation with Qua about the progress and the potential of the trainees. Because Qua was the easiest to talk with, I directed my thoughts to him. "Qua, if you had the opportunity to be an LDNN platoon leading petty officer and had your pick of these trainees, which ones would you choose?"

Qua looked at Manh, then at me, and quickly named ten of the best trainees of the class, which included Ensign Son.

I grinned, then said, "I would have chosen the same men. I hope to have the opportunity to operate with them and you soon.

"Have you ever operated in Dinh Tuong Province in the delta?" I asked.

Qua said, "No."

"Well," I said, "I understand that Tu Ta Hiep will be assigning an LDNN platoon there in the near future. Maybe we'll have the opportunity to operate together with Tu Uy Son." Qua nodded.

I liked Ensign Son. He had a quiet strength about him. He was observant, he controlled his boat crew well, and, most of all, he listened to instruction and recommendations.

As the fourteen trainees who had been sent off for additional climbing jogged toward us after surviving the second hill, I saw that some of them had scratches across their faces. The looks on their faces didn't come close to resembling happiness, pride, or the thrill of victory through teamwork. I chuckled to myself, remembering the outward look and the inward feeling well.

The instructors knew that their men were ready to fold, so they gave the men a break by letting them sit down and have chow for thirty minutes. Toward the end of the timeout, the majority of the trainees seemed to rally, which led to the decision to move them to the beach for a swim while wearing their greens and helmets. That was when two more of the men gave up the chase and quit. About that time I was relieved for the day by the everlively Doc Marshall.

The last three days of Hell Week were strenuous, but only two more men admitted defeat and withdrew from the program. The trainees were put through paddle races of four hours each, footraces, recon exercises, and other tortures. My favorite event occurred on Friday, when the trainees were in IBSs trying to knock one another into the water. All of the officers and many enlisted men were watching and taking pictures. Like the majority of the human race, we navy guys always enjoyed being entertained at the expense of other people. And I must admit, I laughed pretty hard when one of the trainees got slapped in the head with a paddle and was sent flying into the water, his arms flailing and punching at the air.

My least favorite event turned out to be a four-hour paddling race between the IBS crews. I decided to join and help a crew that had had one of its men quit, and I ended up paddling with all my might for the last two hours of the race because two of the men became useless due to exhaustion. I knew we either had to get moving or miss chow, so I paddled like crazy. And even though we still ended up finishing a stunning second in the race, I was burned red all over by the sun except in the one place on a person's body where the sun doesn't shine.

On the last day, Saturday, I cleared with Security for Rio and me to recon a beach about one and a half kilometers southeast of the base. We climbed up a canyon and down into a valley with a most gorgeous beach. On the southwestern edge of the beach, there was an old French bunker which I explored. The main porthole for a machine gun had a surprisingly small field of fire.

While Rio and I walked just below the berm line, I noticed holes in the sand two to three feet wide and a foot deep. I realized that sea turtles had buried their eggs there. We also saw fresh monkey tracks and boar excrement everywhere, along with tree rubbings where deer had shined up their antlers. I was hoping we'd find some tiger tracks; we knew some were around because their roars had been heard a couple of nights earlier. But there were no tracks. In case we did see a tiger, I was carrying an M-14 with several twenty-round magazines.

The next day, all of us worked on the camp, setting it up for the Hell Week party. All but seven trainees had survived the punishing week, and after a restorative half day of sleep, the men were ready to celebrate their collective achievement. They pooled their money and hired a ten-person band from Nha Trang for later that evening. Meanwhile, I took Willis and Manh with an IBS to the south beach to do a little fishing for the party. Since fish, rice, and beer sounded real good to Willis and Manh, they had volunteered to help me.

We paddled out into the bay a couple hundred meters, then I slipped on my fins and face mask. I gave Willis the MK-26 frag grenade I had taped to a two-pound block of

TNT, then, holding my face mask with my right hand, fell over the side into the water.

"Dat's some mighty fine-lookin' bait!" Willis said with a grin as I treaded water. The gold star in his front tooth flashed as he held up the explosive.

"No fish can resist it!" I replied, then moved slowly away from the side of the rubber boat. I continued swimming slowly on the surface, paralleling the beach, looking down and watching for schools of fish. I could see an easy hundred feet into the crystal clear water, until the bottom sloped off into the murky depths. I concentrated my attention on areas that were no more than seventy-five feet deep, which was my maximum working depth.

It didn't take long before I swam over the top of a large concentration of fish. I quickly waved to my mates, who paddled quietly up to me. I grabbed hold of the IBS and pulled myself out of the water, gently kicking with my fins. Sitting on the starboard main tube and near Willis, I reached for the "bait." Still smiling, he gave the grenade–TNT combination explosive to me.

"I've always been a very successful fisherman," I said before pulling the pin on the grenade. I tossed the boosted grenade into the water directly above the school of fish. The fuse delay varied between six and seven seconds, giving the grenade time enough to reach the bottom, sixty to seventy feet at that point.

We looked at one another, then concentrated on the surface where the charge had entered the water. We excitedly counted the seven seconds. Then we heard the underwater *karumph* and felt the reverberation of the detonation through the rubber raft. Shortly, a small blurp of water, bubbles, and gases erupted on the surface where the deadly charge had first entered the water.

I immediately put on my face mask, grabbed my large mesh underwater game bag from the floor mat of the IBS, then eased into the water. Expectantly, I looked down toward the area of carnage. Wow! Fish were lying all over the bottom. Contrary to what I used to think, fish killed that way sank.

I hyperventilated three times, then dove at a slight angle directly toward the dead fish, kicking hard with my fins. Most of the fish were lying on their sides; some were quivering and moving slowly in circles. Some of them weighed as much as five pounds and were very beautiful in color. I kept a watch out because it wouldn't take sharks long to associate underwater explosions with food, that is, fish and humans.

I happily started shoving fish into the bag as fast as I could. "Two for me and one for them, one for them and three for me, four for me and one for them," I thought while giggling. I was especially delighted when I found a nice one that looked similar to our catfish. I knew Bro Willis would want that one.

Suddenly, I felt a terrible desire to get some fresh air. I had forgotten how hard I was going to have to work to get my heavy prizes to the surface. I shoved hard off the coral formation and kicked urgently for the surface, oddly remembering that someone had once said, "The Lord takes care of fools and sailors." As I climbed upward through the water, I thought, "I hope He does, 'cause I'm not leaving the fruits of my labor to waste!" Besides, my image was at stake again! Manh would never let me forget it if I came up empty-handed.

By the time I had made it to within ten feet of the surface, spots were swimming before my eyes, which meant I was close to blacking out. When my head broke the surface, I inhaled and exhaled rapidly while hanging on to the side of the IBS.

"Don't drown yourself, for cryin' out loud!" Willis snapped at me as I gasped for air.

Ignoring him for a moment, I gave him the handle of the bag of fish. After he pulled the heavy bag into the IBS and dumped the contents out onto the floor mat, I said, "I'm just trying to make it look good. This is a piece of cake."

When Willie saw the five-pound catfish as it fell out of the bag, his eyes got big.

"Oh, yeah!" he sang. "Ah splib's treasure!"

Grinning, he handed me the empty bag. I hyperventilated again, then dove. I didn't bother to count the fish or giggle this time, quickly stuffing them into the bag until it was full, then beginning the ascent.

After seven dives, I had picked up about one hundred fish. I was getting the spots before my eyes again during the last two dives. I told Willie, "I'm calling it quits pretty soon. There's only a few little ones left and I'm seeing polka dots pretty bad!"

Willie looked at me and laughed. "Want me da take over?" he asked kiddingly as he emptied the bag for the seventh time.

I sucked in a big mouthful of water, then squirted a stream with perfect accuracy. The water smacked him directly in the eyes and he shook his head, coughing and swearing.

Laughing, I said, "Take over? You can't even handle a few drops of rain!" I reached over the spray tube and grabbed my bag for another dive.

"You honky bastard!" he howled at me. I quickly ducked underwater.

A minute and a half later, I eased back to the surface on the opposite side of the IBS from Willie. Before he realized I was back, I yelled, "Hey, Bro, what's happening?"

"I was hopin' you wasn't comin' back," he said with a big grin, then he asked, "How many fish you got?"

"About half a bag of little ones. The pickin's is gettin' a mite rough an' my po' head is full o' spots." I laughed, handing him the bag, then continued, "I can probably get another half bag of little ones. I know how our Vietnamese brothers love the little fish, huh, Manh?"

Manh started grinning and licking his lips, kind of reminding me of an opossum eating a green persimmon, the way his lips were puckered up. I looked at Willie with a wink, and asked, "Did you ever see a 'possum eatin' per-simmons, Bro?"

I thought he was going to fall out of the IBS. He laughed, spit and sputtered, and finally said, "You best get back on down dere an' get da last o' dem 'possum fish fo' dey gets away."

After one more dive, the ninth, we had enough fish to feed us for two parties.

While we paddled back, Manh was grinning from ear to ear. He finally said, "I like fish with you two! Many fish, many funny!"

"Yeah, this is what I call a hard way to make a living. Can you imagine, we even get paid for doing this!" I said.

As I paddled, I decided to tell a story to reinforce our festive mood. "This fishin' with a grenade reminds me of Demo Dick Marcinko's SEAL Team Two platoon in '67 to '68 at Binh Thuy near Can Tho in the delta. They had a pet monkey." Willie looked at me quizzically. Continuing, I said, "This monkey fought all the time with their pet dog, just in a playful manner, but one day they were bitin' at each other's mouths when they suddenly just stopped and stared at one another. It's like the world stood still for several seconds." I stopped paddling for a minute and moved my fins and face mask away from my left foot.

Straightening up, I said, "Then the monkey just kinda slowly reached into his mouth and slipped out a tooth that the dog had somehow pulled out. He stared at the tooth for a moment, then looked at the dog, the dog looked at him, then the monkey tossed the tooth behind him and the two went back to bitin' each other again."

Willis and Manh laughed.

The three of us giggled over the story all the way in to the beach, happy with our bounty and with each other. Hell Week was over and all would celebrate with a heavenly feast.

CHAPTER SIX

There must have been something in the air. Some kind of head virus. That was the only thing I could figure was causing irritability among the men over the next few days. That was the only possible explanation as to why I would get into a fistfight with Deal, who was eighty pounds heavier than me. Some invisible force had affected or infected my brain. Still, it probably was Deal's temperamental behavior that pushed me over the edge. After all, I had to blame it on something.

Four nights after the Hell Week party, Deal smarted off to me while we were outside the VN trainees' sea hut. "If you guys would get off your dead butts I could get more work done around here. Instead, you're leaving all your crap details for me," he growled. "If it wasn't for me, you guys would still be shittin' behind the sand dunes and sleepin' in a tent. You're nothin' but a lazy bunch of overrated bums."

"What!" I said, feeling my anger turning to rage.

"You heard what I said!"

That was all she wrote. I lost it right there. I had a flashlight in my hand and I threw it at him, hoping to bean him right between the running lights. Deal ducked. The flashlight sailed over his head by inches. Its missing the mark made me even more furious.

Losing control of myself, I flew into Deal and tried to take him to the ground. That was a bad mistake; we *both* fell to the ground, him on top. He was a powerful man and much stronger than me. His weight didn't help me any, either. Instantly, Deal reached down and grabbed me by the throat with both hands. I felt the strength of his shoulders all the way down to the tips of his fingers as he squeezed.

Why was it that I had to lose my temper with a guy who was much bigger and stronger than me? Why hadn't I kept my distance and kicked and punched him until I wore him down? There is always somebody bigger, better, smarter, or stronger than you, but I had to pick on a guy who was both bigger and stronger. Considering my position, he was a dang sight smarter than I was, too. For some reason I remembered an epitaph written on a fellow's tombstone in Arizona:

> Here lies Lester Moore
> Four slugs from a .44
> No Les, no Moore

When I felt cartilage near my voice box break, I began to get concerned. Deal was making mincemeat out of me. That called for drastic measures, and besides, my image was at stake again.

"If I'm not careful," I thought, "this image thing is going to get me killed." Since Deal had my right arm pinned, I raised my left hand and drove my thumb deep into his right eye socket. My thumb was buried all the way to the knuckle. I could've popped out his eyeball in an instant, but before I went that far, I decided to get a big mouthful of his right arm and take a hunk out of it; at least the doctors could sew that up. As my teeth broke through the skin, Deal let out a god-awful scream. "Ahhhhhhhhhhh!" he yelled. "I quit! I quit!" He started trying to get away from me, but I hung on to his arm with my teeth like a badger and maintained my thumb in his eye socket.

Within a nanosecond, we were surrounded by the VN trainees and instructors. Then my image was really at stake! Finally, with a powerful lunge, Deal pulled away from me and ran off into the night, headed toward the base. I didn't know it then, but I would never see Deal again. He had been an administrative fellow attached to us from the Naval Support Facility because he was a good cumshaw man, but he had made his last acquisition in my neck of the woods, so to speak. He must have talked his way out of working for us any longer, which was quite a cumshawing feat in itself. I stood up, spitting the blood from my mouth and wiping the drippings on my shirt. The Vietnamese returned quietly to the sea hut.

As for me, I never heard a word from the top about the fight and I never said a word about it. Besides, I could barely talk for a couple of days. My throat was mighty sore, but I didn't have anybody check it. It was months before the cartilage grew back together.

The next day, Lieutenant Kuhn got back from NavForV in Saigon, and he told me that another LDNN had been killed on Dung Island in IV Corps near the mouth of the Mekong River. BM1 Rogers of SEAL Team Two was the LDNN adviser with the LDNN platoon when they got surrounded by the VC. They finally received an emergency extraction, but not in time to save the wounded LDNN.

That night I was awakened at around 2330 hours by a fight in our sleeping quarters. I thought Willis was involved, so I jumped out of my rack to stop it. Sure enough, Willis was on top of Rio. Doc Marshall was already trying to break up the fight, so there was little need for me to get involved, especially since I really liked both of them. Besides, I could still hear fists hitting home, and after all, my severe throat injury wasn't totally healed yet. "Let Dunlap do the dirty work for a change," I thought. I crawled back into bed. But that fight reaffirmed my belief that there must have been something in the air.

Its effects continued that night as I closed my eyes and saw myself back on the night of June 23, 1969, with the PRU. I was patrolling with seventeen Vietnamese, single file across rice paddy dikes in the Sam Giang District of Dinh Tuong Province in IV Corps. Our mission was to capture the individuals attending a village-level VCI political meeting in a specific hootch. The Communist party secretary of that village was to preside over the meeting.

Our area of operation consisted of two square kilometers that were near the U.S. Army 9th Infantry Division Headquarters at their Dong Tam base. In case sector and subsector Tactical Operation Centers (TOCs) were penetrated, I had also cleared several other AOs about the same time to keep the enemy guessing as to which AO we would be visiting.

We departed My Tho by vehicles just before dark. Sao Lam, my counterpart, was the senior PRU leader. He directed the driver to stop at a particular point on a narrow dirt road. We quietly assembled near the edge of the road in single file and waited for the vehicle to depart the area. The point man was forward, Sao Lam was second, I was third, and the radioman, carrying our only radio, was fourth, followed by the remaining fourteen men. Each man carefully checked his gear and weapon. Most of the PRU were carrying AK-47s and RPD belt-fed machine guns. One man was carrying an M-79 grenade launcher. I was carrying my faithful M-16/XM-148 combination rifle and grenade launcher.

As the last of the evening's orange glow disappeared over the horizon, we started northerly patrol into the coconut trees and secondary growth on a narrow footpath. The Milky Way was very prominent and beautiful. Since my childhood, the Milky Way had always represented mysteries far beyond my imagination. As always, it was an awesome view.

We didn't have a moon that night, but we had plenty of starlight. Shortly, we crossed another dirt road. In the center of it was lying a large-bodied viper about three feet in length. He hissed loudly at us, indicating a bad attitude and temperament, making the hair stand up on the back of my neck. The snake looked like a Malayan pit viper. It reminded me of the bad-tempered cottonmouthed water moccasins in central Texas I saw when I was a kid. During the seven-year drought in the fifties, many stock tanks were going completely dry in the countryside. I had spent many a happy day shooting bullfrogs, turtles, water snakes, and an occasional moccasin. The worst part about retrieving the bullfrogs from the watery muck was worrying that a cottonmouth would bite me. I especially didn't want to be bitten in specific areas of my naked midsection. Hung, who was my interpreter and radioman, stood behind me, leaned forward, and whispered into my ear, "Bad omen. Bad luck for us. No good."

Shortly after that, we reached a series of flooded rice paddies. Sao Lam and the point man whispered to each other while pointing toward a dark wooded area a couple of hundred meters directly ahead of us, or twelve o'clock from our position. We continued in single file on the rice dikes, zigzagging across the paddies and toward the wooded area.

When we were within fifty meters of the wooded area, the point man passed back the word to Sao Lam that the VC were just ahead of us! Within seconds, the enemy opened up on us with automatic fire and grenade or rocket launchers. The point man was immediately shot in the chin and stomach. He was still breathing, but there was nothing we could do for him until we were able to suppress the enemy by fire and movement. We immediately returned our maximum rate of fire and Sao Lam had six men start a right-flanking movement for two reasons: We had to get to the wooded area for more cover and concealment; and we would have to be very aggressive if we were to survive. Surprisingly, the enemy's rate of fire decreased.

Suddenly, an 81-mm mortar illumination round ejected its charge directly over us. The casing whistled on past us and into the darkness while the parachute deployed with the illuminating charge burning brightly as it oscillated over our exposed heads, casting ominous shadows all around us and occasionally emitting an incendiary sputter as it drifted slowly past us. Stunned, we dug even deeper into the rice paddy, which was flooded with about twelve inches of water. Our night vision was gone and our rate of fire decreased.

As the enemy quickly increased their rate of fire, I realized that we were in contact with friendly forces! I shouted to Sao Lam what was happening and told him we must head for the tree line, which was about six hundred meters across flooded rice paddies to our left flank. I quickly grabbed the hand piece to the PRC-25 radio from Hung and tried to radio sector TOC to have the friendlies cease fire. Of course, by this time the handset was wet and inoperable. And we didn't have an extra! There was no way I could communicate with the outside world.

I yelled to Sao Lam over the terrific noise, "We've got to get out of here, now! The friendlies will be calling in 81-mm mortar HE rounds and/or have helicopter gunships overhead in minutes! Have the men cease fire!" At that point we stopped firing. I was sure sorry the PRUs were carrying AK-47s and RPD machine guns. Communist weapons had their own distinct sounds and their tracers are a different color. I knew the friendlies had to be convinced that we were the enemy.

As Sao Lam started passing the word to the rest of the men, 40-mm HE projectiles started detonating above our heads into a tree. Sao Lam, myself, and Hung were directly under that small tree of about ten feet in height and hiding behind the paddy dike. The noise was deafening. Hung was wounded several times. Had I been hit, I wouldn't have known it. I don't believe a big fellow with an eight-pound sledgehammer could have driven a sixteen-penny nail into my butt at that point. It didn't take me long to figure out that this was a true cause with a sense of urgency with a negative twist and to hell with my image. There was a time to fight and a time to be flexible. In the teams we planned, trained, and rehearsed our missions carefully and with as much foresight as possible. However, there were occasions when our best efforts went awry and we had to play it by ear and draw upon hindsight. In other words, we had to be flexible, stick together, and not panic.

We began crawling to our left, in a westerly direction. We barely made out our seemingly impossible destination, the dark outline of the palm trees on the horizon, while the friendlies had to have been having a ball. They kept track of our westward movement through starlight scopes. Each time we came to another rice dike, we had to crawl over it, exposing ourselves and our position. The friendlies started firing M-72 LAAWs at us and continued automatic weapons and 40-mm HE fire. Yessir, it must have been quite a turkey shoot. Fortunately, the friendlies were terrible shots.

We had crawled for about three hundred meters through flooded rice paddies and continuous friendly fire when we heard the *whump-whump-whump* of the Huey gunship helicopters flying over our position. My heart started having murmurs and my gut started churning.

I remembered the nights in the Rung Sat Special Zone when we called in the Navy Seawolf gunships to strafe enemy positions with miniguns and 2.75-inch rockets. What a fearsome sight it was to behold, and I wasn't on the receiving end, either. Well, that night was my night! "This ought to really round out my combat experiences," I thought. If I survived this one, I thought I ought to win a few beers on it. And if I'd known how, I would have been open to a much closer relationship with God. About that time the helicopters were circling almost directly over our position and they dropped a white phosphorus grenade to the ground. The grenade's thirty-five-meter bursting radius then became a reference point from which the friendly patrol leader would give the gunships an azimuth from their position to ours. The gunships established their racetrack pattern at a right angle from the friendlies and demonstrated their firepower at our expense. The gunships continued to circle nearer and nearer to our line of desperately crawling, mud-covered individuals. It was a nightmarish and exhausting experience to crawl over five hundred meters through flooded and muddy rice paddies with weapons and web gear getting in the way and slowing us down while getting shot at the same time.

I could tell that the helos were about to make their firing runs right on top of us by the way they had adjusted their racetrack pattern relative to the position of the friendlies. It was amazing how much a fellow could learn when he was about to die.

We were still about one hundred meters from the coconut tree plantation when I jumped up and screamed in Vietnamese, followed by various expletives for emphasis, "Go! Go! Go! Hurry up! Hurry up! Hurry up!" I sprinted for all I was worth for the tree line. It was every man for himself.

We had just gotten to the tree line when the helicopters made their firing run from south to north along the inboard edge of the tree line. They knew exactly where we were. When I reached the tree line, I dove to the ground as the M-60 machine guns opened up and the 2.75-inch rockets started flying north, toward where I was lying. I wouldn't have bet a Confederate dollar that I'd survive.

I gritted my teeth and buried my face in the mud as the rocket explosions and ground vibrations came progressively closer and got more violent. I knew that the next rocket would be right on target and I'd soon be in hell where I belonged. Strangely, it didn't come! But my delight was short-lived; the helicopters swung around again for another run. Again I lay there waiting for the messenger of death to blow my body into a pink mist.

The helicopters made a total of four rocket and M-60 runs, and when they ran out of 2.75-inch rockets, they continued to shoot M-60s in our vicinity. I was almost tempted to return fire but I couldn't find my weapon in the dark. I had thrown it away from me when I dove into the tree line. There's a dumb shit born every minute and that night I was one of them.

Suddenly the helicopters were gone and there was total silence. All I could hear was a ringing in my ears. It was also totally black. It reminded me of the times I was scuba diving for ship hatches in Da Nang Harbor and Subic Bay in '66. The water was so muddy and dark I couldn't see my hand up against my face mask.

It must have taken me fifteen minutes to find my weapon. When I did find it, I also located a lightweight two-foot-long limb which I used in front of me to probe for booby trap trip wires.

Gradually, my hearing returned. I began to hear voices within a couple hundred meters. I moved cautiously toward them. The closer I got, the more I realized it was the PRU excitedly talking. I knew there was an ARVN (Army of the Republic of Vietnam) outpost nearby but I wasn't sure just how close I was to it. I didn't want to blunder into their claymore mines and trip flares, either. Finally, I recognized Sao Lam's high-pitched voice and his unbroken stream of cursing. It was a sound for sore ears. I yelled to my men and let them know I was coming in.

When I reached them, we were all elated to have survived. Not one of us had gotten killed or wounded by the helicopter firing runs. It was amazing! I then used the outpost radio to call TOC and give them our situation report. I requested they give us continual 81-mm illumination rounds until we could return to the ambush site and get our wounded point man.

I found out that we had been ambushed by an ARVN platoon and a U.S. 9th platoon. Considering that we were far outnumbered, we were lucky we didn't all get killed. It was a long walk back to get the point man. He had died while we were crawling for the tree line.

What I hadn't known was that units of the U.S. 9th and the ARVN 7th divisions nightly saturated the areas surrounding the huge Dong Tam military base with a combination of point and area ambushes. Apparently, TOC was to grant AO clearances of only one and two square kilometers. Considering that a square kilometer is approximately 1,100 yards by 1,100 yards, it was not hard to imagine that two friendly units could inadvertently blunder into each other during a black night and with no prominent land features visible under the best of conditions. In these circumstances one's compass man and pacer* had better not have a margin of error over fifty meters or so.

Shortly after daybreak, we finally made it back to the road where we had inserted the previous evening. We were a sad-looking bunch of men, and very tired. I went to Sao Lam and put my arm around his shoulders as we waited for a company truck to come and get us. We just sat there. No one was talking.

We never did operate in that area again.

After running the hair-raising story through my mind, I was able to relax and fall to sleep. The next day, I and everybody else seemed more settled. We were back to normal. Perhaps it was due to Rio's getting a cat and two of her kittens from one of the Seabees. The mere sight and the playfulness of the animals touched hearts and had a soothing effect on a bunch of macho wired-up he-men. A group of us took but a minute to come up with names for the cats. We called them SEAL 1, SEAL 2, and UDT.

*The man assigned to count paces in order to estimate the distance a patrol has moved.

CHAPTER SEVEN

Everyone's morale greatly improved a couple of days later when the advisers and trainees practiced jumping from a UH-1 Huey helicopter into the water (called "cast and recovery" in the teams) in the southern cove adjacent to the base. The training evolution began with Lieutenant Kuhn, Willis, Louis Boisvert (of UDT-11), and me climbing into the helo from the sandy beach just below the Officers' Club. Lieutenant Kuhn, as the castmaster, carefully briefed the pilot. Kuhn instructed him to fly about twenty feet over the surface of the water at twenty knots. Slowly, the Huey lifted into the sky to begin a day of training, laughter, and fun.

I slipped my fins and face mask straps onto my web belt, which also included my knife and MK-13 day/night flare, and fastened the belt around my waist. I was also wearing my UDT life jacket. I grinned at Willie and Lou as I sat at the edge of the starboard door with my feet hanging out, then glanced down into the clear blue water.

I looked to Lieutenant Kuhn for his hand signal to exit the helo. I had volunteered to go first because I loved to stand in the door and look outside. It excited me. Also, by going first, there were less chances for screwups, especially when we made our night, combat equipment, static-line parachute jumps. Suddenly, Lieutenant Kuhn's right hand pointed emphatically to starboard, indicating that the good times had begun. Placing my feet on the starboard strut, I instantly exited the helo. I kept my eyes parallel to the surface of the water, holding my arms directly above my head and compensating for the forward movement of the helo. After entering the water I immediately returned to the surface, giving a thumbs-up to show that I was okay to Lieutenant Kuhn.

After me, Willis, Boisvert, and finally Kuhn leaped out of the helo with shouts and flailing of arms. We all loved cast and recovery! Then the safety boat, a motorized IBS with Rio in it, picked us up and took us to the beach.

The VN instructors and trainees were on the beach and had been watching our performance. Our purpose for going first was for "show and tell." In other words, we'll show you how to do it, then we'll tell you how to do it. However, some of the trainees were uncertain about the motives of the screams and flailing of arms and legs. The Vietnamese were very superstitious and inclined to look for signs and omens of the past, present, and future for answers to unknowns, and they were prone to develop their own very individual interpretations of these signs and omens.

The helo landed on the sandy beach with its rotors still turning. Lieutenant Kuhn returned to the helo as castmaster, and Willis, as Kuhn's assistant, accompanied the eight trainees aboard and into the air. Lieutenant Kuhn directed the helo to parallel the beach on an east-to-west approach for casting. The trainees then began exiting the helo at about five-second intervals.

All went well until the last trainee came out of the chopper. Just before he jumped, the pilot goofed by starting to prematurely climb and bank to port (left). The trainee ended up jumping from forty feet and he hit the water with a resounding *plop*. He disappeared beneath the water's surface for a few seconds, and when he finally popped up, he inflated his UDT life jacket just before passing out. Doc Riojas immediately directed the motorized IBS to the trainee, and they pulled him into the boat. Rio gave him mouth-to-mouth for a couple of minutes until they reached the beach, where a resuscitator was put on the trainee, all of which revived the man satisfactorily.

Afterwards, we hooked up our 120-foot rappelling line to the helicopter's deck D-rings, with the line hanging out the starboard door and over the skid. Each man was to hook up and step out onto the skid facing the helo, then release his brake and jump out and away from the helo. Lieutenant Kuhn led the way followed by Qua and Willis.

When my turn came, I asked the pilot to fly higher until the end of the line was about twenty feet from the water. I then rappelled down about 110 feet with minimum breaking, slipped off the line, and fell twenty feet into the water. I just had to get in a little free-falling, even if it was only twenty feet. Afterwards, the trainees enjoyed their first rappel from a helicopter, which was lots of fun for all.

Later that evening, everyone had a few beers and played some volleyball. Then we got out our boxing gloves and some of the men boxed a while. A few of the guys got punched around pretty well, but morale was so high that no one complained.

That evening I finally got to check out Willis's gambling ability. At 1930 hours, Willis and a half dozen base personnel showed up in our hut with a pair of dice. I was very interested. I had never watched a crap game. My dad used to tell me about crap games he and his brother-in-law had gotten into when they were in the Civilian Conservation Corps (CCC) in the thirties in New Mexico, so I watched with interest as they laid a GI blanket on the floor, placing it up against the wall.

"Smitty, here, is jus' watchin' an learnin'. He ain't playin'," Willie explained to his guests.

The men quickly determined the order of rolling the dice, then they inspected each man's dice. The only rules were that both dice had to bounce off the wall and the minimum bet was twenty dollars for each person's roll. Side bets were unrestricted.

Willie, being the senior man, had the honor of leading the group. Betting that Willie would crap out on his first roll, a couple of guys threw out twenty-dollar bills. No one took the bet. All of them were holding large rolls of MPC (Military Payment Certificates) in their hands. Willie's bundle was lying on the edge of the blanket. He stooped while holding the pair of dice snugly in his right fist and gently tossed them onto the blanket, where they lightly bounced off the wall. He didn't appear to rattle them in his fist. Seven was the perfect number to roll.

Before the dice had settled, Joe, a Seabee, yelled, "Snake eyes or boxcars!" The dice turned up three points.

"You might just as well have crapped out, Willis," Joe grinned as he looked at me. "There's only one chance to roll another three."

Willis responded by kneeling down. He picked up his dice again and tossed them softly against the wall. They settled on double aces or snake eyes, costing Willis twenty dollars. He left his bundle on the blanket and backed away so Joe could take his roll. I watched Willis closely but he didn't look at me. I noticed that Willis didn't make any side bets on anybody else's roll, either.

The six enlisted men from the base were all kneeling around the blanket, noisily making side bets, when Lieutenant Kuhn suddenly walked in. They looked up apprehensively, as it was illegal to gamble in the military.

Kuhn looked at Willie solemnly and said, "What's a hat full of MPC doing down there on that blanket?" No one answered, moved, or made a sound. After a long silence, Lieutenant Kuhn asked, "What's the limit?" He then broke into a big grin. Everyone relaxed and continued on with the game.

Joe threw forty dollars onto the blanket, which was shortly covered by another fellow. Joe held his dice in his hand, blew on them, shook them, talked to them, and finally threw them hard against the wall, showing an eight.

"Eighter from Decatur, the county seat of Wise," Joe chanted. He was delighted. He looked at me, saying, "I've got two chances, Smitty." I nodded with a grin. He was obviously a Texan, because Decatur was a few miles north of Fort Worth, my birthplace. Joe threw the dice again and made his eight.

Willis eventually got another turn. He rolled a five, commenting, "Ah fiver in da schoo'house, run whores run." He rolled again and got the five. He then started a winning streak by rolling sevens, then his was followed by Lieutenant Kuhn's own winning streak. The gambling continued intensely for over an hour. Willis and Lieutenant Kuhn kept winning big and usually laid a minimum of forty dollars on the blanket for starters. It didn't take long to separate the men from the boys. The money flowed and changed hands to the point that only two individuals—Kuhn and Willie— were left with any money. I began to realize that Willis was a con man and a good one. I wasn't making any judgments about Lieutenant Kuhn.

Surprisingly, the men from the base left empty-handed with no hard feelings. I offered them several beers each before they left. Shortly thereafter, Lieutenant Kuhn departed for the officers' quarters with five hundred dollars in his wallet. Willis's grin was enormous. The gold star in his tooth gleamed brighter than ever as he folded up his winnings and tucked them into his wallet.

"Well, Smitty," he began, chuckling, "how'd you enjoy watchin' da expert?"

I laughed. "I'm not sure I understood all that was going on, but I know one thing for sure, you and Lieutenant Kuhn are slick gamblers." Shaking my finger at him, I added, "You guys are professionals!"

Willis looked at me, still grinning, but he also shook a finger at me. "Now, now," he playfully reprimanded me, "don't go makin' dose nasty accusations widdout proof. Back in da wild, wild West, I'd a shot you by now."

"Well, hell," I countered, "I would've robbed you fifteen minutes ago and stuck a big Bowie knife in you, layin' your guts on the floor on my way out the door."

Willis smirked. "Yeah, right," he mumbled, lifting his

posterior slightly up from his chair in order to shove his wallet into his back pocket. Then, gesturing toward our new table, he said, "Take a seat, Smitty. I tell you how da make money."

I laughed a little, but I sat down.

"What da hell you laughin' at?" Willis asked, acting slightly offended. "I'm da guy wid four hunerd big ones in my pocket, not you!"

I nodded, acknowledging the truth.

He continued, "Now, do you wanna learn da ropes or not?"

I grinned and kept nodding.

"Now, den," Willis began, lowering his voice so only I would be able to hear him, "you gots to learn how da smuggle green money inta 'Nam without declarin' it, den you exchange it on da black market for MPCs." He glanced around, making sure we were alone. "Trade it on da black market for double da value—like, if you got a hunerd-dollar bill, you trade it for two hunerd dollars back in MPCs."

"That's a one hundred percent profit on the exchange rate," I interjected, liking the sound of it.

Willis gave me a silly grin. "I'm glad da see you can figger, Smitty. Dat's right, it's a hunerd p'cent profit, all right."

I leaned closer to my friend. "How do you smuggle in the greenbacks?"

"When da new SEAL platoons arrives in 'Nam, I tries to always meet dem at Tan Son Nhut Airport." Watching me closely, he continued, "I ask dem if dey has any greenback to get rid of and usually dey does. The last platoon that came in-country gave me over five thou!" He grinned. "Another way is to have someone send you hunerd-dollar bills in da mail. Dat's all dey is to it."

"Well, where do I exchange my money at?" I asked with enthusiasm.

"You gonna kick yoself in da butt when I tells ya," he said as he took a long swig from a Pabst Blue Ribbon beer.

"Well?" I snorted.

"Da Indian tailor 'cross da street from NavForV," he whispered, then he started laughing. There was a gleam in his eyes. "All da officers and enlisted at NavForV exchanges their greenbacks dere. B'tween da gamblin' an' da smugglin', I picked up a cool twenty gran' last tour."

I thanked Willie for the information and started to get up from the table.

"One more thing," Willis said, stopping me. "We gonna play a little dice again in a coupla days. You be dere, an' I make shore you wins some money."

I grinned. "How are you gonna 'make sure'?"

Willis grinned back. "Da dice an' me are da best o' friends. We's always loyal ta each odder, if you know wad I mean." He winked.

Just then Rio walked into the sea hut and came up to us. "Hey, man," he loudly addressed Willis, "I heard you made out like a bandit tonight!"

Willis's facial expression changed instantly from a smile to a scowl. He hated it when someone made a direct comment to him that had a negative connotation. I thought he was going to react angrily, but several tense seconds went by and he didn't say a word. I never did know why there were negatives vibes between Willis and Rio.

Finally, Willis pushed his chair away from the table and stood up, staring at Rio. A grin spread slowly across his face. "I wanna invite you ta our nex' game on Monday night, Doc," Willis said calmly. I couldn't help but grin along with him as I realized Willis had decided to take some of Rio's money.

"Thanks," Rio said innocently.

"You bet," Willis mumbled, leaving us. When he was gone, Rio grabbed me by the arm.

"Is he any good at gamblin'?" he quizzed me. "Did you see him throw the dice?"

"Yeah, I saw him."

"Well?" persisted Rio.

I shook my head. "Hey! I'm out of this! I like both you guys. Make your own decisions Monday night."

Having done about all the advising for the LDNNs that I could do, I was getting anxious to leave the Cam Ranh Bay peninsula and go someplace where I could get involved again in actual combat missions. Lieutenant Kuhn must have read my mind, because a couple days later he called me from Saigon and said he would like me to transfer to Sea Float in An Xuyen Province, where I would advise the Vietnamese Navy's Biet Hai personnel and work with Lieutenant Commander Sphinx (an explosive ordnance [EOD] officer). An Xuyen Province was located just over three hundred miles to the southwest, and the Biet Hai were already setting up house on the northern bank of the Cua Lon River adjacent to Sea Float. Since Sphinx was EOD and had no small-unit tactical training, I would be the field adviser to the Biet Hai VN navy lieutenant, which sounded good to me.

Before I left Cam Ranh in a few days, however, there was money to be made and some more diving to be done. First, I won a slick three hundred dollars that night after Willis took me to the side and told me to bet on him on his first two dice throws. I never found out what his trick was, but he tossed a seven on both of those rolls. Rio had to fork out fifty bucks right off the bat, which Willis gladly took from his hand. I was careful never to place any bets against Willis or Doc. If they got into any more fights, I wasn't going to be a part of it. By the end of the evening, Bro walked away with about six hundred dollars in winnings.

The next day, I went free-diving with Lieutenant Kuhn, Manh, and Qua in the coral reefs. On my first dive, when I was in about fifty feet of water with a speargun in my hands, I saw a huge ray coming toward me along the bottom. It was at least six feet wide and almost five feet long with a tail about two feet in length. Following the ray were two remora. My eyes popped open even wider when

I saw the seven-foot big-headed shark behind the trio of fish.

Since the group was moving along quite slowly, I swam beside them for several feet, then took aim at the ray and shot him with a spear. The shaft penetrated only a couple of inches because I fired from the maximum range of ten feet. Upon impact, the ray shifted into fifth gear and headed out, the shaft falling out of its body. I had to strike for the surface to grab some air.

I went back down and picked the spear off the coral-studded bottom, then proceeded to make several more dives in my hunt for interesting fish. Lieutenant Kuhn and I lucked out and found three cuttlefish in thirty feet of water. I shot one of the ten-armed mollusks with my speargun, but the shaft didn't penetrate the cuttlebone because I had had the shaft charged with only one rubber band. Before I could grab the cuttlefish, it got away.

Lieutenant Kuhn wasted no time in shooting a second cuttlefish. His shaft missed the cuttlebone, but buried itself just beneath the cuttlefish's eye. I quickly grabbed the shaft and thereby caught the cuttlefish, which instantly wrapped all ten of its long tentacles around my hand and forearm. I didn't like the feeling of the suction cups, so I manipulated the fish into my mesh game bag and brushed its tentacles off of me. Then Lieutenant Kuhn and I swam up for air with our catch in tow.

When my head broke out into the sunshine, I gasped for oxygen and started laughing. "Hoo-yah!" I shouted, slapping the surface of the water and making a splash. "That was fun!"

"It was great!" Lieutenant Kuhn chimed in, chuckling at my exuberance. Treading water alongside me, he added, "I'm gonna miss diving with you, Smitty." That said, he started swimming toward Qua and Manh, who were diving together about a hundred meters away.

Lieutenant Kuhn's kind words had struck a chord. I paused a few seconds to let the feeling wash over me as I watched the lieutenant's strong strokes take him away from me. I would miss Lieutenant Kuhn, I thought to myself. But still, I knew it was time to move on.

CHAPTER EIGHT

Two nights before I left Cam Ranh Bay, a Vietnamese officer and a black GI shot it out in the village. Somehow a little girl was hit by a stray bullet, then the GI got shot in the head. If the GI lived, I knew he'd have hell to pay because the village was off-limits.

When I hit the rack after hearing the news, I thought long and hard about my upcoming stint at Sea Float. In 1969 the navy had anchored twelve barges together on the Cua Lon River in Nam Canh District, Ca Mau Province, the southernmost district of South Vietnam. The thirty-five-mile-long river, which was up to a half mile wide, cut right through the center of the district from the South China Sea on the east to the Gulf of Siam on the west. The river was called the Bo De River on the east side and the Cua Lon River on the west.

Sea Float was about twelve miles inland from the mouth of the Cua Lon where it opened into the Gulf of Siam. On the top decks the barges had berthing for two Navy SEAL platoons, MST (mobile support team) and boat support people, Seawolf helicopter crews, and other support personnel. There was a helo pad on top, also. Down below were spaces that included a tactical operations center with a variety of radio equipment for communicating with ships, PBRs (patrol boat river), Swiftboats, helicopters, and fixed-wing aircraft. It also had situation maps with overlays and mosaics of Nam Canh Forest lining several bulkheads (walls). The situation map scales varied from 1:250,000 to 1:25,000.

The "Float" was home to several Swiftboats, PBRs, and

usually one patrol gunboat (PG). The PG's largest arma-
ment was a three-inch gun, the rounds of which were designed for piercing armor. Since there weren't any VC ships
or PT boats around, the PGs were used against enemy
bunkers constructed of mud and logs. The PG was beautiful
to look at, but somehow it reminded me of the Ford Edsel,
vintage Robert McNamara. It might have looked great, but
as we soon found out, it just wasn't designed for guerrilla
warfare on the Cua Lon River. Even *Mighty Moe*, the big
LCM-6 that often rescued me from ambush sites during my
1967–1968 tour, was there.

The barges were anchored right in the middle of the Cua
Lon about two hundred meters from either the northern or
southern shore. On the northern shore lived the Biet Hai,
numbering about twenty-five men, on the spot where the
village of Nam Canh had stood until it was wiped out by
B-52s in 1968 during the Tet Offensive. Few trees were left
standing in an area of a half mile or so. The Biet Hai had
built a few shanties for their housing near the riverbank,
along with a ten-by-ten-foot hootch out of scrap wood for
their lieutenant and his new bride. Since I would be advising them, I was expected to live among them. Also living
on the shore were Kit Carson Scouts (KCSs), RFs (Regional Forces), Montagnards (Strike Force), U.S. Seabees,
and RMK-BRJs. This made it all a real mess because the
Montagnards weren't liked by any of the Vietnamese, and
the RFs and Biet Hai hated the Kit Carson Scouts because
the scouts were ex-VC. The RFs also didn't like the Biet
Hai. In the midst of all the animosity, the Seabees worked
their asses off to build everyone else's future housing. I was
supposed to get in there and improve morale as much as
possible.

A few kilometers to the north of the Biet Hai camp was
the beginning of the U Minh Forest. To the immediate
south of the camp was the very tip of South Vietnam. Both
areas were much like the Rung Sat Special Zone, which
was a thirty-by-thirty-five kilometer area of dense mangrove swamp located southeast of Saigon; only the U Minh

and the great swamp were much bigger. Both areas contained some of the most troublesome terrain in Vietnam, and both were havens for the NVA and VC, who used the most impenetrable areas for R & R after operations and for regrouping and retraining. They also used the thickly jungled locations to hide POW camps. Apparently the marines and the army wouldn't go into either area for extended periods of time simply because it would be a low-priority operation and it would definitely reap diminishing returns. They could have eventually destroyed the VC and NVA safe areas but the casualties probably would have been fairly large. Also, American liberals and the news media would have distorted the numbers of those killed and wounded in action, friendly and unfriendly, to further their own agendas. Because of those military and political problems, the SEALs and other paramilitary personnel were ideal for H & I operations deep within enemy-held swamp and marsh areas. I knew that just as I had become rather intimately acquainted with the Rung Sat during my 1967–1968 tour, I would soon be all too familiar with some portions of the U Minh and the great southern swamp. Setting up ambushes to cause death in a place has a way of impressing on the mind every detail of one's surroundings.

I was also informed that since the entire area within a mile on all sides of Sea Float had been bombed out and defoliated, the VC had no cover (trees or brush) in which to attach and conceal B-40, B-50, and 150-mm rockets and launchers against us. A couple of times, a few VC frogmen had tried to swim to the barges with explosives in the night, but all were spotted by the marine security guards and were blown up with grenades or shot. Occasionally, the VC lobbed a few mortar rounds into the area. Thus, having had no success in attacking Sea Float, the NVA resorted to building bunker complexes along the Bo De and Cua Lon riverbanks and several minor tributaries running throughout Nam Canh District where U.S. Navy boats operated. Special NVA rocket squads strung one-inch steel cables across the streams in order to snag and slow down the boats to make them easier targets for rockets. The navy responded by sending in the SEAL platoons and some navy and marine EOD guys from Sea Float to locate and blow up the bunkers. The Biet Hai and I were to become a part of that cat-and-mouse exchange.

After a good night's sleep, I awoke to tackle my last full day at Cam Ranh for a while. I spent most of my time taking care of last-minute details and duties. At 1800 hours, I finished packing gear for my stay at Sea Float.

An hour later, the guys in the sea hut opened up the bar for my farewell party. As always, any excuse for a drink was a good excuse. I was serving the refreshments.

Willis, grinning from ear to ear, held up a beer and offered the first toast of the evening. "Smitty," he spoke loudly, his gold tooth shining, "there be lotta asses to kick at Nam Canh, ol' buddy. I expect you're da man to do da kickin'." I glanced around at the others and saw all of them looking at me, smiling—except for Dunlap, who was still lying in his bunk.

Willis finished his speech, saying, "When we see you back here da first week o' June, jus' make sure your own ass don't got no boot prints on it!"

Everyone laughed, then chugged down some beer together.

Feeling that some good times were about to happen, I said, "Let me tell you a true story about a SEAL buddy of mine named Randy Sheridan." I took a drink of my beer. After swallowing and noting that all eyes were upon me, I continued, "Randy and I were PRU advisers in '69, and he had a seven-foot python in a cage at the PRU office. One day he set up an office party and invited a round-eyed [American] Red Cross nurse that he wanted to impress." At the mention of a woman, the interest in my story peaked.

I took a quick sip of beer, then said, "Anyway, Randy had bought a duck for the python to eat, so he let the python out of his cage during the party with a lot of fanfare, tellin' everyone that the snake would entertain them by eatin' the duck. But the python showed no interest in the duck at all."

"So much for impressin' the nurse!" cracked Rio. Everyone chuckled.

I kept the story going, saying, "Randy sends a Vietnamese down to the market to buy some baby ducks, thinkin' the snake would eat them. Meanwhile, he's drinkin' like a fish, which also didn't overly impress the nurse."

"Man, I can feel a bad endin' a-comin'," interrupted Willis, grinning and hoping for a disastrous result.

Continuing, I said, "The python finally ate one of the little ducks, but he did it real slow. Randy got drunker and more disgusted with his snake because it wasn't showin' some flair in eatin' the poor little duckies, so he grabbed the python by the tail and swung it 'round and 'round in a three-hundred-sixty-degree circle, then slammed it to the floor. He did this three or four times, which naturally killed the python."

"And further impressed the nurse," Doc Marshall interjected sarcastically.

I nodded. "Yeah, and Randy was so tooted and mad about everything that he grabbed the big duck and bit its head off with his teeth!"

"No shit!" howled Rio, laughing. "Are you tellin' the truth?"

"Yep," I answered, "and that's not all. Randy then picked up his dead python and tried to bite its head off, too!" All of the guys roared. "But the snake's head was about three inches in diameter at the neck, and try as he might, Randy couldn't bite through."

Willis cut in. "An' whaddabout da nurse?"

I took a drink of my beer, then replied, "Well, she was so disgusted she left!"

"Poor Randy!" laughed Rio. "His piece left 'im!"

Qua suddenly shouted, "He should eat big duck, forget piece, more better." Everyone laughed harder.

I finished the story amidst a lot of laughter, announcing

loudly, "After the nurse was gone, Randy sat around for a long time tryin' to pick the pieces of meat out of his teeth!"

As the men continued cackling and drinking, I couldn't help but take a good, long look at each of them. They were all fine, strong men. Sure, they were a bit rowdy and coarse, but the heat, the harsh living conditions, and the hell of a swamp war were not conducive to the milksop and the mollycoddle. War was a bitch, and these men didn't refrain from calling it a bitch and treating it as such. And neither did I as I mentally prepared myself to depart from my friends the next day, when I knew I would step right in the middle of the shit hitting the fan. I knew I would meet the enemy once again right on his front doorstep. With those thoughts in my mind, I suddenly raised a not-so-fresh can of beer in salute to myself and bellowed, "If I die at Nam Canh, men, put this verse on my tombstone: 'And when he goes to Heaven, to Saint Peter he will tell: Another Navy SEAL reporting, Sir; I've served my time in hell!' "

"Hoo-yah!" a couple of the men chorused; then we all drank the night away.

CHAPTER NINE

The next morning I awoke with a headache, but a good breakfast soon empowered me to participate with the guys at our daily PT and run or swim. After a hard workout, I took a shower, gathered up my gear, and ate lunch. Doc Marshall drove me to navy AirCoFac at NAF Cam Ranh. I grabbed my parachute bag and field gear, then looked at Doc with a smile. "Doc, you hang in there."

Doc looked at me thoughtfully, saying, "You, too, Smitty. We'll have a cold beer waiting for you when you return."

After a three-hour or so wait, I finally got aboard an old C 117 and was airborne. The flight was short-lived, however, as there was a vibration around the landing gear. We circled back to Cam Ranh and landed without a problem. The ground crew replaced the landing gear cover and gave us the go-ahead for our flight. By the time we finally arrived at Tan Son Nhut Air Force Base in Saigon, a hundred-and-eighty-mile trip, it was after 1800 hours and the day was pretty well shot. I grabbed a taxi to ComNavForV, but everyone there had already left. I headed for the Metropol Hotel, where I got a room for the night.

After breakfast the next morning I saw GMG1 Nelson at NSWG (Naval Special Warfare Group) at NavForV. I asked for and got an M-60 machine gun for use at Sea Float. I was then briefed by Commander O'Drain and Lieutenant Commander Graham about the Biet Hai program. They told me that the enlisted adviser had been PR1 (Parachute Rigger) DeWeise, but DeWeise had accidentally set off a perimeter trip flare in his pants pocket and had to be medevacked. Another "brown shoe" (naval air) guy was going to relieve DeWeise and I was supposed to break him in. Commander O'Drain also reiterated that I was to improve morale among the various factions of men at Nam Canh and to start them operating much the same as the SEALs.

That same afternoon I worked on my tour records, pay records, and shipping over. While I did so, about a hundred VN students staged a demonstration at the Cambodian embassy, located a short distance from NavForV. I assumed they were protesting Prince Sihanouk's hypocritical neutrality of continuing to allow VC and NVA sanctuaries where the NVA established and maintained their COSVN (Central Officer of South Vietnam) military headquarters (similar to our Pentagon) and supply and troop distribution points inside Cambodia. The NVA was also permitted to use Cambodia as an R & R area for battle-weary VC/NVA units and to infiltrate with impunity or exfiltrate when necessary. President Johnson would not allow the U.S. military to cross into Cambodia on preemptive or retaliatory missions against the enemy. President Nixon changed that when he allowed us to strike inside Cambodia for about eighteen miles.

When I stepped outside to get some fresh air during a break, my nostrils were met by the irritating odor of tear gas. The young demonstrators, who appeared from a distance only to be having a good time and not violent, had been walking around the Cambodian embassy. Now they seemed to be dispersing.

When the NavForV offices secured for the evening, I went with BM1 Rogers and some SEAL Two guys to the EM club at the bar of the Metropol Hotel. There we drank some beer and talked until I left them to shower and hit the rack at 2100 hours.

The next day the Vietnamese students were demonstrating again. I watched them for a minute, wondering what President Thieu and his Directorate General of the National Police were trying to accomplish.

After spending a few hours at NavForV, I drove with Rogers in a jeep to Nha Be to see some of the guys at my old haunt. We spent the afternoon talking and watching television in their lounge. I had a good time, then Rogers drove me back to my room, where I crashed for one more night.

The next day was April 30, 1970. I went to NavAir-CoFac at Tan Son Nhut at 0730 hours. It took a while, but PR2 Scott, attached to Naval Advisory Group, and I caught a ride by UH-34 helicopter to Sea Float, where we approached at about 1130 hours. The flight had covered about 165 miles.

As we neared Sea Float I was amazed at the terrain. Most of it was underwater at high tide. It looked like a terrible place to operate.

I leaned over to Scott and yelled teasingly, "Looks like a great place to operate." His silence and the troubled look on his face revealed his thoughts.

I studied Petty Officer Scott as we hovered over the helo pad on the west end of the rectangular float. He stood about five feet ten inches in height and 160 pounds in weight. He was an easy fellow to get to know because of his openness and sense of humor. He was friendly and seemed always to have a smile on his face. He appeared to be motivated without being temperamental and was open to conversation and interesting to talk to. I had liked him from the beginning. Scott was to replace PR1 DeWeise, who had been previously medevacked, and to assist Lieutenant Commander (Tu Ta in the Vietnamese navy) Sphinx. Sphinx was to advise the Biet Hai in EOD clearance operations, coordinate their perimeter security tasks, and do other duties as required by the Sea Float commanding officer. My job was to advise Dai Uy Banh (equivalent to a navy lieutenant), the Biet Hai commander, in tactics and to serve as a liaison between him and Lieutenant Commander Sphinx and other coordination or as liaison between Sphinx and other paramilitary organizations.

After our helo set down on the flight deck (by then Sea

Float was made up of fourteen barges welded together), Scott and I immediately grabbed our personal gear and quickly moved from the helo pad. I asked a Sea Float crewman where the SEALs were located and was given the directions to their berthing space where Echo and Foxtrot Platoons were located. I was anxious to see my teammates again.

Echo Platoon had been in Nam since 28 February 1970 and were to remain in-country until 28 August 1970. The platoon members were: OIC LTjg Christopher H. Ward, AOIC LTjg William M. Tomlin, EN1 David M. Bodkin, AE2 Harry K. Kaneakua Jr., EN3 Kirk D. Scarboro, AMS3 Charles N. Chaldekas, SM3 John S. Durlin, SN Toby A. Thomas, SA John D. Donnely, SA John S. Baker III, FN Robert L. Bunke, SN Robert Conklin Jr., HM Max P. Green, and RM3 Robert J. Wogsland. Echo Platoon was to eventually survive ninety-nine missions and lost Durlin, Thomas, and Donnely KIA in a helo crash in 23 June 1970.

Foxtrot Platoon had arrived in Nam on 28 March 1970 and were to remain in-country until 28 September 1970. The platoon members were: OIC LT Frank G. Winant, AOIC LTjg John L. Hollow, Platoon Chief HMC Wayne G. Jones, HM1 Jim Gillis, SM2 Peter W. Vanflagg, EN3 Kirby "Danny" Horrell, TM3 Alan A. Yutz, SN Paul L. Pittman, SN Thomas M. Haselton, SN Joseph M. Cutrone, PRAN Julius J. Stocinis Jr., SM Michael Martin, SN Roland Green, and SN Gene Wentz.

Once I found the SEAL's berthing space, no one was there. Later I was told that one of Foxtrot Platoon's squads was out on an op. No doubt they were doing their best to locate and eliminate a few more Nam Can VC/NVA communist two-legged pigs. Assuming they were still onboard, there was only one other place they might be—the mess deck. That was always a good place to look for hungry SEALs.

"I should've known you guys would be stayin' where the chow is," I cracked at EN1 Dave Bodkin, Echo Platoon's acting chief petty officer.

"Well, when you operate in a swamp filled with all the pitfalls of hell, chow's the highlight of our day. 'Course, you wouldn't know about that, having just come down from the Cam Ranh Resort," he retorted with a slow country drawl.

"I'm humbled right down to my toenails." I grinned. "I sure hope you guys won't hold it against me." I walked over to shake hands with Dave, Wogsland, Yutz, and the other members of Echo and Foxtrot Platoons.

After introducing Scott, we got our chow and sat down with the guys for a good Navy meal. They were hungry for news from Cam Ranh and Saigon. The rest of the lunchtime was spent teasing, gossiping, and telling war stories. I especially took delight in telling them about my combat diving experiences at Cam Ranh Bay. They really liked the tales about the eighteen-foot-long moray eel and the jealous sea snake.

After lunch I tried locating Lieutenant Commander Sphinx. I was told he had gone ashore to spend some time with the Biet Hai and that he would return to the float at around 1500 hours. It was then that I was told that UDT-11's Golf Platoon had a five-man detachment also at Sea Float assisting LCDR Sphinx in clearing the swampy jungle inland with explosives so that the Seabees could begin building the new Solid Anchor that was to replace Sea Float. The UDT contingent consisted of: PR1 Burt W. Campbell, HM2 Thomas G. Holmes, EM3 Michael P. L. Bennet, SN Gerald S. Boward, and FA Craig R. Danielson. The remainder of the UDT-11 Golf Platoon was onboard the SS Tunny, a submarine; the APD USS Cook, and old converted destoyer; or in Subic Bay, the Philippines. They were as follows: OIC LTjg E. C. Brown, AOIC LTjg J. E. Klinger, BM1 John J. Gracio, HM1 Clyde R. McNew, PO3 Patrick J. Park, FN William P. Parris, SH3 William Ramos-Flores, FN John P. Sager, SK1 Roger K. Sick, SA Frank J. Sobisky, SN Stephen D. Symonds, and FA John Wolfram. In the meantime Scott and I visited with my teammates.

When Lieutenant Commander Sphinx showed up that

afternoon, I quickly studied him. He was a well-built man, about six feet tall and weighing approximately 190 pounds. His uniform was issue jungle greens with his name tag over the right pocket and his master EOD badge over the left.

I walked up to Sphinx, saluted, and said with a grin, "Petty Officers Smith and Scott reporting as ordered, sir."

He returned our salutes with a typical navy salute— sloppy. "Very well," was his reply.

When I handed him our orders he looked at me, then at Scott, and stated, "We've got a lot of work to do. We'll visit your new quarters shortly. Leave your personal gear here. In the meantime let's go to the mess deck and eat an early supper."

After supper we departed Sea Float by small aluminum boat with an outboard motor to the northern side of the Cua Lon River, where the beginnings of Solid Anchor were being developed into a complex of Butler buildings, a docking facility, and a landing strip. RMK-BRJ were bringing in barges filled with sand to be used for the foundation of Solid Anchor.

The Seabees were laying a foundation for the first Butler building. Solid Anchor would be placed at the center of the perimeter. The extreme edges of the northern perimeter were about 335 meters inland from the river. In order to extend the perimeter and eliminate cover and concealment for the enemy, Sphinx had been progressively destroying all brush and trees in a northerly direction from the river.

"The RFs are located on the extreme left flank of our perimeter," Sphinx explained as he pointed to a group of buildings. "I utilize them frequently to patrol the perimeter and set security when the Seabees are working on the new runway." Turning to me, he said, "Smith, you'll be coordinating with Tu Uy [Second Lieutenant] Phat, who is the commanding officer [CO]." I had dealt with the RFs many times when I worked with the PRU. They were similar to our National Guard and were equivalent to the Vietnamese regular army in dress and rank but were normally assigned to and under the operational control of the province and/or district chiefs. Their primary mission was to secure key installations and communications routes and act as reaction forces to assist village and hamlet forces (PFs, or Popular Forces) under attack.

Sphinx, or Tu Ta, pointed to a small plywood shack that was a short distance north of the Seabees, saying, "That is where I sleep. It's also my office."

Scott looked at Sphinx's shack and commented, "Man, I can hardly wait to find out what I'll be sleeping in!"

I broke out laughing, saying, "Any port in a storm, mate."

Tu Ta interrupted, "Smith, you'll be staying in that hammock on the porch of that shack near the stream that runs into the Cua Lon River. The Biet Hai are living in individual shanties between my office and the shack you'll be staying at. Tu Uy Hao, the XO, will be moving into your shack in a week or two with his new bride. You'll have to arrange your own berthing. Dai Uy [Captain] Banh is the CO of the Biet Hai here.

"That is the Kit Carson Scout compound to the east, just across the stream from your location. They are a ragtag group of men. They don't wear standard uniforms and are hated by the Biet Hai. I suppose it's because they are all ex-VC."

"Yessir," I interjected, voicing my understanding. "BM1 Leon Rauch and PO2 Steve Frisk [SEAL Team One] are the advisers. Leon and I worked together for a while as PRU advisers in Kien Giang Province last year. Both of them are good men," I stated proudly.

Unimpressed, Tu Ta turned and pointed to the west. "Scott, there is another small shack near mine that you can stay in. It was DeWeise's quarters. Any questions?"

"Yessir, I've already arranged for Scott and me to stay on the float for the night so that we can do some visiting and clean up and get a good night's rest," I stated. "What time do you want us to report to your shack ... uh, office?"

"Meet me here at 0700 hours," Sphinx said. He turned and began walking toward his shack.

I winked at Scott with a big grin and said, "Let's go to the float, where there's a couple of cold beers awaiting us."

Scott responded with "Say what!" and a smile filled with flashy teeth that spread across his whole face. "You've got the helm, Jack!" he exclaimed.

Scott and I had a good evening with my teammates of SEAL Team One and UDT-11. We discussed the latest rumors from the Silver Strand, new weapon developments, tactics, etc., until taps at 2200 hours. Scott and I were more than ready to hit the sack and get a good night's rest.

Suddenly, at 0130 hours, our good night's rest was interrupted by the float's loudspeakers sounding the alarm, "General Quarters, General Quarters, General Quarters. All hands report to their battle stations. I say again, General Quarters. All hands report to their battle stations." There was chaos in the dark berthing compartment as everyone heaved out of their racks, putting on their flak jackets, grabbing their weapons, and scampering toward their battle stations. All of the team guys were stark naked except for their flak jackets and helmets. No lights were turned on for a variety of reasons; one of the most important was to keep our night vision.

A moment later, I heard the marine security guards firing M-16s on full automatic and several grenades detonating underwater, then another, followed by more AW (automatic weapon) fire. I knew then that we were being attacked by enemy frogmen. It seemed strange to be on the other side of the fence.

With Scott following, I took my M-60 and ran with my teammates to their battle stations. The float maintained ship's darkness. Once outside, we were positioned behind sandbags and facing the south bank of the Cua Lon River. Lieutenant Ward yelled to Dave Bodkin to have two men throw several concussion grenades overboard and to watch closely for heads bobbing on the surface. Fortunately, there was enough moon and starlight reflected off the surface of the water that we could easily see any human movement. Lieutenant Ward yelled, "No pop flares!" just in case an overzealous sailor decided to pop one.

Knowing that we were under attack by waterborne sappers, it didn't matter that we didn't have any flares hanging overhead. The moon and starlight would work very well. If any of the sappers had survived the initial AW fire and concussion grenades of the marines, they were probably underneath the float between the barges trying to attach explosives to anything available.

Suddenly a marine EOD staff sergeant let out a yell and started firing his M-16 down between two of the barges. "I got one of the bastards! He's fish bait now!" he cried.

Lieutenant Ward again gave the order to throw overboard one concussion grenade every thirty seconds.

If there were any survivors left, I doubted that they would survive long due to internal injuries from the concussion grenades. As another grenade detonated underwater, I mentally put myself in the enemy's place, swimming like hell, diving, and swimming as far as I could before I came back to the surface for more air. I would break the surface gently with just my lips protruding, inhale deeply, then go back under and get as much distance between myself and the float as my physical capabilities would allow me.

Suddenly a head popped up about twenty yards out from the barge. The swimmer just barely had time to get a fresh breath of air when about twenty automatic weapons opened up on him. His head literally exploded, leaving tattered skin, hair, and skull bones settling to the bottom of the river.

"Hoo-yah!" I heard someone cry as the shooting spree finally diminished. I stopped firing and stared out into the water, looking intently for any more movement.

We were informed a few minutes later that initially four sappers had been spotted swimming with the current toward the float, towing explosives attached to flotation bladders. We were confident that we had gotten at least three KIAs and that the concussion grenades had killed the fourth sapper. Only time would tell. Their bodies would float to the surface within a day or so if the sharks didn't get them first.

There was little hope of getting any sleep for the rest of the night. We were kept on GQ for several more hours. No one could sleep anyway. The next day I'd be able to get a good night's rest when I moved ashore and my "home" would be a hammock. Sleeping outside under the eaves of a Vietnamese officer's shack was just one more "perk" in a long list of many similar bonuses that I had earned over the years as a Navy SEAL. Lucky me.

CHAPTER TEN

Reveille came at first light, about 0600 hours. I quickly dressed in my issue cammies, etc., shaved, and went to Scott's bunk.

"Reveille, mate!" I yelled as I shook him gently by the shoulder. "Heave out, trice up. Sweep the decks fore and aft. Pipedown in five minutes. Reveille!" Turning around, I quickly went back into the head.

I heard a stomping of feet, shuffling around, then a loud "Shiiiiiit. Maaaaaaan."

Obviously, Scott needed motivating. "Say what?" I exclaimed. "If you want to stay here and clean yourself up, I'll just ditty bop on over to the mess deck and get a big breakfast of bacon and eggs with grits, hot oatmeal, and coffee, milk, apple, and orange and be back here in a whistle."

"Hey, dude, I'm coming!" Scott assured me as he pulled on his boots without lacing them.

We soon finished breakfast, collected our weapons and gear, jumped into Tu Ta's twenty-five-horse aluminum boat, and returned to the beginnings of Solid Anchor.

Scott wasted no time going right to the shack where DeWeise, the previous adviser, had lived. As planned, I got the hammock on the front stoop. The hammock was completely enclosed by mosquito netting, which was an obvious forewarning of things to come.

After unpacking my bags and storing my stuff inside Tu Uy Tran's shack, Scott, Sphinx, and I went to the RFs' camp to see Dai Uy Banh, the OIC (officer in charge) of the Biet Hai. After the initial introductions, Banh told us some of his grievances with the previous navy lieutenant whom Tu Ta Sphinx had relieved.

"He always tell my men what he want to do and not tell me," complained Banh, looking at Scott and me, sizing us up. "I no like! My men work for me. No one else!"

I nodded in approval with what he said. Out of respect for his rank and person, I was careful not to give him too much eye contact. He seemed to be a sincere man and, if what he said was true, he was totally justified in his anger at the U.S. Navy lieutenant's violation of his chain of command.

Banh then told us that Ensign Tranh and fifteen of his men were going out on an ambush that evening, so I volunteered to go with them. I was anxious to observe how the Biet Hai operated. Besides, I was hoping to get back into the groove after all the weeks of LDNN training evolutions. Firing my machine gun at the sappers the night before had revived the itch to get back into the action. For some reason, I felt guilty when I wasn't sharing the bad times with my teammates.

Patting my back once with his hand, Banh invited me and the others to walk with him around the camp perimeter, thus giving us a chance to inspect it. The perimeter was actually a one-hundred-meter-wide belt of land running east and west between the scrubby tree line and the first manned defenses to the south, approximately two hundred meters away. There were numerous illumination grenades set up on stakes to ignite when a trip wire was pulled by anything moving through the area. Also, many command-detonated M-18-A1 antipersonnel mines were placed in such a way as to overlap each other's field of fire. Concertina wire was laid between the minefield and the manned defense bunkers. Thousands of sharp, punjilike splintered tree stumps studded the belt. They were created by priming and detonating old antiaircraft ordnance against trees during extensions of the perimeter. And to add to a sapper's potential misery, the belt was little more than a swamp. It was a formidable obstacle for the VC/NVA to penetrate.

After the tour, I cleared the evening mission by coordinating with NOC (Naval Operations Center) on the float. In turn, it would clear out our AO covertly (in theory) with subsector, which was located at the new Nam Canh District's tactical operations center a few kilometers west of Sea Float. Then I ate lunch with the Seabees at the makeshift chow hall near their construction site. The lunch consisted of canned tuna, vegetables, milk, fruit juice, and fruit cocktail. We even had peanut butter, jam, and crackers for dessert. "A man can't ask for much more than this," I thought.

At about 1500 hours, Dai Uy Banh and Tu Uy Tranh (who soon would be relieved by Tu Uy Hao) came to the hootch where I was busy getting my field gear ready for the night's op. They were friendly and shared some Tiger beer with me.

"You welcome go with Tu Uy Tranh tonight," Banh said, then he pointed at the PRU patch that was sewn on the tiger-stripe cammi shirt I was wearing. That patch had been given to me by the PRU in Rach Gia, Kien Giang Province, in 1969. However, the Biet Hai were more interested in the M-16/M-203 combination rifle and 40-mm grenade launcher I had borrowed from Echo Platoon. I had been tinkering with it when they arrived. I explained that I really liked the weapon's versatility because I could fire 40-mm grenades accurately out to 250 meters with a maximum range of 350 meters. If I had problems with the M-16 then I had the M-203 as a backup, or vice versa. We shot the breeze and had two beers apiece. I had to laugh to myself as the Vietnamese officers put away the beer with no problem, just like a good SEAL. It seemed that drinking beer was a requisite of war.

Afterwards, I got permission to test-fire my weapon from NOC, so I went to the small stream just fifty meters east of my hammock. There I checked the M-16's point of impact from fifty meters to two hundred meters, followed by fa-

miliarization firing twenty 40-mm HE rounds from the
M-203. I sure wished it had a trigger that could be adjusted
a bit forward and outboard of the M-16's trigger, similar to
that of the XM-148. I didn't like having to move my right
hand away from the M-16's pistol grip forward to the
M-203's trigger. With the XM-148 I could continue grasping the pistol grip, move my trigger finger one inch forward, then fire the XM-148. It was simpler, faster, and I
was more accurate with it. But the M-203 setup would have
to do for the time being. Moreover, it beat carrying a heavy
M-60 and 500 rounds of ammo. A feller needed a pair of
vice grips and a come-a-long just to tote the damn thing—
especially when jumping out of a helo ten feet above a
muddy rice paddy.

At 1900 hours I was ready, and loaded to the gills. I continued to use my old nylon H-harness with web belt, magazine pouches, and K-bar knife that I first used when I was
in Nha Be in 1967. My newly made custom vest was worn
over the H-harness and web belt. The vest and magazine
pouches held a maximum of sixty-three 40-mm HE and
40-mm para-flares. I had seven thirty-round M-16 magazines, two M-26 frag grenades, two minifrag grenades, two
mini-CS grenades, two concussion grenades for enemy
swimmers, two white pop flares, two red star cluster pop
flares, two MK-13 day/night emergency flares, a pencil flare
with twenty rounds, lots of mosquito repellent, one LRRP
(Long-Range Reconnaissance Patrol) meal, a two-quart col-
lapsible canteen, first-aid kit with morphine styrettes, strobe
light with red, blue, and IR (infrared) lenses, small penlight
with adjustable red lens, a 1:24,000-scale map of the area
and Silva Ranger compass with preset declination, and a
bright cloth panel to signal FAC (Forward Air Control) aircraft if we got lost, etc. And under all of that I wore my
UDT life jacket. Everything combined was a bit heavy, but
I was ready for bear.

Tu Uy Tranh and fifteen Biet Hai met at our hootch,
where I joined them. Tranh repeated earlier instructions to
his men in the Vietnamese language. I didn't understand all

Banh said, but he had filled me in about the mission while we toured the Solid Anchor perimeter. I knew we were to patrol about a klick (one thousand meters) to the northeast where we would set up a point ambush on a stream in hopes of catching unawares a sampan or two of VC.

In single file, the seventeen of us started moving north, paralleling the creek that was the extreme right flank of Solid Anchor and its perimeter. I was positioned behind the radioman—that is, I was the fourth man in line.

Just before we were to complete our traverse through the last of Solid Anchor's booby-trapped perimeter belt, the line in front of me slowed way down. In the light of the three-quarter moon, I saw Tu Uy showing the radioman ahead of me a trip wire, then he stepped over it. In turn, the radioman in front of me pointed out the wire to me by touching it. Unfortunately, he tripped it! Immediately, a flare started sputtering, emitting a bright light that exposed all of us, destroyed our night vision, and very possibly compromised the mission. I was disgusted. "Nothing like a great start," I thought.

Regardless of the warning we may have given nearby enemy, we continued our patrol. The terrain was muddy and the vegetation consisted of mangrove roots in places, small bushy trees, and an occasional nipa palm tree, calling for slow and careful patrolling. But instead of stealth and concealment, the Biet Hai plowed ahead with close to reckless abandon. The careless sloshing through swampy areas did little to develop my faith in their patrolling procedures. Obviously, the Biet Hai were in need of some basic small-unit training, a la Navy SEALs.

Another mistake the group made occurred at a footbridge that stretched across a tiny stream of water perhaps fifteen feet wide. Rather than follow a standard operating procedure (SOP) for a "danger area," which in this case involved setting up security on right and left flank positions before sending the men across the bridge one at a time, the Biet Hai ignorantly exposed themselves, bunching up and walking the footbridge three or four at once.

To their credit, they did set up at the ambush site properly, hiding nine men, including me, on the bank of the designated stream in a line that reached about fifty yards from left to right flank. The remaining eight men moved back into the brush about ten yards to act as rear security.

I sat a few feet back from the riverbank between a couple of small bushes in the mud. I laid my weapon across my lap, angling the two barrels toward the moonlit stream in front of me. I could see well enough to spot anything moving in the water, since the stream was only twenty to thirty meters wide and the moon was plenty big and bright. In 1966 and 1967, the VC loved to travel on moonlit nights, literally singing songs in the Rung Sat, until we started interrupting their serenades with missiles of death. I was glad to be able to rely on my eyes that evening, as my ears were full of buzzing mosquitoes. As bad as I had often had it with skeeters in various places in Vietnam and Texas in the past, the blood-craving creatures of Nam Canh already ranked up there with the worst. The multiple layers of mosquito repellent I had applied didn't seem to offend too many of the things; I was glad that I'd put on cotton long johns under my tiger-stripe cammies.

I was positioned one man in from the right flank, which made my primary responsibility one of watching for any sampans approaching from the right—in this case, the east. In the event of a sighting, we were to hold our fire until the enemy reached the center of the kill zone, which was right in front of Tu Uy Tranh. As the middle of the kill zone was penetrated, Tranh would initiate the ambush. Upon his firing, the rest of us were to open fire. The enemy, caught in a hailstorm of bullets, would have little or no chance of coming up with the time necessary to kiss his ass good-bye. As my eyes scanned the glittering waters, in spite of the irritating mosquitoes, I felt good about getting back into action.

After twenty minutes, instead of stealthy VC, I was approached by a noisy Tranh, who was moving down the line to check on everyone. His maneuvering was completely unnecessary. Every Navy SEAL who had been through training knew not to move around on an ambush site like that unless absolutely necessary. Instead of motion on the ambush site, we would have used a line between each man for communications. One pull on the line meant "Are you okay?" Two pulls meant "I hear something." And three pulls meant "I see the enemy!" But Tranh had not been properly trained. As he sloshed his way back toward left flank, I imperceptibly shook my head and prayed that his rustling would not be heard by an unseen enemy. It was obvious that the Biet Hai were badly in need of some solid training such as had been given the LDNN trainees.

When Tranh settled back down into his central ambush position, everything grew strangely quiet. I was able to tune out the hum of the mosquitoes, listening right through it for other noises. Besides a couple of wheezes from a nearby crocodile, though, all was still. And with a long silence and period of inactivity, the usual, sudden feeling of sleepiness flooded my body to the outmost parts of each limb. The sensation was almost overpowering, but like hundreds of times before, I knew I could defeat it. After all, a big part of my job was to stay awake all night on ambush sites so I'd be ready to put the unsuspecting enemy asleep for eternity.

To keep my mind active, I thought back to my first mission on a river ambush site in September 1967, in which I helped kill two VC. I remembered the suspension line that was tied to my right wrist jerking hard three times, which meant "The enemy is here!" I raised Sweet Lips, my sawed-off Ithaca model 37 pump shotgun that was loaded with double-0 buckshot, as the figures of two men in a sampan appeared only ten feet in front of me. One of them cried *"Choi hoi"* after the blast of an M-16 rifle sounded at my right side. The words, meaning "My God," were to be his last.

I had squeezed Sweet Lips' trigger again and again, firing six rounds at the two enemy. MM2 Funkhouser joined me with his M-60 machine gun. Tracer bullets streaked across the river through the dark from Funkhouser's gun. M-16 fire, CAR-15 fire, and exploding grenades from an M-79 also tore the hell out of the river as all six of us SEALs on ambush made sure the enemy did not escape.

I remembered how the concussion of sound was ear-shattering and brain-splitting and how it seemed to last forever. And then, after it had finally stopped, a concussion grenade blew up in the river and scared the piss out of me. Lieutenant Meston had tossed the grenade as an afterthought, calling out to the rest of us that he wanted to kill any possible swimmers. That made me laugh, but only for a second. When silence returned, the shrill ringing in my ears gave me an immediate headache.

To my amazement, a few seconds later I heard talking from across the river. Vietnamese language was being used, which meant more enemy existed. I then heard Lieutenant Meston talking on the radio, saying something about Navy Seawolves. He was calling for the helo gunships.

I remembered the men on the flank positions, which included me at left flank, preparing our battery-powered strobe lights with blue-colored lenses. When I heard the Seawolves approaching above, I lay flat in the mud of the riverbank and flashed my light at the black sky. Meston got on the radio and the pilot identified our location via the blue lights, then all hell broke loose. M-60 machine guns strafed the opposite shore just forty meters away. I watched with my head down as tracer bullets zipped through the darkness.

As the first Seawolf flew away, a second one swooped in, firing 2.75-inch rockets at the riverbank. The rockets exploded as another M-60 started barking.

Following a racetrack-in-the-sky pattern, the two Seawolves circled and made a second pass down the river. More rockets demolished the jungle, and more M-60 machine gun fire ripped the air. I was spellbound at the precision of their attack, and I was sure the enemy was hellbound by the accuracy of the strikes.

After several runs, the Seawolves flew away, leaving me

with a severe pressure rush against my eardrums that literally pounded against them. But I didn't mind too much because the Seawolves had also left me with something I cherished: my hide. And that hide was extracted from the ambush site by a two-man crew in a Boston Whaler with a 105-horsepower outboard engine humming full tilt. Little did I realize that night that I would be back for more on a fourth tour of 'Nam with the Biet Hai.

At the end of my reminiscence, I was shocked back into reality by 81-mm mortar HE and M-79 HE rounds exploding four to five hundred meters south of our position toward our camp. The mortaring was obviously being laid in pretty thick by the RFs and possibly the Seabees. They all might have been firing M-79s. I began wondering if one of the VC had been showing another one a trip wire and inadvertently pulled it, setting off a trip flare. Well, no doubt they were paying for their carelessness.

I sat quietly with my own thoughts, eyeing the sparkling surface of the water, until 2300 hours, when Tranh sneaked over to me.

"I think I see sampan opposite side," he whispered, his lips close to my ear.

I whispered back to him, "See anyone?"

Tranh shook his head.

"Let's wait," I suggested softly. "If someone moves out in the sampan, let's open fire."

Tranh nodded his head affirmatively, then he moved a few feet to my left and sat down in the mud. We waited about five minutes, when a couple of parachute flares were shot up by Solid Anchor's perimeter security to the south. I figured that the VC spotted south of us might try to extract at our position, using the sampan Tranh had seen along with other sampans we could not see in the dark.

During the next fifteen or twenty minutes, several more parachute flares lit up the sky in the distance. When no more were forthcoming, the jungle seemed darker than before. I had the ominous feeling of evil creeping up on me, even as the black water overflowed its bank and soaked my behind while the tide came in. I just knew the enemy was coming in, too.

Over the next thirty minutes, I had no trouble staying awake and alert. The chirping of crickets helped, as did the cool water lapping at my testicles, but more than anything it was the smell of lurking death that kept me on edge.

The sudden thud of a paddle against the side of a boat brought my weapon to my shoulder. A few seconds later, I saw the outline of a sampan with two men in it drifting my way in the middle of the stream. They were passing through the middle of our kill zone, so Tranh did not hesitate to initiate the ambush. The instant he fired his M-16, I opened up with my M-203, firing an HE round into the middle of the sampan.

I thought I heard a man's scream out on the water, but then seven other weapons were fired virtually simultaneously from the riverbank, covering up any sounds of life in the jungle, human or otherwise. For twenty or more seconds, the nine of us sang "Now I Belong to Buddha" with machine guns, rifles, and grenades.

Someone down the line shot a parachute flare over the stream, which lit up the whole area like a lighted football field. The sampan was floating past me but no people were in view. Just for good measure, though, I and the VN on the right flank put another twenty to thirty holes in the skiff as it moved rapidly farther downstream with the current.

When the banging finally ceased, as usual, my eardrums ached. My left ear, in particular, felt as though some crazed woman had thrust a knitting needle into it. I walked over to Tranh and used the PRC-25 to call NOC. Using prearranged code words, I notified them that we were departing our ambush site and patrolling back to Solid Anchor.

Our return was uneventful. "Hoo-yah!" I whispered softly so that nobody heard but me. But that was enough. Mission accomplished.

CHAPTER ELEVEN

Sealed off from the mosquitoes, which were stubbornly refusing to give up looking for a way to get at me, I lay in my net-covered hammock at 0230 hours. Just the thought of having to attempt E & E (Escape and Evasion) from the enemy and from the midst of the Nam Canh swamp gave me cold chills. If the enemy didn't get me, the swamp would. The NVA and VC, the sappers and snipers, the booby traps and mines, the crocks and the sharks, the snakes, the heat. The mosquitoes had better grab a claim check and step to the back of the line, I said to myself. Death is everywhere, lurking and easy to find. It hangs every night like the moon, just waiting, so fat and low I could reach out and touch it.

I had been somewhat far removed from Death's presence while with the LDNN trainees, but now I knew I was back in his immediate vicinity. However, I was no longer working with SEAL platoon personnel I could absolutely rely upon. I was forced to place all of my faith in Vietnamese men whom I really didn't know very well. However, I seldom felt vulnerable.

I smirked at the moon for the last time at around 0330 hours before finally falling asleep. I dozed for three hours until I was awakened by Lieutenant Commander Sphinx and Scott, who were making noises as they prepared to head out on a recon to replace trip flares that had been expended earlier that night by the VC in our perimeter.

I ate breakfast then went back to bed again. But Seabee electricians were working inside the hut where my hammock was strung and they were walking in and out of the place so I couldn't fall asleep. All I did was close my eyes and rest for a couple more hours, listening to the distant sounds of boat activity up and down the river, crickets, frogs, and occasional lungfish chasing each other on the mudflats. It was all music to my ears, reminding me of similar sounds I had heard when, as a kid, Wallace Farr and I went camping and fishing at Possum Kingdom Lake, near Graham, Texas.

When I finally got up, I decided to take a walk through a maze of old dikes where there had been some rice paddies before Nam Canh was bombed out during the Tet Offensive. The hike was challenging, as I had to cross each canal by walking eight to ten feet over a bridge that was nothing more than a pole measuring only three to four inches in diameter. I felt like a one-man high-wire balancing act, which made my excursion interesting.

As I shuffled across one particular pole bridge, I noticed a pretty, striped snake, about two and a half feet in length, lying still and unafraid in the mud perhaps three feet below me. I carefully squatted on the pole and reached down with my hand to within two feet of him. He was unimpressed. I made a mental note to look for this snake again on another morning.

At 1145 hours, Sphinx and Scott were returning from the morning's op, so I got up from a shady spot I had enjoyed beside a lone, small tree and worked my way through the dikes and over to Scott's hootch.

"See anything?" I asked Scott as I approached him.

He stood his M-16 against the front wall of his shack, took off his PRC-25 radio, and set the radio down next to the steps. "We found VC footprints on right flank. There must've been a half dozen of them checking out the perimeter defense system."

"Could you tell what direction they were coming from?"

"No, but we found where they sprung the trip flare." He pointed to the north-central area of the perimeter. "After that we couldn't tell where they went. Probably, they jumped in the creek and *di di mau* out of here." Pondering a minute, he shook his head. "We did find millions of damn mosquito bites." He spat, then added, "Man, I ain't never seen bigger, uglier, meaner sons a bitches no place else in 'Nam. They're thicker than shit out there in the jungle."

"I know what you mean, mate. Dawn and dusk are killers. You ought to try living outside and in a hammock with thousands of them hanging on to the mosquito net sucking on my arm and leaving lumps the size of lemons for their calling card."

As we cursed the mosquitoes, one of the Biet Hai came up to me. His name was Nguyen. He was unusually tall for a Vietnamese, but slender like most. He reminded me of Smiley, one of the PRUs in My Tho in 1969. He'd always had a smile on his face, and so it was with Nguyen. He had been on our op the night before.

Appearing anxious, Nguyen said haltingly, "Smitty, I can ask something?"

"Sure," I responded, nodding my head affirmatively.

Nguyen drew a breath, then said, "Smitty, I want start Lien Doi Nguoi Nhia [LDNN] training. Many hard to do?"

"No sweat," I quickly commented. "Do you know when you go to Cam Ranh Bay?"

"Very soon, I think. All Biet Hai want go to LDNN training now!" he stated enthusiastically. "We no like Biet Hai work. No good."

"I understand," I replied, totally agreeing with him. "I hope you and other Biet Hai go Cam Ranh soon. Very beautiful, diving very good, many big lobster, fish, squid, and sea turtles," I said, trying to encourage him and give him something to dream about. A man who doesn't have any dreams is a man who doesn't have any hope! I sympathized with Nguyen and the Biet Hai.

Nguyen seemed to be satisfied with that bit of information. "You come eat five o'clock with me, okay?" Nguyen pointed at his watch.

"Thank you, Nguyen. I'll be there." I was delighted and was looking forward to the diversion.

With a pleased look, Nguyen headed back toward the Biet Hai line of shacks and bunkers to tell his buddies the good news.

Wanting some lunch, I left Scott, but when the Seabees' chow hadn't arrived by 1230 hours, I ate a LRRP (Long-Range Recon Patrol ration). The lunch wasn't very tasty, making me hope that the evening meal with Nguyen would be a good one.

After eating, I grabbed a two-hour nap in the hammock. Then I went to a Biet Hai shack where a makeshift barbell set was available, a length of aluminum pipe and two cement weights, adding up to approximately fifty pounds. I worked out with the apparatus for thirty minutes, doing many repetitions of military presses, bench presses, arm curls, half-leg squats, and everything else I could think of.

As I left the shack after my workout, Lieutenant Commander Sphinx met me outside and asked me to go to the RF camp and talk to Second Lieutenant Phat. I was to ask Phat for five of his men to help with the Seabees' next-day surveying party.

I found Phat talking with two of his men outside his hut. He greeted me pleasantly, but when I passed on Sphinx's request, he adamantly refused. "No one brought my men anything to eat for lunch other day on survey party," Phat explained. "Sea Float Dai Ta [Commander] want our help with no payback, no courtesy. I tell you, Smitty, no food, no work."

I agreed with Phat wholeheartedly, nodding my head and telling him he was right to be upset. I apologized for his not having received any food for his men and promised that I would explain this to Sphinx. I returned to inform Lieutenant Commander Sphinx of the negative results, but he had already departed for Sea Float. Using the PRC-25, with external speaker, near my hammock, I reached Sphinx at the Float's NOC, where the radio operators were located.

"Munster. This is Munster Seven. Over."

"Munster Seven. This is Munster. Over," the radioman acknowledged.

"This is Munster Seven. Interrogative Munster Seven OIC your location? Over," I asked.

"Munster Seven. This is Munster. Wait. Out." The radioman was paging Sphinx to report to NOC.

"Munster Seven. This is Munster Seven OIC. Over," Sphinx replied.

"This is Munster Seven. Be advised, negative results in getting five men for tomorrow. Regional Forces OIC said, 'No food, no work.' Today, the surveying detail received no C rats. I strongly recommend you twist supply officer's arm and get some C rats. Over."

"This is Munster. Roger. I'll discuss the matter with the CO. Over."

I signed off.

I hurried to take a bucket shower before heading for my dinner date with Nguyen. The shower stall was located a few feet from my hammock and was attached to the north side of the shack. Two pieces of plywood were secured to the shack with two-by-fours to form a cul-de-sac. A piece of canvas covered the entrance. A wooden ordnance box was used to stand on while pouring fresh water over the body with a quart canteen cup. I could easily take a bath with no more than three gallons of fresh water.

The supper was everything I had wished for and more. It was especially good with the two warm Tiger beers I had brought to go with the supper. Nguyen served eggs, pork, rice, onions, cucumbers, and *nuoc mam* (a strong-smelling fish sauce). He gave me pineapple for dessert, and by the time I got up from his makeshift plywood table I was stuffed.

"Cam on ong," I thanked my host, bowing slightly to him.

"Very much welcome," Nguyen replied as he bowed even deeper. He stood up with a wide grin on his face.

I excused myself and walked to my hammock, where I intended to write my parents a letter and to read some before dark. I managed to finish the letter, but just as I began reading a paperback, NOC radioed from Sea Float asking for all unit commanders to report immediately to NOC.

In less than an hour, at last light, Tu Ta Sphinx had returned from the Float. He appeared to be in a somber mood as he reached my hovel. "Sea Float received a flash message from NavForV stating they had received intelligence telling them that Sea Float and Song Ong Duc [a small fishing village located about twenty-two miles north of Nam Canh] are targeted by the NVA for complete destruction tonight." He looked out toward the center of the perimeter, saying, "I want you to coordinate with Dai Uy Banh and offer to support or assist the Biet Hai in any way you can. Scott and I will be staying at my hut monitoring the radio for further information or instructions from the Float." Looking at my PRC-25 radio, he said, "Make sure you keep that radio with you. I want to be notified of your tactical situation every hour on the hour."

"Yessir," I responded quickly. A situation with a sense of urgency excited me. After receiving the information from Tu Ta, I grabbed my M-60 machine gun and immediately went to Dai Uy Banh's hut to offer him my support and assistance. He suggested that I stay on right flank and be near Nguyen and several other Biet Hai. He then instructed his men to double up immediately on perimeter watch, one man sleeping and one watching. I returned to my hovel, where I set up the M-60 for the best field of fire and laid out a can of belted ammo. I also kept the M-16/M-203 handy.

"This could be a long night," I thought. I motioned to Nguyen that I would be sitting on the empty ammo can near my weapons. Thank goodness the stars were out and bright. It was a good night for the VC/NVA to attack, though. As usual, the mosquitoes were terrible. I was continually putting more mosquito repellent on my face, neck, and hands. The night was hot and humid. Sweat kept rolling down my face and into my eyes and mouth, bringing with it the repellent I had just rubbed on. For some reason the mosquitoes were worse than in the Rung Sat.

I began wondering if that cocky snake was still under that footbridge. I had just begun planning the liberation of its head when a trip flare went off to the north of our perimeter. Everyone immediately shot the hell out of the hinterland. I grabbed the M-16/M-203 and began lobbing 40-mm HE rounds out at about three hundred meters in the vicinity of the burning flare. Tracers were ricocheting off the ground, floating up and disappearing into the stars. The noise was deafening! Two hand-fired pop flares were aimed toward and over the burning trip flare. Nothing was seen and nothing moved. If there were any enemy in the vicinity they were dead or squirming for their lives and belly crawling to beat the Reaper out of the area.

After five minutes, except for the ringing in my ears, all was quiet on the northern front. Nguyen was cursing in a low voice to another Biet Hai. That was followed by some giggling. I wondered if they were smoking pot. Earlier in the day, I had seen several of them rolling something that looked similar to tobacco in cigarette rolling paper. "Damn their hides," I thought.

I was finally able to get to sleep at around 0300 hours, which made reveille at 0700 seem mighty early. I experienced another one of those illustrious SEAL perks: little shut-eye.

CHAPTER TWELVE

The attempted destruction of Sea Float by the VC continued the next night. At about 0300 hours, the enemy shot a B-40 rocket (RPG-2 rocket launcher) at our PG boat and hit it on the starboard side. The boat suffered little damage, but the hit provoked an immediate response from the U.S. forces. Scores of weapons commenced firing from Sea Float into the pitch-black perimeter. After the response was ended, a total quiet blanketed the area for the rest of the night. We could only hope that one or two VC had been killed by our attack and thereby silenced for the rest of the millennium.

To discourage the VC from persisting in their riverbank rocket attacks against our boats, at 0930 hours I went with Tu Uy Tranh and nineteen Biet Hai, Lieutenant Commander Sphinx, Scott, several men from EOD, and the five-man contingent from UDT-11 to blow some enemy bunkers. We traveled by Swift boat a few miles up the Cua Lon to a point where numerous bunkers were situated near and on the riverbank—as reported by SEAL and Seawolf helicopter pilots. At that point we inserted where a small tributary joined the main river to our right flank. Ensign Tranh, his men, and myself were inserted first. Our job was to initially recon inland no more than one hundred meters and to try to maintain visual contact with Sphinx if possible. Because this area occasionally had some company-size enemy forces in it, Tranh and I decided to spread out in a skirmish line and slowly advance inland while carefully watching for booby traps. This gave all of us maximum firepower at the twelve o'clock position and it would also help keep the men from grouping up and inadvertently shooting each other. Also, I felt this formation was justified because: (1) we were a small unit of men with first squad to the left flank and second squad to the right flank; (2) we had fairly good visibility between all of us; and (3) Tu Uy Tranh and I wouldn't have any problems with command and control.

We advanced through vegetation which generally consisted of small trees of up to twenty feet in height, nipa palm, and shorter undergrowth. We stopped at a small canal that paralleled the river. It was little more than two meters wide. Our new-found canal would offer us cover and concealment if and when the enemy was foolish enough to assault us. We decided to quietly hold our position until Tu Ta Sphinx directed us to pull back to the river by squad, in leapfrog fashion, for extraction.

I could barely see the EOD and UDT guys amidst the mud-and-log bunkers. They reminded me of the time we were tasked to blow up huge bunkers in the Rung Sat Special Zone in 1967. I was in Foxtrot Platoon then, and *we* almost got our butts blown away instead of the bunkers. The lesson we learned then was "Never let your guard down."

The bunkers were generally small and could comfortably hold two or three men in the prone position. In each there was a rectangular porthole that was about four by six inches and faced the river. Some of the bunkers had insulated wires that were laid to a rocket launcher pod holding two or three rockets that were electrically initiated. The rockets, which were the B-40 or B-50 or a more crudely made 150-mm type, were carefully secured and concealed in a bushy tree that was usually in the edge of the water. If the first rocket missed, another could be quickly fired by simply touching another set of wires to the battery. The VC's ordnance and tactics were incredibly simple and very effective. One man could fire three rockets at any boat that entered the kill zone, crawl unseen several meters to his sampan, paddle out of the immediate area, and lay low before the Navy Seawolf helicopters could arrive on scene from Sea Float.

I was carrying a PRC-25 radio and my M-16/M-203, which meant that I was carrying a heavy load. I hated carrying radios when I was in the field. It seemed that the folks at Sea Float and other powers-that-be were always curious about the whereabouts of me and the Biet Hai and generally insisted on diverting my attention from our perimeter security responsibilities to answer their sometimes unimportant questions. Of course, that was the privilege of command; there was little hope of maintaining a quiet presence in the bush because of the continual chatter on the radios.

"Munster Seven Alpha. This is Munster Seven. Over," Sphinx called.

"Here we go," I thought. "This is Seven Alpha. Go."

Sphinx continued, "This is Munster Seven. We'll be setting charges soon. How much longer before you are set up? Over."

"This is Seven Alpha. We're set up now. Over."

"This is Munster Seven. Roger. As soon as we have all of the charges set I'll notify you to start returning to my location followed by having everyone else load the boat except Ellis and me. When you reach my location, Ellis and I will prime the charges [sensitized detonation cord] and ignite the time fuse (M-60 fuse lighters), then we'll all extract. Any questions? Over."

"This is Seven Alpha. Roger. Out." I immediately relayed the information to Tu Uy Tranh.

"My men much hungry," he commented while rubbing his stomach.

I could sure emphathize with that! I had lost approximately ten pounds since I had been at Sea Float. Reinforcing his comment, I replied, "Maybe we will have some extra C rations that we can share with the men. I could eat at least two meals myself."

Tranh nodded his head in approval. "Good!" Tu Uy

commented with flashing eyes and a stern look on his round face.

I was hoping that I would be able to locate a few rations from the Swift boat crew and or the EOD and UDT guys for the Biet Hai. It was hard to build rapport with the men if they weren't well led and, especially, well taken care of.

Suddenly I received a call from Tu Ta Sphinx. "Munster Seven Alpha. This is Munster Seven. Over."

"This is Seven Alpha. Go. Over," I quickly replied.

"This is Munster Seven. Return to my location immediately. Over."

"Munster Seven, this is Munster Seven Alpha. Roger. Out." We quickly began our alternate leapfrog movement, by squad. I stayed with the second squad as Tu Uy led the first squad back to the river. Within fifteen minutes the Biet Hai were loading aboard the Swift boat as Tu Ta Sphinx and Petty Officer Ellis, who stayed behind, yelled, "Fire in the hole!" They pulled the two M-60 fuse lighters that started the explosive chain of events. We had ten minutes to move out into the river to a safe area and watch the fireworks—approximately two hundred pounds of C-4 plastic high explosives.

I immediately got the Biet Hai's C rats and gave them to Tu Uy Tranh to issue as he wished. There were two cases with a total of twenty meals. At least we had gotten one meal each. I asked the Swift boats' chief petty officer if he had any leftover C rats that I could give to the Biet Hai. He went down below and came out with a box of assorted cans of ham and lima beans, peanut butter, cheese and crackers, etc. I thanked him and took the box of vittles over to Tranh to issue as he wished. The Biet Hai were delighted. They were all talking excitedly as they pillaged the box. They sure loved C rats.

"Ten seconds to go," Ellis yelled. "Nine, eight, seven, six, five, four, three, two, one, zero, crap, crap, crap."

Kabooooooom! Logs, mud, and debris went flying out over the river and fifty feet up into the sky. Unfortunately, the VC would have the bunkers rebuilt within a week.

"You were three seconds off, Petty Officer Ellis," Tu Ta Sphinx commented with a slight grin.

"Yeah? How do you like me so far?" he quipped in reply. "That means you owe me three beers because you timed and measured the time fuse. I'll be over to your villa this afternoon to collect. I suppose you'll have some cake for me to eat, too? Huh?" Ellis was referring to the old joke that some officers (especially administrators) are "cake eaters." All of the EOD and UDT guys respectfully burst out laughing and hee-hawing.

Tu Ta grinned weakly without saying another word. He kind of reminded me of myself.

Shortly afterward, the Swift boat officer relayed to Tu Ta that the Biet Hai would be needed to accompany his boat out to the mouth of the river to rendezvous with a Coast Guard WPB and another Swift boat that was loaded down with fourteen Vietnamese detainees. Two PBRs (in this case, "patrol boat, river") soon arrived to offload the EOD and UDT personnel and return to Sea Float. That meant that myself, Tu Uy Tranh, and the men were to remain onboard and escort the Swift boat with detainees back to the Float. It was a beautiful day and I enjoyed the ride and the scenery. We didn't even get shot at.

It was late afternoon before we returned to the Float. Back at my shack, I showered with a bucket, which refreshed me. By this time it was after 1730 hours. I was so hungry I didn't care what I ate or what it tasted like, I just wanted some food.

I ended up eating sun-dried fish (heavily salted), boiled rice with *nuoc mam* sauce, and hot tea with the VN enlisted men and Tu Uy Tranh. The fish heads and rice were very good, and I made sure I ate plenty. I minded my own maxim, which was "quantity, not quality." The bloated feeling of a packed stomach was what scored big points with me.

After dinner, I felt tired. Two nights in a row of dealing with the Vietcong's attempted advance against us and Sea Float had taken their toll. I climbed into my hammock at dusk, beating the mosquitoes to the draw. Despite the commotion and noises made by the other men throughout the area, I quickly fell asleep.

When I awoke at about 2330 hours with an all-too-familiar pressure in the bladder, all was still. I slipped out of my net-covered hammock and drained my lizard beneath a partially visible moon and a small, scrawny scrub tree. I glanced around as I stood there, noticing the reflection of the moon in the receding waters of the nearby creek that drained into the river. The sound of the rippling water and the starry reflection was mesmerizing and reminded me that I needed to go back to bed and get more rest.

When I secured my position back in my hammock, I couldn't help but grin. The night air was a bit cool, perfect for sleeping. I had already managed a few hours' sleep, and now that I had emptied myself, I was looking forward to several more. My delight was short-lived, however, as a trip flare went off just as I dozed off again. Our perimeter security began reconning by fire. Two more flares were set off, probably by our M-79 HE rounds that were exploding in the swamp. However, I didn't hear any enemy fire coming our way. I guessed it was a crocodile that had set off the first flare.

Watching the fireworks for a couple of minutes, I sat up in my hammock. Then I lay back and covered my ears until the banging ceased. It was obvious that the VC were determined to get through our trip flares and claymore mines some night and attack us where we lived. But since that particular night looked secure enough, I decided to forget about potential danger and grab some more shut-eye. I finally fell asleep at around 0100 hours, getting the rest my body and mind needed.

I awoke at 0545 hours, as Nguyen brought me a glass of hot French coffee mixed with raw sugar and thick cream. *"Com on ong,"* I said, thanking him for his kindness. Nguyen smiled and left without saying a word.

After my coffee, I elected to check on the striped snake under the distant footbridge. When I reached the bridge, I didn't see the varmint. My curiosity being what it was, I gingerly moved out to the middle of the pole bridge and stopped. While carefully balancing myself on the four-inch-diameter pole, I closely examined the shadowy bank area, as the sun hadn't risen above the horizon yet. All two and a half feet of the beast lay curled up in the dark recesses.

I stealthily moved across the pole bridge to the opposite side of the canal. There I looked for and found several stones, which I picked up, to be used as missiles. I cast the messengers of death at the snake with determination. However, each of them just missed being a direct hit on his plated head. The serpent didn't move an inch.

Since the snake seemed so secure, I recrossed the bridge and headed back to my hammock, where an ax was leaning against Tu Uy Tranh's shack.

I grabbed the ax, which had a blunt end to be used as a hammer or to bludgeon and a wide, deep blade for cutting wood or assorted appendages and to perform decapitations. Just the weapon I needed.

I hurried back to the snake's lair. I almost went too fast, stumbling over my own feet while crossing another pole bridge and barely making it across.

When I finally reached the inhabited canal, I stepped onto the bridge as my eyes skirted the crevice for the snake. There he was, only a couple of feet from his den. He lay directly beneath the pole on which I stood, which was the perfect place for my planned strategy. No doubt he was waiting for his next innocent victim.

I took four or five steps out onto the rail-thin pole, positioning my feet less than a yard above the snake, balancing myself as though on a high-wire, with the ax handle in my right hand.

Finally, I decided that the time had come to deliver the reptile of his beguiling head, but as I lowered my body with my legs to guide the ax to its target, I lost my balance and flipped upside down, falling down and on top of the previously torpid snake and the ax. I splashed into the canal's polluted water and mud that carried Vietnamese excrement and urine to the river.

I was beginning to wonder who was getting crapped on there. I quickly determined that I'd make that decision later. Without hesitation, I rolled over and away from the snake, which more than likely was poisonous. Throwing mud, I thrashed my way toward the bank of the canal, stumbling over the ax and grabbing it on the way by. Placing my hands with the ax on the top of the bank, I pulled my right boot out of the sucking hole it had created, dragging a heavy clump of clinging mud into the air. I gave my foot a hard shake, which threw off half the weight of the noxious muck, then swung my leg up onto the bank. I hoisted myself out of the canal and stood up on dry ground, wet and coated with Vietnamese crap.

Angry and humiliated, I spun on my heel and started back to my hammock area thinking of the cleaning up I had to do and how the muck reminded me of the mud pit during Hell Week.

About the time I was halfway "home," I replayed my awkward fall into the canal in my mind. After doing so, I couldn't help but lose my anger and begin to chuckle to myself. By the time I reached my hammock, I was laughing, outwardly, at myself.

Nguyen looked at me and my muddy, smelly clothes and asked, "What you do?"

Laughing, I said with exaggeration, "I got into a wrestling match with a seven-foot snake, and he won!" Nguyen laughed with me, then I added, "But if you think that I look bad you should see the snake!"

Nguyen inquired, "What kind snake he was?"

"A big one!" I fibbed. We both guffawed some more.

After my initial douse in the creek, I stripped off my clothes and stepped into the bathing stall, where I took a great four-gallon bucket bath. Afterwards, I hung my wet cammies out to dry on a rope I had strung on one end of the porch near and downwind of my hammock. I put on a fresh pair of cammie bottoms, a blue-and-gold T-shirt, and coral booties, then went to breakfast.

Shortly afterwards, I cleaned the M-16/M-203, then took the weapon with me as Scott and I got in a small, motorized boat and went to Sea Float. I returned the weapon to TM3 Yutz, the weapons petty officer of Foxtrot Platoon, SEAL Team One. I explained to him that I didn't like the M-203 nearly as well as the XM-148 grenade launcher. I just wasn't comfortable with it. Surprisingly, he had a couple of extra XM-148s in the platoon weapons conex box available. Even though he was short of time, as Foxtrot Platoon was about to depart on an operation, he had an XM-148 installed within five minutes. "Thank goodness for teammates," I thought. I now had another of my old tried-and-true VC terminators again. I then arranged for the loan of a .50-caliber machine gun with tripod, ammo, and cleaning equipment from BSU for perimeter defense. I also had to arrange for gas, oil, etc., for the Biet Hai.

When Scott and I got back to shore, it was nearly time for lunch. We ate together with the Seabees, then I lay down for an hour or so. It was so hot that I couldn't sleep a wink.

I finally got up and gathered five Biet Hai, who went with me to several bunkers to collect ordnance and ammo that I had made arrangements for that morning. We stored the ammo in the Biet Hai bunkers on the defense perimeter. We then got aboard the Biet Hai junk (about thirty feet in length) and went to Sea Float, where we picked up the .50-caliber MG, ammo, and gear.

While I was at Sea Float, Petty Officer Rob Wogsland of Echo Platoon told me that they had been shot up pretty badly earlier in the day; however, Rob wasn't hurt badly. He said the platoon had been hit by the VC with B-40 and B-50 rockets, automatic weapons fire, and claymore mines. They had been traveling up a dead-end canal by Mike boat and MSSC (Medium SEAL Support Craft) a few klicks to the southeast just after noon when they ran into large cables stretched across the stream by the VC that significantly slowed down their progress and enabled the enemy to open up on them. Eighteen of the twenty-one men in the boats were wounded, but only one SEAL and one of the BSU personnel were hurt badly, which was a minor miracle. The area in which they were moving was a hot one, and they broke an old rule that SEAL Team One learned in 1966 and 1967 in the Rung Sat Special Zone: "Don't fart around in a hot area in the daytime."

After returning by junk to Solid Anchor, the Biet Hai and I soon had the .50-caliber MG set up and our defense perimeter well organized and ready for a formidable assault. As we worked, I was troubled about Echo Platoon and its casualties. I was also intent upon making the VC pay for the damage they had done to Echo Platoon. "What comes around, goes around," was more than just another cliché to me and my teammates. When the enemy messed up one of us or some of us, then he had better get prepared to deal with the rest of us.

I took the M-16/XM-148 to the old rice dike area and practiced shooting the weapon. After a couple of minor adjustments, I shot so well with it that it looked as if I had been born with the thing in my hands. Since we were scheduling a mission two days away, I thought I might soon find out how well the weapon and I could make some unfortunate VC wish one Gary R. Smith had never come out of a womb.

CHAPTER THIRTEEN

The next evening almost ended up being my last as I found myself in the middle of a heated showdown between our own "friendly" troops. Shortly after dark, about thirty Kit Carson Scouts, ex-Vietcong assigned to Naval Special Warfare (NavSpecWar), were angrily facing off against twenty or so Biet Hai, each side yelling accusations at the other. By the time I hurried upon the ugly scene, which was just across the creek from the KCS camp and a short distance from my hammock, everyone had his machine gun or rifle loaded, off safe, and aimed.

Nguyen, my friend the Biet Hai squad leader, was screaming expletives at his former communist enemies and claiming that they had murdered his mother and father and were descendants of dogs that weren't fit for consumption (dog meat is a delicacy in Vietnam and much of the world). Memories die hard in war zones, and Vietnam was no exception—especially when one's relatives and immediate family members had died under the sword of Ho Chi Minh and his power-hungry goons.

The Scouts were not about to accept any accusations that they were sons of dogs and "once disloyal, always disloyal." Both sides were quickly working up to a no-return confrontation.

Another Scout shouted a string of counteraccusations and then waved his AK-47 automatic rifle menacingly, ready to open fire.

The two opposing groups had spread out in skirmish lines, yelling at one another across ten yards. It was into this space between the incensed sides that I stepped, waving my arms in overly demonstrative circles. I was unarmed and knew that I must get between them if I was to stop a bloodbath and save my SEAL career.

"Son of a bitch!" I cried in Vietnamese, looking back and forth between the men. My strategy was to throw a temper tantrum in which I appeared madder and meaner than anyone else. "Stop this!" I screamed at both sides. "This is no good!" Neither side budged from its confrontational position.

"There is no future in the past! We must be brothers!" I exclaimed. With as much emotion and courage as I could muster, I continued, "Our enemy is the VC, not each other. We must fight the enemy side by side, not fight against each other."

I looked toward the Biet Hai. "Nguyen, you are my brother. All the Biet Hai are my brothers." Then I turned to my right and faced the senior Scout, saying, "Duong, you are my friend. All of the Scouts are my friends."

With finality, I turned to Nguyen and emphatically ordered him to take charge of the Biet Hai and to return them to their huts immediately. As his adviser I had hoped that he would obey my command. I could see the indecision in Nguyen's face, but he said nothing and made no move.

Again, I faced the Scouts and demanded that Duong order his men to return to their compound immediately.

I was not sure why, but both sides lowered their weapons and began to disperse. Apparently, both sides were unwilling to be the first one to kill me. They also knew that their punishment would have been swift and severe, i.e., the firing squad.

Tu Uy Tranh wasn't anywhere to be found. It was just as well, for I would have been poor company. I decided to "hit the hammock" rather than endure the mosquitoes' continual harassment. I lay in my hammock for a couple of hours, pondering the recent South Vietnamese history of war and its fight for independence. As I had just witnessed, the Vietnamese temperament changed like the weather. Gradually, my stomach stopped churning and the hum of the mosquitoes around my hammock net made me drowsy.

The next morning, Tu Ta and Scott came to get me to go with them, EOD Ellis, and several Biet Hai to extend our defensive perimeter by cutting down trees with old antiaircraft projectiles. Since some of the trees were on the opposite bank of the creek that separated us from the Kit Carson Scouts camp, we used a couple of sampans for the task. In one of the sampans, which was powered by two devil-may-care men, we loaded fourteen projectiles to cross the stream. The coxswain was PO1 Ellis with yours truly stroking from the bow.

Ellis took charge by sounding off, "Let us give way together, Herr Schmidt."

Being the good sailor that I was, I replied, "Aye, aye, matey!" With a strong back and a powerful arm, I pulled with a long stroke that would've pleased Hercules.

"Watch out!" Scott exclaimed amidst the laughter of the Biet Hai. But it was too late. I didn't even have time to look at Tu Ta, either. It was probably best, anyway. No doubt he was contemplating keelhauling both of us.

The results were incredible! The sampan was so overloaded with ordnance that the river came rushing over the gunwale. In less time than it takes to yell "Abandon ship," we were left floundering in a whirlpool created by the overladen boat that had settled on the bottom of the creek at about three fathoms.

Scott, being quick to encourage us, stated matter-of-factly, "Man, that's what I call takin' the wind out of y'all's sails."

Tu Ta looked at Ellis and me and commented, "Fine job, Seamen Ellis and Schmidt." The way he said "Schmidt" made me think of something that comes out of the south end of the body.

"Why, hell! You're the one in command," Ellis yelled at him while we were swimming for shore. "I was just following orders. If we'd had decent leadership your boat and ordnance wouldn't have sunk. With due respect, sir, it's all your fault."

When I reached the muddy bank I looked up at Sphinx, then Scott, and meekly commented, "We may not look like much, but we've got good hearts." I flashed a goofy grin.

"Does this mean the day's evolution is canceled, sir?" Ellis continued as he stood up from the muddy water. Tu Ta didn't bother to answer. He and Scott were already headed for his office/shack. Obviously, we were done for the day.

I told the Biet Hai that we had no more work for them. Ellis returned to Sea Float to change his clothes while I returned to my temporary quarters to clean up.

I ended up eating supper with Tu Uy Tranh and the boys, then I wrote some letters to my family and friends back in the States. I also prepared my gear for the next morning's op, which was another bunker-busting mission. Since we were going into a hot area, I figured we'd have contact with the enemy. Just for them, I decided to carry the M-60 machine gun and five hundred rounds of ammo.

Reveille came at 0615 the next day. I ate breakfast at the Seabees' mess, then Tu Ta and Scott showed up at my hammock at 0800 hours. Each of us drank a cup of coffee while we waited for the Swift boats to arrive.

The boats came for us about forty-five minutes later. Tu Ta, Scott, and I, along with Ellis, six UDT-11 guys, and fifteen Biet Hai with Tu Uy Tranh in charge, boarded Swifts 63 and 35 and traveled seven kilometers east of Sea Float. We inserted in an area where a dozen VC with weapons had been spotted. Our mission was to blow three or four large bunkers about a quarter mile from the river that were being used by a dozen VC.

Scott and I were part of the point element, which consisted of three Biet Hai in wedge formation, Tu Uy Tranh, myself, Scott with the radio, followed by twelve Biet Hai, Tu Ta Sphinx, Ellis, and finally, the UDT-11 men following as rear security. Right away, the Biet Hai point men began moving too fast for my liking. They weren't taking enough time to watch for the ominous, almost invisible monofilament line leading to a grenade in a camouflaged can.

After about half an hour, the point element veered slightly to the left to check out an old hootch. Afterwards, they returned to our original course. A few minutes later we discovered that Divine Providence must have guided us to swerve, as the main element behind us found seven VC grenade booby traps set up directly in the path of the area the point element had sidestepped. VC tracks around the booby traps indicated that they had probably set them when they realized that we were patrolling in their direction. Feeling fortunate, we waited a bit while Ellis disarmed the traps.

We finally moved forward into terrain that was surprisingly dry. There were only a few areas where the swamp prevailed. The vegetation was mostly small trees four or five inches in diameter, dense underbrush, and secondary growth sporadically scattered throughout the area. We found another recently inhabited hootch that was well camouflaged by the natural cover of the swamp growth. I walked up to it where the lower edge of the thatched roof was level with my neck and stooped to peek inside.

Suddenly, Nguyen yelled at me and pointed to the apex of the roof, where a long, slender, grayish green snake about six feet in length was lying next to the crest. It reminded me of the coachwhip/prairie racer that was common in Texas.

Tu Uy Tranh leaned over to me and said, "Cobra."

While I stayed frozen, one of the Biet Hai shot the cobra with his M-16. The snake was only wounded and, crawling toward us, began hissing and acting very aggressive. The hair on the back of my neck promptly stood up, followed by goose bumps up and down my back. We quickly retreated from the first cobra I had seen in Vietnam.

Tu Uy then ordered the men to burn down the hootch. I

DEATH IN THE DELTA:
Diary of a Navy SEAL

EN LEN !!! LAM CHỦ THÀNH PHỐ

"Go forward to master cities," says a Vietcong poster captured near the Dinh Tuong Province (My Tho city) PRU, 20 August 1969.
(Gary Smith)

Al Huey, Trung Uy Loc (PRU Team Chief), and Embassy House staff, summer of 1969.
(Gary Smith)

Ian S. (center) was the POIC at the Embassy House and Col. Dao was the Province Chief of Dinh Tuong Province during my 1969, 1970, and 1971 tours.
(Gary Smith)

My good friend Sao Lam, the PRU Assistant Team Chief of Dinh Tuong Province.
(Gary Smith)

PRU Special Operations Training Camp Billy Machen near Cuyamaca, CA, January 1969. The camp was named for the first SEAL to die in Vietnam. *(Gary Smith)*

I'm standing in front of my defunct tent at Camp Billy Machen, January 1969. *(Gary Smith)*

U.S.S. *Benewah* (APB 35), a barracks flag-ship of CTF 117's Mobile Riverine Force, anchored in My Tho river, just offshore of Dong Tam in January 1968. *(John Odusch)*

LDNN trainee helo cast and recovery just offshore of the Naval Support Activity. *(Gary Smith)*

Left: LDNN Instructor Qua and Doc Riojas free sparring. Good block, Doc! *(Gary Smith)*

Middle: A good example of a Cam Ranh lobster. The LDNN training camp is in the background. The instructors' hut is on the right. *(Gary Smith)*

Below: One of the better foot bridges near Solid Anchor. Nguyen, the Blet Hal Leading Petty Officer, is in the center. *(Gary Smith)*

Patrol Gunboat (PG) *Ready* or *Antelope*.
(Gary Smith)

Bright Light op, 30 July 1970. Bottom left is Lt. (jg) Tom Norris, Medal of Honor recipient; Lt. Ski and Ken Peck of SEAL Two's Fifth Platoon; Dong Tam. I'm standing top-center with M-60 and bandoliers. Photographer Mate Clinton is next, with Tu Uy Son to his left.
(Gary Smith)

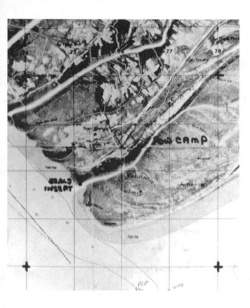

The 1:25,000 scale map of the 30–31 July 1970 Bright Light operation carried out by Lt. Todd's Hotel Platoon on the tip of the Thanh Phu peninsula. *(Gary Smith)*

That's me (left) as a SEAL Basic Instructor at Camp Niland after my LDNN tour. On the right, dressed as a VC abductee, is my old UDT 12 Fourth Platoon LPO Joe Gary Thrift. A tough man to interrogate, VC Thrift was known to coldcock trainees and take off into the night. *(Gary Smith)*

Members of SEAL Team One's Echo and Golf Platoons. Sea Float, Nam Canh, An Xuyen Province. (Standing, left to right) Lt. (jg) John Hollow, Tommy Hatchett, Chester Craig, William Armstrong, Joseph Cutrone, Lt. (jg) William Tomlin, Toby Thomas or Dave Brinkley, Paul "Lee" Pittman, David Bodkin, Matt Ferrez or James Martin, John Baker III. (Middle row, left to right) unidentified, Lt. (jg) John Huggins, Robert Conklin, Thomas Haselton, Roland Gerson, Julius Stocinis. (Front row, left to right) Robert Sparks, Wayne Jones, Peter van Flagg, Alan Yutz.

(Paul Pittman)

figured I had better radio Tu Ta and let him know what was going on. "Munster Seven. This is Munster Seven Alpha. Over."

"This is Munster Seven. Over," Sphinx answered.

"This is Munster Seven Alpha. Be advised that one of the men shot a cobra and my counterpart is having the hootch burned down," I explained. "Any instructions or recommendations? Over."

Tu Ta answered, "This is Munster Seven. Negative. Continue on our course. We'll be taking a lunch break soon. Over."

"Munster Seven. This is Munster Seven Alpha. Roger. Out." I relayed Sphinx's message to Tu Uy Tranh. While the hootch behind us went up in flames, the point element again started moving toward our objective. Within fifty meters we spotted another cobra in the branches of a tree and about fifteen feet from the ground. This time the Biet Hai rifle fire was more accurate. In short order, the cobra was lying dead at our feet. I didn't bother getting very close to it; I had great respect for the cobra's neurotoxic poison.

The cobras bothered me, but the burning hootch and the shooting made me feel even more uneasy. I generally felt very insecure when tactically compromised, especially when I was in Indian country and didn't have air support directly overhead. There was always someone bigger, better, smarter, and stronger waiting to humble you.

With two cobras down and out, we continued on our course toward the bunkers. There were numerous human tracks in the area. I was a bit apprehensive because of the lack of training and experience of the Biet Hai, who were still moving too quickly. I finally had to caution Tu Uy Tranh to tell the Biet Hai to maintain noise discipline and slow down. They simply didn't have that sixth sense that only comes from good training and combat experience.

At about 1130 hours, we paused for a rest. I was delighted at being able to sit on dry ground, a couple yards from Scott. The point element was spread out about twenty yards ahead of the main element. On the march, we generally fanned out rather than congregating closely.

I was preparing to eat from a can of beans when I heard a chopping noise no more than a hundred meters ahead of our point man's position. I looked at Scott and a couple of the others, and I saw by their sudden attentiveness that they, too, had heard the sound. I grabbed my M-60 that was lying on its side to my right and softly clicked off the safety. I clutched the M-60 with sweaty hands and held my breath as the sound of high-pitched voices drew closer. I gently caressed the trigger with my shooting finger and prepared myself mentally for an immediate ambush.

I scanned the brush for movement, but saw nothing. I heard nothing for a few seconds, then the sucking noises of people walking in mud reached my ears. Since we were operating in a free-fire zone, I knew that I could open fire at any time, as no one but the enemy was to be out and about in this godforsaken place.

As I looked and listened intently, the noises began growing more distant. Obviously, the people had turned away from us. I glanced at Scott, then at Tu Uy. Both of them were sitting high on their knees, Scott gripping the radio handset with white knuckles and Tu Uy with his M-16 at the ready.

Suddenly a chopping noise shattered the air from about fifty meters away. Several more chops followed, with a couple of them ringing out simultaneously, indicating at least two axes being worked at once. At first, the bramble of underbrush and small trees broke up their silhouettes and prevented me from seeing them. Gradually, I began to make out one individual.

I recommended to Tu Uy that we should quietly move forward all of the Biet Hai and prepare for offensive action. He quickly agreed. As Tu Uy was quietly moving his men into place, I checked with Tu Ta Sphinx to see if he wanted to withdraw or advance on the woodcutters. He motioned for me and the Biet Hai to go ahead and take the woodcutters as prisoners.

"Good man," I thought, as I returned to Tu Uy Tranh's position. Tu Uy had Nguyen and his squad take left flank with Ut and his squad on right flank. That way Tu Uy and I would remain in the center of the formation to better command and control the advance and assault.

While Tu Uy gave final instructions to Nguyen and Ut, I couldn't help but think about the thousands of occasions that military men of all ages had prepared to do the same thing. There was something very exciting about advancing on the enemy when you had the element of surprise. It was similar to skydiving from fifteen thousand feet or shooting at a seven-point bull elk, or having a fifteen-foot shark swim by you during a night underwater compass swim, or being shot at and missed. Maybe it was the adrenaline pumping through one's veins. If we were still fighting with swords it would really be exciting or spooky—depending on one's outlook. Imagine slashing your enemy's neck and having his heart pump blood through his opened left carotid artery and squirting it all over your face. One on one combat becomes very personal. Combat troops have to see and face the consequences of war in a very real and personal way. When you watch your enemy's pupils suddenly dilate, the finality of knowing that at that very second the dead warrior is either in heaven or hell, paradise or darkness, causes one to ponder his own destiny.

We began moving slowly forward, trying to be as quiet as possible. Finally, I spotted a fellow squatting behind a hardwood tree that was masked in a cloud shadow. He was so intent on cutting down the tree that we got within ten meters of him before he saw us. When he did, he let out a scream that would've given most men a sudden dose of the squirts.

Realizing we were compromised, we let out our own screams and assaulted the enemy. Lo and behold, there were the three bunkers we were looking for, also. Suddenly men were running all over the place. They were screaming; we were screaming. Within a minute we had rounded up thirteen suspicious fellows who had been playing around in a free-fire zone. We had no idea how many, if any, had gotten away.

Once we gained control of the situation, I left Scott and his radio with Tu Uy Tranh with a reminder to insure that the Biet Hai searched the bunkers and maintained perimeter security. I then quickly returned to Tu Ta to fill him in on the results of our assault and to receive further orders.

"Tu Ta, we've found the three bunkers," I reported excitedly. "The situation is currently under control. Tu Uy is taking care of the thirteen prisoners and interrogating them. Do you still want to blow the bunkers?" I asked.

Looking at Ellis and the UDT-11 men, Tu Ta said, "Ellis, I want you to take the rest of the men and start setting the charges as quickly as you can." Turning toward me, he said, "Smitty, I want you to stay with the Biet Hai and be ready to return to the river when I give you the word on the radio. The Utes [UDT-11 guys] will be rear security. Any questions?"

Ellis and I quickly answered in the negative. I immediately returned to Tu Uy and filled him in on Tu Ta's decision to blow the bunkers and for us to be especially watchful for any enemy probing activities. Tu Uy, Nguyen, and I got busy interrogating the woodcutters. Several were old men and were legitimate woodcutters trying to make a living. They told us that the VC had been taxing them a percentage of their woodcutting as payment for letting them come into the Nam Canh Forest. I wondered just how much the South Vietnamese government was taxing them. The VC were taxing them, the government was taxing them. It was no surprise that all of the people in the Nam Canh area were incredibly poor.

"Munster Seven Alpha. This is Munster Seven. Over," called Tu Ta.

"Munster Seven. This is Munster Seven Alpha. Go," I quickly replied.

"This is Munster Seven. Ellis will be pulling the fuse lighters shortly after this transmission. Make sure your men take cover. Immediately after the shot, myself and Ellis will check the bunkers. If all goes well, we'll then depart for our extraction point. Any questions? Over."

"Munster Seven. This is Munster Seven Alpha. Roger. Out," I said.

Within a minute or so I heard Ellis yell "Fire in the hole!" three times. That meant that he was pulling the firing mechanisms of two M-60 fuse lighters that began a timed chain of events. The fuse lighter's primer ignited the time fuse's black powder core, which started burning its way to the non-electric caps that were crimped onto the opposite ends of the time fuse and buried inside the main charge of C-4 (two-and-a-half pound blocks of an explosive that resembles putty). When the burning black powder reached the sensitive non-electric caps (filled with PETN high explosives), the heat caused the caps to detonate. Within a picosecond after the caps exploded, their detonations caused the less sensitive C-4 high explosive to detonate, thus destroying the bunkers.

I hunkered down behind a small tree with my fingers in my ears. I looked at Scott to see how he was doing. He had his radio removed from his back and leaning up against another tree. Behind it was Scott, lying down and peeking around the right edge of the radio. *Kaboom* went the charge! Scott jumped about a foot off the ground. I was laughing until mud and sticks began raining down on our position.

"Munster Seven Alpha. This is Munster Seven. Head for the extraction point. Over."

"Munster Seven. This is Munster Seven Alpha. Roger. Out," I replied.

I turned to Tu Uy Tranh and passed the word to him. He immediately directed the point element to start patrolling toward the river. The thirteen prisoners had been individually tied, then tied together, blindfolded, and escorted back to the river. Once we arrived at the river, Tu Uy released all of the prisoners but two. He had decided that they were

VC. The two oldest men were crying and continually bowing up and down, thanking Tu Uy and Nguyen for their release. I couldn't help but feel sorry for them.

Shortly after our arrival at the extraction point, we loaded the whole menagerie aboard the two Swift boats and headed for home. The two prisoners were signed over by Tu Uy Tranh and Nguyen to the RFs at the newly built hamlet of Tran Hung Dao. The probable VC were initially interrogated by the RFs' Vietnamese intelligence officer, followed by their being turned over to the district's (subsector) S-2 or intelligence section for further interrogation, exploitation, and disposition. If the two prisoners decided to accept the Chieu Hoi ("Open Arms") program and defected to the South Vietnamese government, they would be sent to the sector/provincial capitol (Ca Mau) where the Chieu Hoi center was located. At that point they would be known as a Hoi Chanh, or one who has seen the error of his ways, and would be reindoctrinated into the South Vietnamese system.

Once we were back at Sea Float, we all sat around and drank two beers apiece from UDT-11 guys' supply, then we headed our own ways.

I cleaned my gear, took a shower, and lay in my hammock, glad that we had chosen to round up the Vietnamese woodcutters for interrogation and had not just shot them. According to the "rules of engagement" for this area, shooting them would have been justified as they were caught in a free-fire zone. But blasting away at people who might be innocent and simply in the wrong place at the wrong time always carried with it some unpleasant and disturbing memories. Fortunately, I knew that my memories of that day would be good ones.

I relaxed completely in my hammock and enjoyed a nice afternoon siesta. I had to grab the rest while I had a chance, as we were preparing a big op for the next day. Two dozen of us were going to patrol Rocket Alley, which was twenty or thirty klicks east of Sea Float in a free-fire zone. We planned to destroy all the bunkers, hootches, and booby traps we could find, which would harass the VC and serve as a bit of a payback.

CHAPTER FOURTEEN

Reveille came the next day at 0545 hours, but I had already been awake for half an hour. I had been dreaming about one of my missions in July 1969 with the PRU, and the end of the dream brought full consciousness with it. But the visions which had unreeled during my slumber continued to fight for attention after I awoke.

Lying beneath a blackened sky, I saw myself in tiger-stripe cammies loaded down with my M-1D Garand sniper weapon, web gear, thirty-five .30 caliber (.30–06) eight-round clips, first-aid kit, water, etc., and sitting in one of three UH-1 Huey slicks, reinforced by two Huey gunships from the U.S. Army's 9th Infantry Division helicopter unit. About twenty-five of us were going in shortly after first light, ready to insert on the edge of a village in the Cho Gao District of Dinh Tuong Province. Our objective was to capture or kill Nam Phen, the My Tho party committee's military proselytizing section chief; his assistant, Hai Nhien; Nguyen Thi Toai, the commanding officer of the H-10 artillery unit; and other members of the Vietcong infrastructure who we knew, through intelligence, to be in that specific area.

As the slick approached the village at tree level, I glanced at Randy Sheridan beside me. He and I were the SEAL advisers to the rest of the men, all of whom were PRU. Randy saw me look his way, so he flashed a nervous smile at me.

Just as the helo began to flare for the landing, when we were the most vulnerable, gunfire erupted from below us and one of the PRU was hit in the left shoulder. The army gunner immediately began firing the M-60 mounted on the port-side door. Bullets hit the ground at the base of a hootch just fifty feet away. They were ricocheting upward and tearing through the palm frond walls of the hut. I had little time to wonder why the gunner was blasting away in that manner as I prepared to jump out of the helo with my scoped sniper rifle.

When the slick was a few feet from the ground, the gunner was suddenly wounded and fell back. I leaped out of the helo and broke into a run with PRU members right beside and behind me. I spotted VC darting across the rice paddies one and two hundred meters away at twelve o'clock—directly ahead of me. There was no doubt that we had caught them with their pants down.

I quickly stopped running and got into a solid sitting position beside a hootch. The PRU began firing on full automatic with their AK-47s and RPDs, and I fired my Garand on semiautomatic. Since I was using red tracers and the humidity was very high, I saw the trace of my bullets ripping through the early morning air. Every time a bullet connected with human flesh and bone, it exited the body at an angle different from that at penetration, so I knew I had scored. Of course, every time a VC dropped, I had conclusive evidence of a hit.

When the third body had fallen in the distance, the PRU around me started hollering and laughing while pointing toward another would-be escapee at about three hundred meters. He looked to be a young VC and was really hoofing it for the tree line. My first shot was behind the VC and seemed to encourage him to run a bit faster. My second shot was a little low and just in front of the unfortunate fellow. The PRU considered the event hysterically comical and continued to scream obscenities at our exposed and unfortunate enemy. My fourth shot reached its mark, traveling through the VC's upper body and ricocheting upward and toward the tree line. His momentum and adrenaline carried him another three steps before he collapsed.

Sao Lam, my everpresent counterpart, friend, and assistant PRU chief, yelled that more VC on the other side of the hootches were running posthaste toward the tree line about five hundred yards away where their bunker complex was located. While the remnant of the VC and VCI ran, and while Randy and Sao Lam concentrated on ferreting out and rounding up several VC and VCI within the hamlet, I quickly got on the PRC-25 radio to the helo gunships, who were chomping at the bit to swoop in and fire their 2.75-inch rockets and 7.62-mm machine guns.

It was time to let the helicopter gunships have some fun, too. "Prairie Dog Twelve. This is Dog Face Ten. Over."

"This is Prairie Dog Twelve. Go," the pilot answered.

"This is Dog Face Ten. Request a rocket strike at twelve o'clock, five hundred meters from my position. Victor Charlie and bunkers are at that location. I will mark their position. You identify. Over."

While the helicopter gunships circled over the hamlet and watched for my signal, I fired three tracers into the tree line where the VC had run and the enemy bunker complex was located.

"Dog Face Ten. I see your three red tracers impacting under a prominent palm tree. Is that where you want the first strike?" the pilot asked.

"This is Dog Face Ten. Roger. That's within ten meters of Victor Charlie's position. Give 'em hell. Over." A few PRU and I moved toward the tree line to improve our view while still maintaining some cover from sniper fire.

When the first gunship began its shallow dive toward the tree line, he started receiving AK-47 small arms fire that included green and red tracers. But the VC fire only served to identify their exact location. The lead helo fired four 2.75-inch rockets right on target and both door gunners sprayed the area with M-60 machine guns. Tracers were flying up and down and all around.

"Hoo-yah!" I howled, knowing that some VC had just experienced a real ass kicking. There was a secondary explosion and a fireball shortly afterwards. Both helos struck the tree line and the bunker complex for two more runs, then departed for Dong Tam. My excitement, however, ended abruptly when I heard an all-too-familiar sound—an agonizing howl. The voice was that of a woman, and it sounded from the area where we had inserted with the helo.

Randy, Sao Lam, and the PRU had captured six VCI (we failed to capture Nam Phen, however) and were parading them past me toward the sound of the screaming woman. Our mission was basically over, so I turned and followed along. I looked beyond our small group to the hootch that the helo gunner had initially shot up and spied an old Vietnamese woman. She was dressed in traditional black pajamas and was wailing and flailing her arms in the air around her head.

As we approached the old lady, she eyed us with a look of ageless sorrow and anguish—reaching toward us with her hands and pleading with her eyes while mumbling incoherently. The PRU ignored her, simply walking by, but I wanted to find out what was wrong with her.

I walked to the opposite side of the hootch, where I saw two children. There was a boy about five years old and a girl perhaps seven lying next to the hootch who were unconscious and motionless. I stepped around the bodies to where I could see their faces and the gruesome results of our helo gunner's random spraying of the hootch with the machine gun. The boy's chin was bloody and partly torn away where a bullet had drilled him, while the girl had suffered an ugly head wound. They were both still alive, however, and in desperate need of medical attention.

Randy Sheridan walked up beside me, glanced at the children, and started away. The old woman, who I judged to be their grandmother, jumped in front of him and cried out to him.

"Help!" she moaned. Then, as Randy shook his head helplessly and departed from the scene, she pleaded loudly, "Help! *Bay gio day!*" She wanted help right away, and I certainly understood why. An expressionless old man walked up to the old grandmother, then to the two children.

I assumed he was the grandfather. Initially, a thirty-mile stare on his face, he looked like a man suffering from shell shock, resigned to the tragedy with little sign of emotion. However, within a couple minutes his face reflected total despair and grief, a complete loss of hope, as he wept bitterly.

Two Vietnamese men from the village, about thirty to forty years of age, hurried over with a hammock which had its ends strung to each end of a long pole. They set the pole down and spread the hammock out on the ground beside the wounded children. As they carefully lifted and moved each child onto the meshed netting, I got the attention of the PRU radioman, who hastened to my side. Using the radio, I called in to subsector at Cho Gao District of Dinh Tuong Province and requested a medevac for wounded personnel, to include wounded children, either from the U.S. 9th Division or the ARVN 7th Division. I was told that there was nothing available to come to our aid. Apparently, all medevac aircraft were currently involved in combat operations with both divisions.

Sadly, I could only look sympathetically at the grandparents and shake my head. The grandmother had been watching me as I talked on the radio, but once she understood that I would be of no use, she drew her hands over her face and shuffled to the two men handling her grandchildren. She gave quick instructions, interspersed with wailing. It was at that time that I began hoping that I hadn't shot the children's father, thereby multiplying the grandparents' grief over the death of a son. "Lord help us all," I thought. It was easy at that moment to believe in the total depravity of mankind.

"Let's go!" Randy called to me. I looked in his direction and saw that our men were leaving in single file. I knew from my map and our briefing that our extraction point was a dirt road about three thousand meters (three klicks) from the village. There we were to catch any available vehicle and be transported to a ferry to cross the river to My Tho.

"Come on, Smitty!" Randy shouted, beckoning with his

arm for me to hurry. His voice seemed rough, and I saw and heard no compassion from Randy toward the distressed grandparents. His disinterest in the wounded children bothered me momentarily until I grabbed hold of my senses and realized he had no choice, and I had no choice. We had to get on the move before the local VC unit started serious sniping or attempted a counterattack. I had to harden my heart enough to turn away from the children and get the hell out of there, just as Randy was doing. Besides, I comforted myself, the children now had help from the two Vietnamese men, who would carry them to the nearest medical facility, which I knew was located far down the dirt road to which we were patrolling.

I quickly joined Randy and the others and we left the village with our captives. The mission would go down as a success in the books of those who kept track, but it was carved into my heart as an unfortunate calamity. I was stung even more deeply when the two men bearing the hammock urgently passed by our troops after the first thousand meters with the grandmother and apparent mother and grandfather scampering after them, also weeping.

The grandmother's eyes rested on me for a moment as she went past, then she quickly looked away to the ground in front of her and continued to wail. I focused on her small, bare feet, moving as fast as the old woman could shuffle them. They were pointed inward, and even the toes were turned toward the inside, making them look like monkey feet. I guessed that they were the feet of one who had spent a lifetime working hard in the rice paddies to help feed the family. And now they were the feet of one running and stumbling toward help at a distant hospital where perhaps a poorly qualified nurse or two would attempt to deal with the dreadful situation. That is, if either of the children were still alive by the time the entourage made it there.

I looked at the horizon where the sun was perched, promising a bright, new day, and I cursed under my breath. "You liar," I whispered toward the sun. "This is a dark day. This is a stinkin', rotten, sad day."

"Smitty!" Scott's voice carried me away from my remembrance and back to the present day. The sun, as it was on that day almost ten months ago, was radiantly peeking over the edge of the earth. "Let's go to breakfast," Scotty said with a grin on his face.

"Yeah," I mumbled, sitting up in my hammock, "breakfast."

"We're patrolling Rocket Alley this morning, remember? It's a free-fire zone, man!"

I nodded my head, remembering. And remembering the two wounded children once again, I hoped I would encounter no kids in the jungle on this bright, new day.

CHAPTER FIFTEEN

At 0830 hours, Tu Uy Hao (Tranh's replacement) and twenty Biet Hai, three UDT-11 guys, EOD Ellis, Scott, and I loaded our gear and explosives onto two Riverine Force boats, then boarded them ourselves and headed toward Rocket Alley. We knew the VC had built many bunkers along the three-kilometer waterway because our boats were often shot at by NVA rocket squads when they entered the area. The CO of Sea Float had determined that we had put up with the attacks quite long enough. Our group of twenty-seven men inserted a few meters west of the first of a long string of bunkers near the south edge of the river. Ellis and the Utes quickly started readying their explosives and equipment. I left four Biet Hai with them to assist as needed. That left Tu Uy Hao, sixteen Biet Hai, Scott, and myself to set up a skirmish line perpendicular to the river and inland of the EOD/UDT demolition crew. Our chore was to advance with the demolition group as its security element, to protect them from lurking enemy, and to notify them of booby traps in the area. We were also to be careful to maintain visual contact between all personnel. As usual, Tu Uy, Scott with the radio, and I were positioned in the center of the skirmish line for command and control.

"Munster Seven Alpha. This is Munster Seven. Radio check. Over," Ellis called to confirm that our commo was five by five (loud and clear) and ready to begin our march of destruction.

"Munster Seven. This is Munster Seven Alpha. I hear you loud and clear. How me? Over."

"Munster Seven Alpha. This is Munster Seven. I hear you same. We're ready to roll. We'll be moving out smartly. When you hear 'Fire in the hole' there will be a five-minute delay before the detonation. Watch out for those snakes! Over."

I was impressed with Ellis's concern.

Ellis's "Fire in the hole" came in less than a minute. Ellis and the Utes were very well organized and moving fast. Most of the bunkers would accommodate just one or two men, each not much more than a shallow hole dug out near the riverbank, covered with mud, logs, and sticks, and provided with a good view of the target area. The bunkers were well camouflaged and very difficult to spot from a boat.

I was kept busy trying to watch and advise Tu Uy Hao, maintain commo with Ellis, and insure we didn't trip any booby traps. There were numerous human tracks in the area, meaning we could expect just about anything.

Nguyen was rapidly improving as a platoon-leading petty officer. He was the first to find a standard-type booby trap in this area. It consisted of a Chinese grenade (with the safety pin pulled) placed inside a tight-fitting tin can that was secured to a tree at ankle level. Monofilament line had been tied to the grenade's fuse assembly and ran for ten feet or so across a trail to a bush where it was tied securely. The fuse was of the instantaneous type—in other words, no delay. If Nguyen had walked into the monofilament line unawares, body contact with the line would have pulled the grenade from the can, the spoon falling away and releasing the spring-loaded, cocked striker. The cocked striker would have struck the detonator, which in turn would have caused the main charge within the grenade to detonate in a microsecond. Fortunately for us, the Biet Hai had learned their booby trap lessons well, for we found six more before the day was over.

The demo crew blew the bunkers while we burned the hootches. Explosions were going off every few minutes and burning hootches were darkening the sky. It reminded me of Sherman's march across the South in 1864–65. It was great fun and good for our morale. We felt as if we were getting even with the enemy—and accomplishing something, to boot.

When all was said and done, we had destroyed thirty-nine bunkers, twenty-five hootches, and seven booby traps. We also killed three snakes, one an eight-foot cobra that was corkscrewed in a tree. It was grayish brown with a light yellow belly.

When we arrived back at our camp at about 1600 hours, I drank four beers and three slugs of Scotch. Needless to say, I felt rather merry.

After a supper at which I ate like a pig, several VNs brought out an old, battered guitar and tried to get me to pluck a few notes and sing a song or three. I apologized and told them that I couldn't play any songs on any guitar, but that I would be glad to teach them some Texas Spanish. So there I was, feeling no pain, trying to teach my Biet Hai brothers how to speak Spanish when I had never mastered English. In spite of my shortcomings and feeling hospitable, I tried to teach the men how to pronounce the Spanish phrase *Mi casa es su casa*, then I attempted to translate the sentence into Vietnamese. Everyone laughed when they finally understood the meaning to be "My house is your house." Apparently they weren't too impressed with my hammock. I thought to myself that it was great to be alive even with the conditions that we were all living under. What a joy it was to have had so much fun with Nguyen and my Biet Hai friends.

As darkness descended upon us, I noticed how still and lovely the tropical evening had become. The mosquitoes hadn't even come out in their usual cloud yet.

"How pleasant to be alive," I spoke to my comrades, then I repeated the comment to their nods of approval. "With the right attitude, almost anything is pleasant," I added, and my friends smiled.

That night as I lay awake in my hammock, I thought about the cobra we had killed earlier that day. My recent involvement with snakes reminded me of the time in 1969 when Leon Rauch and one hundred PRUs and I inserted by helos and captured or killed a dozen or so VCI. After the initial mission, Leon and eighty PRU returned to Rach Gia while my Vietnamese counterpart, named Diep, and I and twenty PRU traveled by motorized sampans to the Three Sisters area, near the coast and between Rach Gia and Cambodia in the province of Kien Giang. Diep was the assistant PRU chief and had fought with the French against the Viet Minh.

During our waterborne trip we stopped at a small café for some iced French coffee or a variety of coconut milk, lime, and papaya juice mixtures with a sprinkling of raw sugar and mixed with crushed ice. The place of business was small, about fifteen feet square, with four small tables made from U.S. artillery-round boxes and some chairs. The young lass that served us was approximately five feet in height, about eighteen, and had a very pleasing body and face. Her glossy black hair was long and rolled into a large bun on the back of her head. She had a delightfully bold and charming personality. She spoke in a musical manner—literally singing her conversation. It was beautiful to the ear and a sight to behold. This was the only woman I had ever seen or heard about who communicated in such a manner. The PRU and I were absolutely mesmerized in her presence. I believe any of us would have married her at that very moment. War tends to make its victims live for the moment and not think too much about the future.

My counterpart, Diep, leaned over to me and commented, "She is much woman." I wholeheartedly agreed.

We continued on our way, and later that evening I ate a late dinner with an old, white-bearded hamlet chief, whose cuisine included duck, python and python eggs, boiled rice, vegetable salad, *nuoc mam*, *ba xi de* (Vietnamese rice whiskey), French coffee, and Oriental tea. As I tried to ignore the python eggs, the chief informed me (through my interpreter) that he had never seen any man eat more than two python eggs. "I can't imagine why," I thought, as I eyed them suspiciously. Looking for an escape route, I turned to him, saying, "It's kind of like a side of water buffalo—a feller doesn't want to consume it all at one sittin'."

Ignoring my attempt at subterfuge, he began instructing me to take one egg and bite a small hole through its leathery covering with my teeth. The situation was hopeless. My image was at stake again, and since I had already proven my manhood by chewing and swallowing a cockroach in 1967 at Nha Be, and since I was, after all, an elite Navy SEAL, I accepted the chief's challenge and picked up an egg about the size of a medium-sized fist. It was soft and felt like it was full of something I didn't want to discuss at the dinner table.

I bit into the egg gently with no results. I bit a little harder with little results. I finally had to bite as hard as I could, simultaneously pulling hard to complete the task. Its contents, which had the consistency of mashed potatoes, squirted out onto my right hand. Not wanting to appear disrespectful and wanting to display satisfaction, I quickly slurped it up, followed by a smacking of my lips. It was all a facade, of course. However, the chief was very pleased at my good manners. Somehow I had managed to eat that one egg, followed by several shots of *ba xi de* to kill the aftertaste. "Snakes and image, image and snakes," I thought. I wondered which was worse.

After dinner the chief offered me a place to wash up and a bed to sleep on. The bed was made of a dark tropical hardwood with thin, narrow slats running from the head of the bed to its foot. The pillow, covered with a lightweight cotton cloth, was filled with rice husks and sewed tightly into a cylindrical bundle that was about five inches in diameter and eight inches in length. A mosquito net was draped over the bed. Knowing that it was an honor to be invited to sleep in the chief's home, I bowed and said *"Cam on ong"* ("Thank you, sir"). That hard bed and pillow never felt so good.

The next morning I felt like puking when I left the hamlet, and things only seemed to get worse for the next two days when the PRUs and I ran out of water while looking for bad guys near the Three Sisters Mountains. It was a good thing we didn't encounter any NVA or VC units, for by the end of the first day all of us had no water. Because we were near the coast, there was only brackish water in the area.

By the morning of the second day the situation was critical. The PRUs started climbing to the top of coconut trees to get coconuts that were filled with milk. Others cut down banana plants of a foot or more in diameter and carved a concave hole down into the stump in hopes of finding water filling the cavity. The coconut milk relieved our thirst for a short while, then it seemed to intensify. When the banana stump cavities failed to produce any water, we knew we had to return inland to the main irrigation canal that ran the length of the province.

We patrolled out of the Three Sisters area in grim silence for the better part of the day, headed toward the canal, where drinking water would be found. It reminded me of the Bataan Death March in 1942, when the Japanese captured thousands of U.S. soldiers, Corregidor, and most of the Philippine Islands. The main difference was that none of us were tortured by the enemy and none of us died.

When we got to within a hundred meters of the canal, where hootches were built nearby, those of us who could began running toward the canal. I managed to get to a hootch first and quickly asked a Vietnamese lady for a glass of water. I didn't care if the water had come out of the canal or not. It was the best water I had ever tasted. It also turned out to be the most unhealthy water I ever drank.

The following day I came down with diarrhea. Talk about the "back door trots"! Within two weeks I had to be medevacked from the U Minh Forest, during a mission, to the army's field hospital near Can Tho because of acute stomach cramps, dehydration, and diarrhea. I spent six days in that hospital. That ended my eating python eggs and lapping canal water.

* * *

I awoke the next morning at 0615. At 0730, Tu Uy Hao told me we were going on an operation in forty-five minutes. I told him I hadn't been informed about this earlier, but he just grinned and assured me I had. I quickly readied my gear just in case an op really was about to happen, and sure enough, at 0815 Tu Ta and Scott came to get me.

Tu Ta said he'd told me about the op at 2030 hours the previous night and that I had carried on quite a conversation with him about it. Of course, this all happened after I had downed the four beers and three slugs of Scotch. At any rate, Scott and I headed out with Tu Uy Hao and fourteen Biet Hai, Petty Officer Bennett of UDT-11, and one Vietnamese Navy EOD (LDNN), bound for an area where the VC had shot B-40 and B-50 rockets at the PG boat *Antelope* the previous day.

Prior to the boats' arrival, we organized into two squads. Myself, Petty Officer Bennett, Nguyen, and six Biet Hai comprised the second squad while Tu Uy Hao, Scott, the VN EOD, and six Biet Hai filled the first squad. I was the radioman for my squad and Scott was the radioman for Tu Uy. Shortly afterwards, my group boarded the U.S. Navy's PCF 40 (Patrol Craft Fast) and Tu Uy's group boarded the Vietnamese navy's PCF 09.

Our mission for the day was to proceed to the mouth of the Bo De River and escort a U.S. Navy AKS supply boat to Sea Float for replenishment of food and supplies. PG (Patrol Gunboat) *Ready* joined us on our return trip to Sea Float. *Ready*'s single three-inch gun, 40-mm guns, and dual .50-caliber machine guns were a big addition to the escort's repertoire.

We hadn't proceeded for more than a hour when PG *Ready* spotted rocket pods set up on the beach. The lieutenant aboard PG *Ready* (apparently the senior lieutenant) ordered us to insert west of the rocket pods. I quickly identified the insertion point and requested the PCF lieutenant ease in to the beach so that myself and second squad could make a jump from the bow for the riverbank. Tu Uy and first squad were to remain aboard their boat for reinforcement if needed. Then we would move in and search the area while the PG, acting as a blocking element, covered the eastern flank and the PCFs supported us.

Just as we were moving near to the brushy beach for insertion, we spotted two more separate rocket pods (three rockets per pod) from only a few yards away. The PCF lieutenant quickly reversed course and moved the boat over a few meters to get us out of the line of fire of the multiple rockets.

After we safely inserted and determined that there were no recent signs of enemy activity, Tu Uy and first squad inserted and set up our security perimeter a few meters inland. Bennett and the VN EOD fellow began rendering safe the rockets and clearing all other ordnance-related equipment from the area while I maintained commo with all three boats and with Tu Uy Hao.

The area NILO (Navy Intelligence Liaison Officer) had been receiving intelligence information that there were several specially trained NVA rocket squads assigned to the Nam Canh/Bo De River area specifically to blow our boats out of the water. What we found that day definitely confirmed the reliability of his source. Well-camouflaged mud-and-log bunkers were spaced all along the river. Interconnecting trenches zigzagged between them. There were also trenches used for escape routes that eventually led inland to a canal where a sampan was concealed. The NVA rocket squads had stashed D-cell flashlight batteries in the strategic bunkers and had run electrical firing wires from the bunkers to the rocket pods, where the firing wire was connected to the rockets inside the pods. The rocket pods had been carefully aimed to hit any boat amidstream at near the hull's water level. When the NVA had information that the SEALs and BSU boats or other desirable targets were heading up- or downstream, they would simply send one or two men to interdict and harass and sometimes destroy thousands of dollars of equipment and/or highly trained personnel with only a couple of rockets. They would then crawl back to their sampan and *di di mau* (head for cover in a hurry) for a safe haven in the Nam Canh swamp before aircraft would have time to arrive overhead. Their tactics were simple. Their weapons and ordnance were simple. No doubt the NVA rocket squads' morale was very high. That was what I called simplicity of mission and job satisfaction. I was envious. However, we did find one grenade, four undamaged B-40 and 150-mm rockets, two damaged B-50 rockets (from .50-caliber MG fire), two trirocket pods, electrical firing wire, and batteries. Somehow, it didn't seem like much.

Afterwards, we went to the VN annex, located at the New Nam Canh village, and waited for the AKS until it had offloaded the provisions at Sea Float and was returning to the mouth of the Bo De River.

While we were escorting the AKS, we received word that a SEAL squad and two Kit Carson Scouts had had an encounter with a company (sixty men) of VC and got the short end of the stick. Both KCSs were wounded. Navy Seawolves (HAL-3) were called in and two PCFs extracted the men. Shortly afterwards, two Navy Black Ponies (VAL-4) came in and shot the hell out of the area with five-inch Zuni rockets and .50-caliber machine guns. They did such a good job that it was likely that at least a couple of VC had kissed their butts good-bye.

When we got to the mouth of the Bo De River, our escort duties were completed. Spotting some unusual items on the beach, we inserted on the south bank and investigated a sampan. We also located a booby-trapped 155-mm artillery round. Interestingly, hundreds of Japanese glass fishing net floats of all shapes and sizes littered the beach. I could have spent the whole day combing the beach for hidden treasures.

Sunburned and tired, but still in one piece, we finally returned to Solid Anchor at 2045 hours. After I had drafted my sitrep (situation report) for NavForV, I was about to crawl into my hammock when Ton, Thu, and Nguyen, three of my Biet Hai buddies, decided to disturb me with their joking and laughter. They informed me that Tu Uy Hao's new wife, who was presently visiting Dai Uy Banh, had arrived at my hut, and my buddies were sure that the Haos would be turning up the radio real loud for the duration of the night. No wonder Tu Uy Hao had seemed to be in a hurry to get cleaned up and head for Dai Uy's pad. I shook my head and dismissed Vietnam's Larry, Moe, and Curly.

"We no Tree Stoogies," Thu chuckled as he finally started walking away with his friends in tow. "You will see, Smitty, we no Tree Stoogies. No way, Jose."

I lay down in my hammock and giggled into my pillow. But my amusement was short-lived. An hour later, after Tu Uy and his wife had returned, a radio began to blare.

CHAPTER SIXTEEN

Two days later, the VC hit our PCF 35 at the waterline with a rocket. The boat crew had to beach and patch the hole, then they were escorted in by our other PCFs.

The next day, I took six Biet Hai on PCF 694 while Scott took five Biet Hai on PCF 63. We served as an escort for two tugs and two barges out to the mouth of the Bo De River. Then we inserted and swept the area where PCF 35 had been hit. We searched for any remaining rockets that might have been set up on the beach, but all we found was a large, dead monkey about fifty meters inland. It was apparent that firing from a boat had accidentally killed it.

After we returned to the base at 1300 hours, I washed my clothes and rested a bit. I then went to Sea Float and found out that the Kit Carsons had been hit hard while trying to insert by PCF. Doug Hobbs, a photo interpreter who was assigned to the SEAL advisers with the Kit Carsons, had been killed. One SEAL was wounded, as were two PCF personnel and two Scouts.

The next day, May 18, 1970, Tu Uy Hao told me that it was Buddha's birthday and that a truce would start at 1200 hours. Somebody should have told the VC. One of our Tango boats, an armored MK 8, was shot at with B-40 rounds. By way of response, our Black Ponies said to hell with the blubber-belly's birthday and blew out all the candles, as it were, that possibly could have been lit in that area. The Tango boat and all our men returned from the fracas without so much as a scratch.

We weren't so fortunate the following afternoon. After

lunch, I went to Sea Float to get the mail and the commanding officer saw me and asked if I would go on a VR (visual reconnaissance). He was sending a psychological operations officer, a Lieutenant (jg) Sherry, along with his chief petty officer up in a helo to do some aerial reconnaissance of an enemy base camp about six klicks north of Sea Float. Since I had nothing else scheduled for the remainder of the day, I agreed to accompany the others on the scouting trip. The commanding officer loaned me his .45 automatic pistol and wished me luck.

The three of us boarded an Army UH-1 Huey slick with a pilot and co-pilot. I sat on the edge of the port-side door, dangling my feet outside the slick and resting them on top of the left strut. Lieutenant Sherry sat behind me and to my right, while the chief sat on a seat to my left and behind me.

It took less than ten minutes to locate the enemy camp. We circled three hundred feet above it as the helo pilot executed a counterclockwise, continuous sharp turn. Looking straight down from my perch, I spied several reinforced bunkers of mud and logs. I also saw five hootches and one sampan.

Wanting to move closer, the lieutenant asked the pilot to go lower. No sooner had we dropped a hundred feet than someone on the ground took a couple of shots at us.

"Damn!" exclaimed the chief from behind me. "Shouldn't we get outa here?"

I looked at Lieutenant Sherry and giggled a little. As a battle-experienced jungle fighter, a couple pops from what sounded to me like a pistol weren't enough to put the fear of death into me. However, the situation was beginning to get exciting.

"Relax, Chief," Sherry shouted above the roar of the helo's engines. Then he told the pilot to keep circling the VC position. "Let's observe things a little more here."

We made the circuit over the enemy base camp two more times, asking for trouble. We got it. A moment later AW fire erupted from the ground. A bullet zipped by my face, missing me but hitting the chief on the right side of his forehead. The bullet made a small indentation in his skull, leaving a mushy hole and knocking the chief screwy. He began rocking back and forth, babbling incoherently.

"Shit!" I spat, looking at the lieutenant. "We're takin' heavy automatic fire!" As bullets ripped into the side and bottom of the helo, I reached back and steadied the chief with one hand and touched his forehead with the other, checking the wound. I felt a softness where hard bone should have been.

In a sudden hail of bullets, the lieutenant clutched at his chin and slumped over behind me. I grabbed him and laid his head on my lap.

"Get outa here!" I hollered at the top of my lungs to the pilot, who was already doing exactly that. Lieutenant Sherry was bleeding profusely all over me from a bullet hole somewhere around his neck, but there was so much blood flowing onto both of us that I had difficulty finding the wound.

When I finally was able to pull Sherry's hand away from his chin, I saw a large hole on the right side of his throat, located just about where the jugular vein was positioned. Guessing that he had already lost at least two pints of blood, I knew I had to do something drastic, and do it quickly.

I reached over my head and grabbed the back of my blue-and-gold T-shirt with both hands, then jerked the shirt up and off. I rolled the shirt into a ball and shoved it into the lieutenant's neck wound, using it as a pressure bandage. I simply didn't know what else to do under the circumstances.

"How's the lieutenant?" the co-pilot shouted over the clanging and banging of the shot-up engine, which sounded as bad as Sherry looked.

I stared at my patient. He was pale and obviously in shock, if not dead. As a matter of fact, I thought right then that he was dead, so I yelled back to the co-pilot. "I think he's dead!"

Lieutenant Sherry slowly raised his right hand and clenched his fist, then he raised his thumb and gave me a thumbs-up to inform me that he was still with us. I was instantly distressed with myself for having announced that he was dead. A message like that, I knew, could convey a hopelessness that would put a man into a deep shock from which he wouldn't recover.

"Hang in there, Lieutenant," I said to him, trying to wipe out my careless words with a quick gush of positive thoughts. "You're gonna make it. I've got the bleeding stopped and you're gonna be okay."

As the helo labored toward Sea Float on a wish and a prayer, sputtering and shaking, I continued pressing the makeshift bandage against Sherry's injury. I glanced at the chief a few times along the way, noting that he had finally shoved a handkerchief onto his own wound and held it there as he sat hunched over on his seat. His face was still flushed, so I figured he'd be all right.

"It's gonna be close!" the pilot yelled back at me over the noises the faltering helo was making. "Be ready to crash!"

I shouted back at him, "How much further?"

"One klick, but it's a long one!" he hollered.

The helicopter engine seemed to be gasping for breath. I was sure by the sounds of things that the pilots were also dealing with hydraulic problems, among others. I was also sure that our landing, wherever it occurred, promised to be a butt-kicker.

"Hang in there, Lieutenant," I repeated, holding him a little tighter. "Medical help is only a minute away. We're almost back to Sea Float."

From my seated position in the slick, I couldn't see Sea Float, but when I saw water out the port door, I realized we were almost there. But "almost" doesn't count in helicopter rides. The slick was bouncing up and down so much that I felt like I was back in Texas trying to hang on to a bucking bronc. The two situations were the same in that in both of them I had to hit the ground sometime.

"Hang on!" the pilot yelled at me, indicating my "sometime" had arrived. I held the lieutenant close, then looked at the chief. He was gripping his seat with only one hand, but that would have to be enough, I decided.

With a distinct wobble, then a halfhearted flare, the helo stalled in the air, coughed, then lurched forward. In the next instant, it dropped hard onto the pad at Sea Float in a controlled crash. The helo shook for a moment, took its last puff, and was dead.

I immediately yelled, "Get a corpsman, quick! Lieutenant Sherry needs medical help now!" No sooner were the words out of my mouth than Doc and two men were alongside the helo door with a stretcher. They were obviously prepared.

"I've got my blue-and-gold over the wound to help stop the bleeding," I explained.

"It's all right, Smitty. He'll be okay," Doc counseled as he checked the wound, bleeding, and other life signs before his assistants loaded Sherry aboard the stretcher. Doc was already preparing Sherry for a blood transfusion. Fortunately, the army helo pilot had radioed Sea Float that Lieutenant Sherry was badly wounded and had lost a lot of blood.

When they took the chief and Lieutenant Sherry away, they left my blood-soaked blue-and-gold lying on the deck. As I stood there bare-chested on the helo pad, I gingerly picked it up and carried it over to the side and started rinsing the blood out of it in the cleansing waters of the Bo De River. "It'll need a good washing before I can wear it again," I thought. I still had Sherry's blood on my stomach, as well as all over the front of my jungle pants.

The CO approached me and extended his right hand to shake mine.

I hesitated, saying, "Ah, I'm full of blood, sir."

He shrugged. "Doesn't matter. You saved Lieutenant Sherry's life." His hand remained outstretched, so I shook it firmly.

"I hope you're right, sir," I replied, not convinced that

the lieutenant would pull through. He was alive a minute ago, for a fact, but I wondered if he would still have a beating heart in an hour or two.

"Well," the commanding officer stated confidently, "if Sherry can take a round in the neck, then survive a helo crash, I have to believe he'll somehow manage to survive the corpsman's diggin' around in him." He grinned and gave me a pat on the back.

I nodded and smiled. "You're probably right," I said, feeling a little better about the whole situation.

"Now, then," the commanding officer said, starting to walk but looking for me to follow him, "let's go find you a shirt."

"Yes, sir," I replied, breaking into a walk behind him. "Oh, by the way, Captain, here's your .45. I never had a chance to use it."

After I handed him his pistol, the commanding officer said with a chuckle, "I guess it's safe for me to assume for purposes of your scouting report concerning the enemy base camp that you found a great deal of activity there."

His remark dumbfounded me for a moment, but after he chuckled again, I answered, "Slightly." Then we both laughed.

As it turned out, the commanding officer's prediction was correct. Lieutenant (jg) Sherry was patched up by the corpsman on Sea Float, was medevacked to Saigon, then to Japan and on to the U. S. of A., where he received excellent medical care, and his life was spared. I did hear later that he suffered some kind of disability as a result of his injury, but I never found out exactly what it was. All I knew then was that he had lived, and I thanked God for that.

CHAPTER SEVENTEEN

The next morning I went out with Scott and nine Biet Hai on my last PCF escort mission. The escort went without a hitch, then we joined Tu Ta and two UDT-11 guys and headed for Solid Anchor's perimeter outskirts to cut and blow trees. There were no signs of any VC nighttime activity along the perimeter and the tree line.

When we got back to camp at around 1600 hours, I took Tu Uy Tranh to Sea Float. There we got some gasoline and oil for Tu Ta's outboard engine. While we were there I talked to a good friend of mine, nicknamed Tiny, whom I hadn't seen since 1969 when I was a PRU adviser in My Tho. He was called Tiny because of his height, six feet four inches, and weight, 250 pounds. He had just arrived in-country as a member of BSU-1 (SEAL boat support folks) for another tour. I had first met him at Binh Thuy during Tet 1968 when he was a PBR sailor. Seeing Tiny reminded me that it was a small world sometimes; it was always good to see an old friend again. I finally had to say good-bye as Tranh and I got a ride back to the Biet Hai camp.

While eating supper, I found out that Tu Ta was planning to lead twenty-two Biet Hai the next day up a canal where the VC had built a blockade across the water. The blockade was located at a point near the enemy base camp where Lieutenant Sherry had been wounded. Naturally, I was interested in going along on this mission, but my time was up with the Biet Hai. I was scheduled to leave for Saigon in the morning.

"You be careful tomorrow," I warned Scott after supper when I found myself shaking hands with him, saying good-bye.

" 'Careful' is my middle name," he replied, grinning. "You just take care of yourself, Smitty."

"You can count on it, mate. I sure wish I could go with you guys tomorrow, though. However, I'm going to recommend to Tu Ta that he request a SEAL squad go with y'all to support the Biet Hai and act as a reactionary force."

"Do you think he'll do it?" Scott asked.

"If you guys run into that NVA/VC rocket-and-sapper group, you'll probably find yourselves in the middle of a swamp, up to your noses in the muck, and surrounded by bloodthirsty crocodiles," I said. "If Tu Ta doesn't ask the SEALs for support, then I strongly recommend that you stay close to Nguyen. He's alert, he listens to recommendations, and he's a good LPO. Tu Uy Hao seems to be working out well, also."

As a final word of friendship, I said, "Well, if you ever get to San Diego, give me a call. I've always got a couple of cold ones in the fridge and the room and board is free."

"Hey, man, keep it cool, now," Scott said as he turned and headed back for his hootch.

I walked back to my hammock and quickly began packing my gear before the mosquitoes chased me to bed. Several of my Biet Hai friends came by to shake my hand and say farewell. One, Ton said to me, "I miss you, Smitty. You good friend."

"You're a good friend, too, Ton," I assured him. I reached down and took a couple of extra twenty-round magazines and a bottle of mosquito repellent from my operating gear and handed them to Ton. "You keep this as a gift from me," I told him.

Ton took the magazines and repellent with a smile. "Tank you, Smitty!" He walked away feeling very happy.

Then Nguyen surprised me with his tears. "Hate to see

you go," he said as he grasped my right hand with both of his. Tears streamed down his cheeks.

Lord, how I hated good-byes. I was having a hard time controlling my emotions, too. I bent down and picked up two hard-to-get thirty-round M-16 magazines from my gear. "From me to my good friend, Nguyen," I said.

"I never forget you," Nguyen replied as he held my right hand in his.

Shortly after Nguyen departed, Tu Uy Hao returned to his shack, where I was still busy packing my gear. "Dai Uy Banh and I are sorry you go. We like you for our *co van* (adviser). Maybe we Biet Hai see you at Cam Ranh Bay for LDNN training soon, for old time," he said brightly as we shook hands.

"I hope so, Tu Uy." I then pulled two thirty-round M-16 magazines, two white and two red parachute flares, two MK-13 day/night flares, two sets of pencil flares, four M-26 fragmentation grenades, and two morphine styrettes from my web gear and vest and set them on the steps to his hootch. "I want to leave these with you and Dai Uy Banh. I hope you and your wife will have a good stay here until you can go to Cam Ranh Bay." I hesitated, then added, "Please thank Dai Uy Banh for me for his being a good officer and taking good care of the Biet Hai. You are a good officer, too. I will miss you both."

After Tu Uy left, I returned to my packing and was just finishing as the mosquitoes showed up in a cloud. That's when Tu Ta Sphinx stopped by for a minute.

"Good luck," he said, also shaking my hand.

"Thank you, Commander," I replied. "And the same to you tomorrow."

Tu Ta smiled. "After we blow their little blockade away tomorrow, our morale will be much higher."

I grinned, setting up a suggestion I had been wanting to offer for the past hour. "You know, sir, I think it would be wise for you to request at least a squad of SEALs to go along so you will have some extra firepower and experienced people in the field."

What had remained of Tu Ta's smile vanished. After a moment of hesitation, he muttered, "We'll see what develops." Then he forced half a smile and repeated, "Good luck, Smitty," before walking away.

I shook my head, tired of all the games some folks play—professional jealousies, hidden agendas, facades of one form or another, vindictiveness, etc. And the folks who specialized in these areas generally operated covertly. As near as I could tell, their motives revealed a total lack of integrity and honor. They simply weren't trustworthy because of their self-serving and self-centered values.

At 0630 hours on the morning of 21 May, I crawled out of bed. After a great cup of heavily sweetened Vietnamese coffee that Nguyen brought me, I packed the rest of my gear. I carried two heavy loads of gear to Tu Ta's pad, where I shook hands and said good-bye one last time with Tu Ta, Scott, Dai Uy Banh, Tu Uy Hao, and many of the Biet Hai. As they left camp to go on their mission, I got on a small boat for the short trip to Sea Float, hauling my gear with me.

At Sea Float, I said good-bye to my teammates and BSU friends and returned the XM-148 I had borrowed from Echo Platoon. Then I filled out a "change of address" card for the postal clerk.

"Hey, Smitty!" a voice called to me as I dragged some of my gear towards the helo pad. I recognized the voice immediately as that of Tiny.

Turning back toward him, I dropped my bags and waited as he walked up to me. "Hi, Tiny," I greeted him. "What's up, mate?"

Shaking his head, Tiny said, "The UH-34 isn't comin' today." This was bad news, as I had been planning to fly in the helicopter to Saigon.

"That sucks," I said disgustedly.

Tiny just grinned. With a shrug, he offered, "Why don't you just bum a ride on the CH-47 to Ca Mau, then catch another ride or two from there?"

I was interested. "When does the '47 leave for Ca Mau?"

"In about five minutes," Tiny answered, still smiling. Suddenly I was more than merely interested.

Picking up a couple of my gear bags, I looked at the other bags, then at Tiny. He took the hint and grabbed the bags for me, and both of us headed for the chopper. "I owe you a cold one, Tiny," I promised.

"No sweat, Smitty. I'll collect when I see you back on the Strand in six months."

Five minutes later, I was airborne and leaving Sea Float in my past. I looked back once for a long half minute and watched as the barges grew smaller and smaller. Then my eyes fell on the Biet Hai camp near the shore of the Cua Lon River. I realized that once again I was leaving behind some friends I would never see again in this lifetime, and that thought made me sad. I fought the sentimentality, as I didn't want to allow mawkish feelings to overwhelm me. But I couldn't help myself.

As the camp disappeared from sight, my thoughts drifted back to the evening of October 2, 1969. I was finishing a long, hard tour, which I was reflecting over while sitting alone on the roof of the Embassy House, an old French colonial villa, in My Tho.

Senior Chief Al Huey and I had shared some good missions together as PRU advisers in Dinh Tuong Province. Al, who had relieved Randy Sheridan as the Senior PRU adviser, had been one of my UDT training instructors in 1965 and was my senior as a PRU adviser. He was not only a loyal teammate but a good personal friend. We had worked well together, and the PRU really liked both of us.

The next day I would be leaving for Can Tho, where I was to pick up my personal and pay records, then go on to Saigon and Tan Son Nhut AFB for departure to CONUS on the sixth of October at 1945 hours.

There was little I could do now other than cumshaw gear for the PRUs, food for the Embassy House, and shuffle papers. I had already taken most of my operating and cumshaw gear to SEAL Team One's Golf Platoon that was operating out of Ben Luc. They were a great bunch of guys and operated in-country from May through November 1969. The members of Golf Platoon were: LTjg G. R. Gray, LTjg J. M. Horst, SF1 Adams, GMG1 Raper, QM2 Ako, HM2 Silva, ETR2 Cheatam, ETN3 Hicks, RM3 Hedge, SN Nolan, SN Passyka, AN Werner, RMSA Bruce, and SA Berta. I had previously taken QM2 Ako, SN Passyka, and SA Berta on a couple of PRU ops. All three of them were great for morale, and not suprisingly, the PRUs loved them.

Another reason time went by so slowly was that the Company-run one week meeting of all Delta PRU advisers at SATC near Vung Tau in September 1969 notified us that there would be an abrupt end to all combat PRU advisers (and SEAL platoons) accompanying the PRU on any counter-VC/VCI/NVA cadre operations as of 30 September 1969.

It was a heavy blow to the Phoenix Program's effectiveness at the provincial and district levels. Regardless, the PRU had been turned over to the Ministry of Interior and down the chain of command from the Directorate General of the National Police at the national level to the provincial national police chief, who had administrative control of the PRU, and the province chief (usually an ARVN lieutenant colonel), who had operational control. Trung Uy Loc (an ARVN first lieutenant) was the Dinh Tuong Province's PRU chief, and Sao Lam, who was a member of the PSB (Police Special Branch—equivalent to our FBI) a subdivision of the National Police Force and subordinate to the police chief at the province and district level), was the assistant PRU chief. Trung Uy Loc and Sao Lam were very good operators and worked surprisingly well with each other. I was especially close with my friend Sao Lam.

"Gary, your going-away party is about to begin and it's 1600 hours already," Al reminded me as he stepped up on the roof where we had occasionally enjoyed a Cuba Libre (rum and Coke with a twist of lime) together during the cool hours of the evening.

"Yeah, I'm ready," I replied reluctantly, "but I hate good-byes."

"Well, let's go. Hung [our PRU interpreter] is already

waiting for us down at the creek crossing," Al added impatiently.

The Embassy House was only a block from the creek, which was called the Rach Bao Dinh and which drained into the My Tho River at the southern edge of town. Across from it was the little hamlet called Ap My Phu, which consisted primarily of PRU and National Police homes and families. I had spent many nights there at Sao Lam's house where he and his wife graciously fed me with wonderful Vietnamese dishes. One night Sao Lam had a pretty lass come over and sing beautiful Vietnamese ballads and love songs. The conversation, the food, and the companionship had always been the best. I knew that night would be an emotional one for me.

Sao Lam's house was a modest hootch of two rooms with a porch. The PRU had set up several tables and chairs outside and under the numerous palm trees. On the tables were bowls of vegetables, dried fish and squid, eel, and other forms of hors d'oeuvres with many bottles of Japanese whiskey, rum, and Scotch; there was also soda and Vietnamese 33 Beer for the timid at heart. It was time for the party to begin.

"*Co Van* Gary," Sao Lam began with his glass of whiskey and soda raised in salutation, "we wish you a safe journey to your home across the sea. We hope to see you again soon, and until the time of your return and for the next few hours we invite you to share with us this food and drink in appreciation of your service with us. *Chin, chin* [Bottoms up]!"

I lifted my Cuba Libre and downed its contents, as did the PRU. Al was already mixing both of us another rum and Coke for the next toast. I went over to Sao Lam, bowed slightly, and shook his hand with my left hand also touching his hand. This was showing him greater respect, not only as my counterpart, but as my elder.

"Thank you, Sao Lam," I said, "for this great honor and for being my good friend. May you have long life, good health, and many children."

Next I turned to Trung Uy Loc, bowing slightly, shaking his hand also and thanking him for the privilege of serving with him in combat.

There was a bilateral bond of camaraderie between myself and those PRU. It was a trust that had been sealed in combat through loyalty and a special closeness that comes from the sharing of the physical, emotional, and spiritual stresses of combat. In my opinion, those PRU were as good as the best troops in the world.

Progressively and individually, a PRU would lift his drink up toward me and then to Al, "the elder," and say *"Chin, chin."* It didn't take very long before the effects of the rum and the whiskey caused everyone to relax and start putting their arms around each other as only good friends would. We were one very happy family.

After the main dinner of roast pig (luau style), rice rolls, and other delicacies were served, we settled down to what was to be the unexpected final phase—the presentation of gifts. Sao Lam first presented me with a painting of two pretty Vietnamese ladies with black silk slacks and their white *ao dai*s flowing in the breeze as they walked alongside a riverbank. Not having expected a gift, I was beginning to have problems controlling my emotions. In spite of that, I presented my .38 Special S&W M-60 stainless steel revolver, holster, and ammo to my good friend Sao Lam. I wasn't able to speak, nor did I try to, for the tears were flowing down my cheeks.

I then gave Trung Uy Loc my wrist compass and two thirty-round M-16 magazines. I didn't see a dry eye in our midst under that beautiful grove of palm trees. It was a special time and a special place between friends and brothers-in-arms. I have no words to truly describe what we experienced together that night.

Later that evening, the PRU escorted Al and me back to the Embassy House. The next morning I was on my way back to the Silver Strand.

* * *

"Ca Mau, comin' right up!" the helo crewman announced, which brought me back to the present time. Since Ca Mau, also known as Quan Long, was only thirty miles by air from Nam Canh, the flight had gone by in a hurry.

When we landed on the helo pad at the airport in Ca Mau, I unloaded all my gear and ended up moving it onto a Caribou, a two-engine transport plane similar in shape to the C-130 but much smaller. I rode the Caribou seventy-five air miles to Can Tho, along with a lieutenant (jg) from UDT-11.

From Can Tho, the lieutenant and I caught a navy flight at 1700 hours which took us eighty-five air miles to Tan Son Nhut Air Base. Upon landing, we gathered up our gear and got a jeep ride to NavForV in Saigon, where we arrived at 1900 hours.

To my delight I met SM1 Tommie Hatchett in the main SpecWar office. Tom had just arrived with Golf Platoon from the Silver Strand as their senior enlisted. LT Richard E. Dill was the OIC with LTjg John R. Huggins the AOIC. The remainder of the guys were as follows: TM2 Lester J. Moe, HM3 Chester R. Craig, EN3 Ray C. Smith, GMG3 Frank Sparks, RM3 Robert E. C. Sparks, EM3 James R. Gore, GMG3 William S. Armstrong, SM3 Hulit R. Weatherford, FN Thomas J. Gade, SA Matthew A. Ferrizz, and SN David A. Brinkley. Golf Platoon was to remain in-country until 10 November 1970, survived seventy-five missions with Mr. Huggins and Tommie Hatchett earning their Purple Hearts. Tommie was a black man who was about six feet two inches and 250 pounds. He was one of the nicest guys in the teams and one whom I considered a good and dependable friend. Because Golf Platoon was on their way to Sea Float, I gave Tom a "heads up" on what to expect there, which he appreciated.

Afterwards, GMG1 Nelson and I ate supper at the Sing-Sing Restaurant. Then we went to the Metropol Hotel, where we had rooms reserved and called it a night.

The next morning, after eating breakfast at the Ky Son mess, Nelson and I got a ride on a VN motorbike to

NavForV. Once inside, I asked Commander O'Drain if he was ready for my report on the Biet Hai. He asked me to see Lieutenant Rasmussen, who was a member of the Naval Special Warfare Group (NSWG) staff.

Before I could say very much in Rasmussen's office, he gave me a document he had written which concluded that the Biet Hai were good only for perimeter defense and sweeps. I read the paper, then chose to explain to the lieutenant that I could easily train a few of the Biet Hai to set up ambushes on VC crossings on canals and rivers.

Rasmussen challenged me, saying, "In other words, you say the Biet Hai are as good as the LDNNs?"

Carefully choosing my words, I replied, "No, sir. I'm saying I can train these men to simply set up ambushes. This type of training is fairly basic and takes a minimum of training when working in conjunction with Swift boats."

Rasmussen, who had no concept of what was really happening in the field and who had no personal experience with the LDNNs or the Biet Hai, persisted in knocking the Biet Hai. He said to me, "Do you realize that if you tell Commander O'Drain that the Biet Hai have this capability with a minimum of training, you're dooming the LDNN program?"

Suddenly I thought Rasmussen might know something which I didn't, probably something involving "professional jealousy," so I simply muttered, "I understand." I was tired of discussing the issue. "Why," I wondered, "can't we all just accept one another and remember we're all fighting on the same side?"

I left Rasmussen's office and again went to see Commander O'Drain. Without mincing words, I explained many of the problems I had encountered and why we were experiencing them.

"To be blunt," I said, "most of the problems are due to very inexperienced naval officer advisers who don't understand the definition of *advising* and who fail to understand the Vietnamese."

Commander O'Drain nodded his head. Looking me right

in the eye, he said, "I was afraid of that." After a slight pause, he concluded our meeting by saying, "Thank you for your report."

As I walked out of his office, Lieutenant Commander Graham stopped me in the passageway. He was holding a piece of paper, which he stuck under my nose.

"Got a message," he told me. I started to read it, but Graham stopped me with his next words. He said, "Scott was wounded in his head by shrapnel and medevacked to 24th Evac in Vinh Long."

I was instantly pissed off. "Dammit!" I blurted. "I asked Tu Ta to take some SEALs along with him, but he didn't do it!" Before I said anything else in front of Graham, I bit my tongue and walked away.

"They believe he'll live," Graham called after me, which did nothing to curb my anger for the moment.

"Thank you, sir," I replied. I was sick of being put in a position of advising U.S. naval officers who were far less experienced than I, only to watch them do their own thing in spite of my recommendations. And I was sick of all the side issues. The only real thing that mattered, and it mattered a lot, was winning this war as quickly as possible with the smallest number of casualties.

A couple of hours later, mentally drained and physically tired, I boarded a flight to Cam Ranh Bay. I was going back there for a short stint, and I was looking forward to seeing my old buddies.

CHAPTER EIGHTEEN

A half hour after I had arrived at Cam Ranh 14th Aerial, Chief Willis and Chief John Fietsch came to pick me up and take me to the naval base at the southern tip of the peninsula, which was the same place where I had served earlier as an LDNN trainee adviser.

"What it is, Brother?" Willis greeted me as he approached me in the airport terminal, his eyes and the gold star imbedded in his right front tooth flashing. "Smitty! I thought you wuz dead!" He reached out with his right hand, palm facing upward.

I slapped my hand down onto his, grasping it for a healthy shake. "Say what?" I answered in surprise. "Well, hell, it just wasn't my time, Bro!"

"All right! All right! Good man," Willis agreed with a smile. "We's glad you're back, Smitty." He let go of my hand so that I could shake hands with Fietsch.

"Dad blame, John! I didn't think the command would ever get you back over here," I teased as I shook John's hand.

"Good to see you, Smitty," Fietsch said.

"Good to be back," I replied, meaning it. I sure was glad to see my mates.

The three of us toted my gear to the jeep Willis was driving, and off to the base we went.

There wasn't a cloud in the blue sky, and the South China Sea was crystal clear, with beautiful waves rolling up onto the white sandy beaches. It had been an enjoyable day so far and I was relishing the thought of five days in Hawaii when John broke the silence by saying, "Willis tells me that you're going to Honolulu for R & R."

"Yeah, I'm going to check out the round-eye broads on Waikiki Beach and the famous Davy Jones Locker bar with its swimming mermaids. You want to come along?"

The normally garrulous John was sitting silently, staring at the sandy beach as if brooding. Willis, sensing John's indecision, mockingly asked, "What's da matter, John? Can't you handle it?"

"What? Oh, I was just thinking about the first time I pulled liberty in Pearl Harbor," John reflected.

"Well," I explained, "the main reason I'm anxious to visit Davy Jones Locker is because of the story Joe Thrift told me about the time in '61 that the 4th and 1st platoons (UDT-12) pulled liberty there after completing a tour of swimming four hundred miles of hydrographic reconns in 'Nam from the DMZ to Ha Tien. It was a hard tour and all of the guys were bone dry and determined to wet their whistles thoroughly on their first night of Cinderella liberty. All was going well until about 1800 hours, when the beautiful mermaids began their swimming performance in the pool behind the clear glass window in the bar." I paused for a moment and grinned. "Naturally, everyone was lined up at the bar with a beer in each hand and all eyes glued on the voluptuous maidens."

"Uh, oh," laughed John, "I know what's coming next."

"Well," I continued, "Chief Paul McNally, LPO [Leading Petty Officer] Lloyd Cob, Doc Beaver, PO1 [Petty Officer First-Class] Layton Bassett, and Joe bet Seaman Skinner Divine that he didn't have the balls to jump into the pool and give everybody a brown-eye. They each put up front a dollar and a quarter for the completed act. Skinner gladly took them up on it by figuring that he had five free beers coming if he didn't get thrown in jail. In short order, Skinner disappeared from the bar and suddenly reappeared in the pool with all of his clothes on."

"Dat must've been like a wolf among the sheep," Willis cackled.

"Yessir, I reckon he was," I commented. "Continuing on his tangent, he headed directly for the mermaids, disrupted their graceful act, swam down to the bottom of the pool where the glass plate window separated the pool from the bar, dropped his trou', spread his cheeks, and plastered his buns up against the plate glass."

All of us broke out with uncontrolled laughter. "Yessir, it looked like a giant abalone with an ugly brown eye in the center, a sort of cyclops," I exclaimed as I broke into another laughing spell.

"Well, at least he had his clothes on when he entered the pool!" John yelled between laughs.

"Man, dat must've looked worse dan ah 'possum tryin' ta shit ah peach seed," Willis howled.

Our lightheartedness continued until we finally arrived at the advisers' sea hut just outside the base's main gate. We carried my gear to a spare bunk next to Doc Churchill's, which consisted of a simple cot.

"Not much to call home," Willis giggled after dropping a parachute bag on the floor beside the cot.

I shook my head and chuckled. "No, but it sure beats the hammock I had in Mosquitoville at Sea Float!"

Joined by the team legend Senior Chief Corpsman Joe Churchill, the three of us ended up going to the chow hall and sitting around and talking into the night. I told them all about Sea Float and even griped some about the side issues and jealousies I had encountered. Finally, at 2400 hours, we all hit our racks for some shut-eye.

The next morning after breakfast I carefully cleaned the M-14 rifle and M-60 machine gun that I had checked out from the armory for use while I was at Sea Float. At 1030 hours I returned both of them to the base armory. Then I got a haircut and bought a couple of items from the exchange.

About 1330, I went down to the Beach Cabana, where the NSF administration office personnel were serving grilled steaks, chicken, and beer. A Philippino band, which was exceptionally good, was playing, and they stayed for about two hours. Willis, Fietsch, and I hung around, enjoying ourselves immensely, until 1630 hours.

As we started back toward our hut, we ran into a few of our LDNN trainees who had just been in a big fight with U.S. Shore Patrol personnel at the EM Club. Evidently, a 1st Class Shore Patrol guy used poor judgment in trying to control one of the trainees instead of asking the Vietnamese SPs to deal with their own. When the fight erupted, the U.S. guys made the mistake of getting it on outside of the club, where the VNs were not shy about picking up and using rocks and two-by-fours. The Americans got the stuffing knocked out of them, with one guy ending up with a broken shoulder. On the other side, not one VN was badly injured.

"We kick ass for you, Smitty!" Thanh told me, grinning widely.

"For me?" I blurted, surprised at the comment and not quite sure what he meant.

Explaining himself, Thanh said heartily, "We your boys, Smitty! We honor your return with kick ass!"

I tried not to laugh, but I couldn't refrain. I found myself cracking up over the fact that some U.S. fellows had overestimated their power against my scrappy VN buddies, whose toughness and reserve I had helped to instill.

A little later, I picked up my R & R orders from the administrative office, as I was on my way to Honolulu in two days. I had a week of rest and relaxation coming to me, and I'd decided Hawaii was a good place to do just that. I couldn't wait to get away from Vietnam, even though my "getaway" would be so short and would pass by before I knew it. That was the way it was with all vacations.

After killing most of the next day and a half with preparing my gear for R & R, on Monday, May 25, Willis took me to 22nd Replacement to check in for my trip. I boarded a Boeing 707 which got me to Honolulu at 1530 hours. All of us were hauled by bus to Fort DeRussy for a quick briefing on the local dos and don'ts, good deals, etc., then I headed for Cinerama's Reef Hotel on Waikiki Beach.

At about 1800 hours, I visited a couple of restaurant bars in the hotel, then decided to go to Davy Jones Locker. Because of its history, the Locker was like a sacred place to me.

When I arrived there, I sat down behind the bar, ordered two beers, and visualized the good time that my old UDT platoon had had on that evening just nine years ago. That Skinner was meaner than a ring-tailed tooter and wilder than a March hare. Unfortunately, he drowned while inserting from a boat in Kien Hoa Province in July 1968. He was a good man. "Well, it's better to die in combat than from the piles," I thought.

I bought a round of drinks for the few people seated at the bar, then held up my own beer for a toast. Addressing the walls, which had seen everything and witnessed all of the visitors of the past, I said loudly, "Here's a salute to my old UDT-12 fourth platoon and teammates, some of whom have crossed over the bar—lest we forget: 'Dog Breath' Allen, Chief Reynolds, Fast Joe Thrift, Bud Juric, Chief McNally, Lonnie Price, Al Flud, Lloyd Cob, Tis Morrison, 'Bear Tracks' Allen, Chief Joe Jenkens, Chief Dick Allen, Chief Bassett, 'Chicken' McNair, Ensign Odusch, Al Huey, Doc Beaver, Monk Holland, Mad Dog Burgess, Funky Funkhouser, Leslie Funk, Muck McCollum, Lieutenant Meston, Doc Brown, Moki Martin, Apache Williams, Herr Von Goerlich, Friendly Frederickson, Whop-a-Hoh Olivera, Dorfi, Van Winkle, etc.!" Then I chugged my beer in a single guzzle. And that was what my week in Honolulu amounted to: a quick guzzle.

I bounced around from place to place, shopping at the International Market Place, where I bought a T-shirt that read "Visit Fascinating Vietnam"; taking the Pearl Harbor tour and the Hawaiiana tour; enjoying Paradise Park and the Oceanic/Sealife Park; sunbathing, swimming, and sailing on a catamaran. I caught some nightclub acts, going to Duke Kahanamoku's place to see Don Ho, where Lucille Ball was in the audience, and hitting the Royal Hawaiian Hotel to see Martin Denny and his band.

Besides the T-shirt, I purchased some hippie-type peace signs for the bar back in Cam Ranh. They would be used as targets for a variety of missiles. I despised the hippies and the baggage that went along with them, especially their drugs, their antiwar and antimilitary sentiments, and the long hair that represented their liberal beliefs and social and spiritual rebellion. But I did think their peace logos would go nicely in each toilet stall. We could then occasionally wipe them out without worrying about the consequences, I thought.

With my new T-shirt, peace signs, and gear in tow, I left Hawaii on May 31, but as soon as I crossed the 180th meridian it became June 1, 1970. After a two-hour stop in Okinawa, I arrived at Cam Ranh at 1900 hours. A Philippino and I rode in a jeep back to NSF.

It was good to see my buddies again. Lieutenant Kuhn, however, had departed. The word was that he had gone with LDNNs and a SEAL Team Two platoon that had recently arrived in-country to Cambodia. I was very disappointed that I didn't get to go with them. As an LDNN adviser with almost four tours under my belt, I felt slighted that no SEAL Team One LDNN advisers were taken. I especially wanted to get in on the destruction of the NVA COSVN headquarters and supply bases that were located just across the Cambodian border from the Vietnamese delta. I was thrilled that President Nixon had the guts to take a stand against the liberal democrats and to give us permission to finally invade Cambodia and to destroy as many of the enemy as we could.

I didn't have to stay disappointed for long, as it turned out. A dozen days later I was on my way to the U.S.S. *Benewah*, an LST (Landing Ship Troop) anchored only about six hundred meters south of the Cambodian border. To start my journey, I went to NavForV in Saigon. There I ran into Lieutenant Kuhn, who told me he was recommending me for the Navy Marine Corps Medal for saving Lieutenant Sherry's life.

At 0930 hours the next morning, I flew by a C-47 to

Long Xuyen, about ninety air miles west of Saigon in the
province of An Giang. From there I was taken by helo
about thirty-five miles southwest to a Special Forces camp
near Ha Tien on the Gulf of Siam. The camp was situated
just miles from Cambodia's border. I boarded a Mike-6
boat for the quick trip to the U.S.S. *Benewah*.

As I unloaded my gear bags from the Mike-6, Chief
Watson from SEAL Team Two came over and introduced
himself. He was of slender build, about five feet ten inches
in height, and easy to get to know. The chief took me down
to the berthing space where the LDNNs were staying and
said that I should get my battle gear ready for the next
morning. Reveille would come at 0330, at which time we
would be leaving on a mission into Cambodia in an attempt
to capture a VC tax collector.

As tired as I was feeling from my travels, the mission
sounded thrilling to me. After all, I had always detested tax
collectors, both at home and abroad. I mused over the
thought that the next day we would switch roles, with me
playing the auditor and the tax collector having to pay up
or cough it up—information, blood, or otherwise.

CHAPTER NINETEEN

Reveille, as promised, came at 0330 hours. Five LDNNs, Chief Watson, and I boarded a STAB (SEAL Tactical Assault Boat), which was a low-silhouette boat that drew only six inches of water on-step and was powered by a Chevy 427 V-8 engine. It had a crew of two or three and would carry a seven-man squad of SEALs. The coxswain and crewman took us about fifteen miles upstream, traveling in a northwesterly direction beneath the Cambodian shoreline under the cover of night. The moon rose but was hidden by haze, giving an eerie cast to the riverbank.

As we went, I replayed the chief's briefing in my mind. He had explained that we were to insert at coordinates WT253314, move inland a few meters, and seek cover until first light. Then we would move about seventy-five meters inland, just to the edge of a road and outside a little village. There we would attempt to capture or kill a particular VC tax collector as he rode his bicycle down the road toward his collection points. Immediately after the taking or extermination of the target, we would backtrack to the Mekong River and extract via the STAB.

I looked through the darkness at the five LDNNs riding in the boat with me, thinking about how often I had been changing and acquiring new teammates and friends on this tour. It suddenly struck me that I didn't know crap about any of these guys, yet here I was headed into Cambodia, of all places, seeking intelligence on VC/NVA movements and with unfamiliar and unproven fighters, at least as far as I was personally concerned, who were of a foreign personality. That was the way it was for people like me, the special warfare guys who accepted the risks and did whatever it took to take the party to the enemy's own backyard. And so I smiled to myself, discounting the daredevil aspects of the mission for the proud feeling of asking not what my country could do for me, but rather what I could do for my country, to paraphrase a president I admired very much. What I could do, I was doing, and that was simply putting my butt on the line for my country, the country that I loved, so that all the protestors and the academics and liberal intelligentsia back home could enjoy the right to demonstrate against people like me, the hated middle class, who were engaged in a fight to give others who wanted independence from oppression the same freedom. With all that in mind, I held fast to my CAR-15 (XM-177-E2) with an XM-148 40-mm grenade launcher under its stubby barrel as the STAB slowed to a crawl in the water, which in itself warned me that insertion was near.

With its engine just above idle, the STAB eased toward the ominous shoreline. As the boat crept toward the bank, Tam, the LDNN point man, and myself moved forward to the bow and crouched down. At the instant the bow nudged the bank, we leaped onto the muddy shore. The others followed behind us.

As we crawled our way up a twenty-five-foot embankment in the dark, I heard the drifting away of our support boat. "That's it," I thought. "We're on our own in Cambodia." I kept thinking about a turtle I found on top of a fence post right after a terrible Texas thunderstorm. There was no way he got up there all by himself.

At the top of the steep bank, I realized we had found a banana grove described in the briefing. I hoped it was the right one. The chief had us take cover and wait for first light. While we sat, the smell of ripening bananas filled my nostrils. The odor reminded me of the countless times when, as a kid, I sliced a banana over a bowl of Wheaties in the morning before heading off for school. The remembrance made me smile. "Now look at me," I thought, "a hairy-chested SEAL sitting on a jungle trail with my CAR-15/XM-148 lying across my lap and waiting for a communist-loving, pro-tax dork to come to a hootch near a log roadblock so that we can capture or kill him." Incredibly, I thought, "I'm even getting paid to do this!"

After several minutes had passed, the eastern skies began to brighten a bit. About that time I heard the sound of human voices coming from where a dirt road was supposed to be, about seventy meters from our position in the banana grove. I squinted and stared hard between the bushes and trees, trying to get a glimpse of the people. My effort was rewarded with the sight of one bicycle and rider after another, barely visible as they went by. I counted twenty-two bicycles, but I was pretty sure I had missed a few that had made it past me in the dark. "Crap!" I thought. "I hope they're not all tax collectors!" With so many riders all together, I guessed I had witnessed an enemy troop movement. "Bring 'em on, boys," I snickered. "We're not far from the river and we have the element of surprise."

Our gutsy squad of seven waited five or six more minutes, then the chief motioned us to move through the grove toward the road. Tam and I led the way, cautious and watching for booby traps and anything unusual, while the rest of the men stayed behind us in single file. As we neared the road, Tam and I crouched lower and lower until our noses and our cods were almost dragging. Our last bit of cover was only twelve feet from the tortured jungle trail of a road that eventually led downstream to the Vietnamese border. Tam and I were on left flank and lay prostrate on the damp, smelly ground behind a nice plump bush that was our only cover. Chief Watson crawled behind a banana plant a few yards to my right with one LDNN positioning himself to the chief's right. The last three LDNNs set up a skirmish line about ten meters behind us to act as rear security.

It was a bit unnerving to be sitting on the edge of an enemy road as the sun started to peek over the horizon. It wouldn't be long before its rays started penetrating the palm trees and illuminating our position.

I could clearly see several hootches to my left. They were but fifty meters away. Then several people began milling around outside their homes, adding to the tension of the moment. It was inevitable that someone would spot us soon and we would be compromised. The only question was whether we would neutralize a VC tax collector first.

My attention was suddenly drawn back to the road in front of me. A small Vietnamese boy, perhaps five or six years old, was walking barefoot toward Tam and me. He stepped off the road, came closer, and stopped on the other side of our bush, where he slipped his shorts down to his knees. A few seconds later, we heard his urine splashing against the foliage.

I looked at Tam. Tam looked at me. We both knew that the show was about to begin. Tam turned his gaze to the boy and demanded softly, *"Lai dai."* Startled at Tam's command to come, the boy jumped back a foot, then tried to run and pull up his pants at the same time. Without a second of hesitation, Tam dashed from behind our bush in hot pursuit of the frightened lad. The chase lasted only a few seconds and fifteen yards. Tam grabbed the boy by one arm and hoisted him into the air, making the mistake of leaving the boy's mouth uncovered. The kid let out a horrific scream as Tam ran back with the little guy in tow.

By the time Tam had placed a hand over the boy's face and muffled the hollering, the mamma-san and papa-san began shouting and running from their hootch toward their child's cries for help. On their heels came two others, a man and a teenage boy. Fortunately, I saw that none of them was carrying a weapon.

When the four people scampered in front of me on the road, I charged out from behind my bush with my CAR-15/XM-148 pointed at them.

"Lai dai!" I barked. Scared squirtless, they stopped in their tracks and gawked at me with eyes as big as saucers.

Only the teenager looked as though he might attempt to flee, so I trained my weapon on him.

"Lai dai!" I repeated as two of the LDNNs moved from behind their cover in a show of force. Their presence was the clincher, causing the four Vietnamese to walk into the bushes with us. When the two parents saw that we had their little kid and he was completely okay, some relief swept across their faces. The relief was momentary, however, disappearing when one of the LDNNs began interrogating them.

They were asked where they lived: *"Ong o dau?"*

Too frightened to speak, the papa-san simply pointed toward the village with a trembling hand. However, the teenager quickly volunteered that two hundred VC had come through the day before and that the village had to feed all of them.

"Ong o dau toi?" the LDNN hammered on. Again the father motioned in the direction of the many hootches. I looked that way and saw a man step out of another hootch. I watched him as he started walking toward our little group.

"Damn," I thought, "here comes another one!" I had a feeling our entire mission was about to unravel.

When the fellow reached a spot about fifty meters from us, he took a couple steps away from the road, lowered the front of his black pajama bottoms, and started peeing. The thought crossed my mind, ludicrous though it was, that perhaps we had set up our ambush site in the village's favorite watering hole. I began wondering what all Tam and I had been crawling through.

While the man was urinating, Chief Watson blurted *"Lai dai!"* Instantly, the man caught in midstream whirled and started running away from us with everything flapping in the breeze ahead of him. One of the LDNNs took off after him with me several steps behind.

When it quickly became evident that no one was going to catch the fleet-footed exhibitionist, the LDNN pulled up, took aim with his M-16, and shot the man in his right leg.

As the victim went down in a heap, the mission went down with him. The sound of the rifle shot had compromised everything and put us in an unhealthy, hairy spot. If there were any VC nearby, such as the twenty-two to thirty men on bicycles, they would respond to the blast. That surely meant we had to move swiftly to gather up our prisoners and get the hell out of there.

I ran to the fallen captive and saw that he wasn't bleeding badly, yet he was moaning due to a lot of pain. I also noted, just for the record, that he had pissed all over himself.

I dug into my first-aid kit for a morphine styrette, which I found quickly. As I prepared the styrette for injection, the man's daughter began wailing when she saw the needle. The LDNN told her to shut up, but that didn't work.

Before I jabbed the needle into the man's leg, I said to the family, *"Cong sao,"* which translated as "No sweat." I gave her a little smile, and she quieted down. Then I gave the shot.

The man's wife showed up with a battle dressing and I let her put it on the wound. All the while, I kept my eyes peeled for any sign of approaching enemy forces. They were coming, I was positive, but I was just as certain that we were leaving.

When the woman finished with the bandaging, the LDNN grabbed the wounded man by his arm and helped get him to his feet.

"Di thi di!" the LDNN demanded, telling the man to go with us. The morphine had taken its affect—the captive was relaxed, smiling, and enjoying himself. The LDNN's directive, however, caused the man's family to begin sobbing again, but this was no time for family consolation. The LDNN and I escorted the hobbling but happy prisoner back to the others, who were waiting for us at the edge of the road.

"I've radioed for the STAB," Chief Watson informed me. "We'll take your man and these other three men with us as detainees." I looked at the three standing with the LDNNs. One of them was the teenage boy, who I figured to be about fourteen years old.

"Let's go!" Chief Watson ordered. Our squad with the four detainees moved back into the brush and the banana grove, leaving the women and the little boy to go home.

We covered the seventy-five meters through the grove in but a minute or two as we went back to the river on a slightly different tangent. I took one last deep breath before we reached the steep bank to the shoreline, drinking in the smell of fresh bananas. I felt like grabbing a handful of the fruit, but decided that would have to wait for another time.

While Tam and I remained above, the rest of the men scurried down the embankment with the prisoners in tow, then waited at the water's edge for a few minutes until two STABs came sailing in for our rescue. Tam and I joined the others and we loaded two of the detainees in one boat with three of our men and two in the other boat with four of us. Then we left the story of our visit behind for the villagers to share with each other and with the late arriving VC. I knew it would be a tale that would irritate our enemies.

"Hoo-yah!" I said with a grin. Tam grinned in return, but the other LDNNs just looked at me. "Never mind," I thought. "One day they'll understand."

We ended up dropping the wounded VN at a camp where the Vietnamese marines were headquartered. There he would be attended to and questioned. If all went well for him, he would satisfy his interrogator and get a quick release.

The other three men, of whom two were VN detainees and the other was a Cambodian, we left with a U.S. Marine gunnery sergeant for interrogation. Then we stopped at a friendly Vietnamese village before returning to the U.S.S. *Benewah*. There we traded a case of C rats for some Tiger beer, which tasted mighty fine, too. It was "bottoms up" for a safe and somewhat successful mission. The only problem was that the tax man was still free to do his dirty work.

"Isn't that the way it always is with the tax man?" I thought. "Yep," I answered my own question, then I drank another delicious beer, thinking, "Ain't war hell?"

CHAPTER TWENTY

Back on board the ship, I cleaned my gear in our living quarters. Our space was crowded with eleven LDNNs, myself, and all of our individual weapons and operating gear collected and organized in every niche and corner. After a shower in the local head near our berthing space, I hit the rack, dead tired. My nap was short-lived, however, as it was too hot to lie in any one place or position.

Chief Watson found me and told me we were going on another mission into Cambodia that night with ten LDNNs and Chief Luom. The plan was to set up on some trails and wait for targets of opportunity. We would be leaving at 2000 hours.

I got my gear ready for the op, then attended the briefing/PLO (Patrol Leader's Order) by Chief Watson with the LDNNs, then ate supper at the mess decks near the center of the ship. At 1945 hours, I gathered with the twelve other men on the flight deck. The chief and I visually checked the LDNNs, minus Chief Luom, to see if they had their gear in order before we boarded our STAB and drifted off into the early evening.

The sun was making its long, slow dive into the horizon as we speedily traveled several miles toward our insertion point of WT238252. I sat in the boat, wishing the coming evening coolness would soon drive out the suffocating heat of the day. As the sun disappeared, I was able to concentrate on the mission at hand.

After inserting on target just after dark, we patrolled up

a draw and set up an ambush site on a road parallel to the river. I positioned myself on right flank with three LDNNs.

At 2320 hours, I thought I saw two men fly by me on a bicycle. My field of fire was so small, though, that I didn't even have time to raise my weapon. No one else fired a shot, either.

Fifteen minutes later, Chief Luom called off the mission. He was totally pissed because no one had shot the bicyclists. He quickly tried to blame me.

"Why didn't you shoot, Smitty?" he challenged me with a sharp voice.

"No time to shoot, Chief!" I responded. "Why didn't you?" I retorted, noting that he had had a much larger field of fire than I. He gave me no answer.

We extracted. Back on the STAB, I commented to Chief Watson, "Win a few, lose a few." He nodded in agreement. We then decided that next time we would string some communication wire across the road to snag the first wiseacre riding a bicycle.

I chuckled. "It'll be our luck that twenty VC will come walking by and we'll be forced to fire on them," I said. "Then we'll have one hell of a firefight."

The next morning, Watson and I decided we'd set up an ambush with just two SEALs and Lieutenant (jg) Bentley, who had been a SEAL-2 pecker-checker. He had recently been promoted to lieutenant (jg) as a physician's assistant and was assigned on board the *Benewah*. We planned to tie the wire across a road and wait for someone to walk, run, or ride a bicycle into it. Admiral Mathews seemed to think we were nuts when we asked for his permission, but he approved the mission.

After lunch we went by the STAB to Chau Doc. There we went to the *Chieu Hoi* center to see if we could wrangle up a Hoi Chanh, usually a former VC/VCI/NVA, with knowledge of some good and timely intelligence information. We found one, and I questioned him through the local PRU interpreter. The Hoi Chanh cooperated, but he made it clear he wouldn't accompany us as our guide. In an attempt

to change his mind, I offered him money, then I proposed
a move of his family to a safe place. My offers went for
naught. The guy simply refused to go with us.

Chief Watson and I returned to the U.S.S. *Benewah* at
about 1730 hours. After dinner, I prepared my gear for the
evening op. I gathered up my CAR-15/XM-148, web gear
and vest with two quarts of water, two LRRP meals, and
lots of 40-mm HE and 5.56-mm ammo, frag grenades, a
medical kit, pop flares, and plenty of commo wire. I was
heavy on ammo and short on food. However, I decided I'd
rather be hungry and thirsty than be out of ammo when surrounded by bloodthirsty commies.

At 2030 hours, Watson, myself, and Lieutenant Bentley
boarded a STAB and took off for our insertion point. When
we inserted an hour later, we lay quiet for about ten minutes, listening for any human sounds. Then, confident of
our clandestine onshore entry, we moved up to the road
which paralleled the river.

The chief and Bentley watched the road while I doubled
communication wire about waist high across it. I secured
the far end of the wire around a tree and tied it securely.

Right after I finished and settled into position on right
flank, a dog at a nearby hootch to my left started barking.
We lay completely still, waiting to see what would happen.
The dog's incessant yipping increased the tension in the air.

Soon I saw a man step out of the hootch near the dog. He
was smoking a cigarette, the hot ashes of which enabled me
to track the man in the ever-increasing darkness. I watched
him bend over, then stand back up. He made a throwing motion toward the dog and I knew he had thrown a stone. The
dog quit barking. The man went back inside the hootch.

Less than a minute passed before another man, on a bicycle, approached our position from my right, riding
slowly. I readied my weapon, training both barrels on the
bicyclist. When he hit the wire, he was stopped dead on
the road. I immediately charged out from behind the bush
which had concealed me.

"Lai dai!" I demanded in a low tone as the guy strug-

gled against the wire in an attempt to stay upright on his bike. My sudden appearance scared the man so badly that he dropped the bike and clumsily fell to the roadway over the top of it.

As he scrambled to get back on his feet, I saw that the guy was an older man, probably in his forties. Bentley covered me while I carefully searched him for documents and/or weapons. Surprisingly, he had none.

"No sweat, mister," I told him in Vietnamese. He faced me and grinned weakly. I then said softly but firmly, *"Di di mau,"* instructing him to hurry up and get lost. He wasted no time in picking up his bicycle and turning it around. He climbed onto the bike and rode off into the night in the direction from which he had come.

Since we were compromised, I cut the wire as Chief Watson radioed the STAB for extraction. Then we slipped quietly through the brush to the river, where the boat picked us up a few minutes later.

We decided to go south about one klick and insert again. After inserting, we had to sneak in the dark among several hootches in order to get to the road. I didn't think we had one chance in a hundred of making it without being compromised by a dog or someone's taking a piss. Sweat poured off my face as we passed one hootch after another. My body was tense in anticipation of a screwup. Yes, we're nuts, I decided, agreeing with Admiral Mathews's assessment of three guys going in alone against a potential world of crap. Yet I thrived on the excitement.

Surprisingly, we made it to the road. I pulled up the green neckerchief that was around my neck and wiped the perspiration from my eyes, taking note of the fact that my hands were perspiring also. Then Watson and I took up positions on the edge of the road while Bentley acted as rear security, watching the hootches behind us.

Sitting quietly in the still of the night, I thought about how dull it was staring at an empty road compared to watching a stream or river. In the Rung Sat Special Zone during my 1967–1968 tour, my platoon's ambush sites were almost always set up beside a waterway. There I was able to observe moonbeams dancing on the surface of the water. Crocodiles making whistling sounds and drawing air kept my attention. The croaking of frogs and splashing of lung-fish and other unknown varmints made music for my ears. During high tides, when I was halfway immersed in water, schools of tiny fish swam around my hands and nibbled on them, as did small crabs, which helped me to stay awake. Those recollections, glamorized though they were in my mind's eye, made me smile for a minute. But as I focused my eyes harder on the dark road in front of me, my smile was wiped away by the harsh reality of my current situation. I was being dead quiet beside a dead road on a dead night, hopeful of a successful mission in which none of the good guys ended up defunct, pushing up banana plants.

Fighting off the boredom for a half hour, I wished for some excitement. It finally came by way of a dog which walked out of the darkness on the road. When the medium-sized, near-hairless canine stepped to a spot right in front of Watson and me, he suddenly stopped and gazed at us. He only stared for a few seconds before losing his nerve and running away in haste back toward where he had come. He didn't bark even once, so we stayed put.

After another hour and a half of boredom during which time absolutely nothing at all happened, we extracted, and headed for the U.S.S. *Benewah*. Because I was a radioman, Chief Watson logically concluded that I should draft the rough message for the Tran Hung Dao eleven spot report and take it to *Benewah*'s communications center. Not surprisingly the three of us were a bit disgusted with our bad luck, as I had hoped to nail an enemy or two in Cambodia right away. After all, the purpose of invading Cambodia was to come in contact with the enemy and destroy him, not just sit on a roadside and watch men ride bicycles and piss on the veggies.

"Oh, well," I thought, "maybe we'll unzip a zipperhead tomorrow night."

CHAPTER TWENTY-ONE

The next morning at about 1000 hours, Chief Watson, Lieutenant Bentley, and I were called up to the flight deck. A Navy Seawolf helicopter crew had reported about one hundred men on bicycles riding north on the nearest road to the east of us. All of the bicyclists were toting duffel bags. The helo crew somewhat amazingly had swooped down out of the sky and nabbed one of the riders. The captive stood before us on the flight deck as we were filled in by Chuoi, an LDNN who was of Cambodian, Indian, and Chinese descent and spoke good English.

I joined in on the questioning of the bicyclist, who was Chinese. He spoke Vietnamese, Cambodian, and a Chinese dialect. He claimed that all of the bicycle riders had simply brought beans to a village located a klick north of us on the east bank and sold them. I thought his explanation ridiculous and told him so; still, he wouldn't budge from his story. But since we already knew that there were supposed to be close to three thousand VC/NVA located five or six klicks northeast of our position, we suspected that the bicyclists were troops moving up and down the road.

Watson took me aside and said, "Let's go in tonight and snatch some people for more intelligence." I liked the idea.

That evening I found myself inserting with Watson, Bentley, and five Vietnamese LDNNs. I was carrying a CAR/XM-148. Watson had his Stoner machine gun and Bentley an M-60 machine gun. The LDNNs had four M-16s and one M-79. We patrolled in the dark to a road junction near a burned and partially destroyed hamlet we had observed by VR. The VN marines were making heavy contact with the enemy about six kilometers southeast of that location, and we figured the VC to vacate their hot area this night. We hoped they would use the road on which we would be waiting in ambush.

We set up our interdiction at the junction and the eight of us sat in silence, anticipating a spectacular strike against the unsuspecting enemy. After a long, boring night of negative contact, however, we decided we were not on the main road and quickly hid as a Cambodian man and his wife appeared. When the couple walked in front of us, Watson jumped out of the bush beside them. The poor people almost fainted from fright. We quickly interrogated them for any intelligence information we might act upon immediately, but we had negative results. The only thing we got out of the male was that six VC had visited his home, about a thousand meters south of our position, during the night and forced him and his wife to leave. He said the VC were regularly harassing the villagers.

We decided to take the Cambodian couple with us as detainees to be questioned further by experts. In single file, with the couple walking in the middle of our platoon, we patrolled to our original insertion point and extracted via STAB boat. On the way back to the *Benewah*, I was disappointed because we had set up on an untraveled road. Having been prepared to kick ass and take names, I felt a little let down. Some days were smooth sailing and some were filled with heavy seas. We thrived on success, not failure. However, such feelings were normal for SEALs who loved the challenges of their line of work, especially when combat was directly related to heavy surges of adrenaline through our veins. Sometimes I wondered if career SEALs' professional motivation to continually perform hair-raising tasks might be closely related to an addiction to the adrenaline that our bodies created during those times.

The seas were a little rough over the next few weeks. I hung on tightly to my seat as my orders changed and I flew with eleven LDNNs to the Binh Thuy naval base in III

Corps on June 21. When I arrived there, I realized that my seabag with all my clothing had been left behind on the U.S.S. *Benewah*. I radioed the *Benewah* and asked the chief master at arms to locate the bag for me. Later in the day, the bag was found aboard the U.S.S. *Satyr* and I was told someone there would take care of it for me. I asked that the bag be forwarded to Navy ATCO, Tan Son Nhut.

After a couple of days of doing little, the LDNNs and I went to the air force terminal on Binh Thuy Air Base and checked in. The LDNNs had dozens of boxes filled with loot they had taken on ops from the indigenous people of Cambodia. I had not been with them on those ops and I definitely did not condone looting. I had seen looting before, and it always disgusted me.

At 1430 hours, we took off in a Caribou C-123 for Tan Son Nhut. When we departed the plane, Tu Ta Hiep (commanding officer of the LDNNs), Chief Watson, Chief England, Rio, and Willis were waiting with iced-down beer for the troops, which was a pleasant surprise and certainly gladdened my heart. We loaded up a couple of pickup trucks and guzzled the beer as we headed to the VN navy base, where we dropped off the LDNNs. Chief Watson, Jerry Waters, and I then split from the rest of the group and headed for the naval base at Nha Be. A new SEAL Two platoon had just arrived there from the States. My old pals Drady and Finley were with the platoon. Drady had been in Richard Marcinko's platoon when I operated here in January of 1968. He had also come over as a PRU adviser in 1969. Finley had served with Lieutenant Boink's platoon in My Tho in 1969 when I was a PRU adviser there. Glad to see one another again, the three of us went to the Acey Deucey Club and celebrated our reunion and caught up on the latest news from stateside and Vietnam.

During the next two days, I concentrated on trying to get my seabag back from the U.S.S. *Satyr*, which was at the Cambodian border on the Mekong River. No one seemed able to help me, however, which was quite frustrating.

On June 26 I talked turkey with Lieutenant (jg) Gainer, the NSWG supply officer, concerning my not receiving a new pair of coral shoes I had requested four months earlier, as my pair was completely worn out. I had failed to receive new shoes, and yet the NSWG administrative personnel people all wore new coral booties. I was pissed and respectfully told the lieutenant that I felt team operators had priority over desk squatters. I also let him know that I was upset with Lieutenant Commander Carruga for the way he had handled the situation and for his curt attitude toward me. Mr. Gainer agreed and said he would try to get a pair of new shoes for me. I then told him I had only six weeks in-country to do and could wait until I got back to the States for the shoes. I ended my beef by stating that I was sensitive about the issuing of field equipment to noncombat personnel at the expense of combat personnel and that I expected respect and support from rear echelon personnel. Again, Gainer agreed. I left him, still clad in my worn-out coral shoes, but feeling better and certainly justified.

Later that same day I went to 8th Aerial, then flew to Cam Ranh with WO1 Bud Thrift of SEAL Two. After failing to reach anyone at the SEAL camp by phone, we hitchhiked there in lieu of getting someone from camp to pick us up. Only Joe Churchill and Louis Boisvert met us when we arrived. Fietsch, Ostrander, and Hollenbeck had all gone to the Philippines.

The next day, which was June 27, I worked mainly on getting ammunition for Lieutenant Diryx in Thailand. I also typed some orders authorizing me to go to the Philippines the next day. Then, at 1500 hours, Louis and I went freediving for cones.

As we swam in water about thirty-five feet deep, a shark about six feet in length (but that appeared to be about eight feet long through our face masks) suddenly appeared toward the end of our underwater vision and was in a feeding frenzy. We never could tell what he was eating because of his moving so rapidly and thrashing around his victim. Suddenly, it dawned on us that we might be his next dinner as we were only about twenty-five yards from him. We quickly swam toward shallower water, nearer the beach.

A little later we came upon a bed of about twenty-five eels in perhaps twenty feet of water. The eels, each of which was striped black and white and the diameter of a pencil, hid themselves in holes in the sand, out of which they would rise and bite at aquatic life floating by, then slide back into the sand. When Louis and I dove to within six feet of them, they withdrew into their holes and would not come out.

After our swim, Louis, Joe, and I sat around in the early evening and listened to music on the Armed Forces radio station. Louis told me that a couple nights earlier a trainee had heard a tiger rustling around in the brush near camp. When the trainee approached the sounds, the noises grew louder, causing the trainee to guess that the tiger had killed a wild hog. It had been a boyhood dream of mine to some-day hunt lions in Africa. Reading Robert Ruark's book as a teenager had served to intensify my dreams. And now the news that a tiger had roamed but several meters from my bunk made my heart pound with excitement.

There was no opportunity to indulge my aspirations of stalking a tiger, however, as the next morning Louis drove me to 14th Aerial, where I caught a flight to Clark Air Force Base in the Philippines. Unfortunately, there was no transportation available to take me from Clark to Subic Bay until the next morning. I ended up eating supper, reading a newspaper, and getting little sleep during a long night of waiting.

A bus finally picked me up the next day at 1100 hours, and I arrived at Subic Bay two hours later. I went to the UDT area and reported in and saw Lieutenant Tom Nelson and some of the other guys. PO2 Bert Campbell was down in the maintenance barn, so I visited with him for quite a while.

Later I went to John Odusch's car sales office near the

navy exchange. John—a former lieutenant (jg) who had gotten out of the navy and UDT-12 two years earlier—and I had gone through UDT training together in 1965. We had kept in touch since then and were good friends. However, he wasn't there, so I left a message for him with one of his fellow salesmen.

After supper, I headed for the main gate. When I reached the bridge over the Kalaklan River (renamed Shit River because the city of Olongapo's raw sewage was dumped directly into it), I noticed that the Philippino boys and an occasional Philippina were still begging merchant marines, sailors, and marines to toss coins to them as they swam in the filthy water on both sides of the bridge. "Hey, Joe, give me money," they all called. Being a softhearted sucker, I tossed a quarter toward a teenage lass who made a lunge for it with two boys lunging just over her shoulders. All of them missed the coin and disappeared beneath the surface of the filthy water. I quickly left the scene and headed for the money changers who were just on the other side of the bridge.

My first stop was at the Rainbow Club, where I found a few of the guys drinking San Miguel beer. No sooner did I order a beer than John Odusch walked in. Man, it was good to see him. After I was transferred to SEAL Team One in March 1967 our trails had never crossed again. A reunion with old teammates always called for a celebration, especially when it took place in Olongapo. Shortly afterwards, we decided to visit our favorite haunts of the past.

After consuming all of the San Migoo we could stand, we drove to John's house near Half Moon Beach. Sitting in the living room of his very nice home, we talked away half of the night.

John began describing to me his Vietnam experience in January 1968 with Team Twelve's commanding officer, Lieutenant Commander "Buffalo Bob" Condon. Commander Condon, John, and I were graduates of the UDT training class 36 of December 3, 1965. Within a year of graduation, Buffalo Bob Condon was the commanding officer of UDT-12.

"It started like this, Smitty," John began. "I was the OIC of a small UDT-12 detachment under the opcon of CTF 117's Mobile Riverine Force. We were berthed aboard the U.S.S. *Benewah* [APB 35] at Dong Tam near My Tho to test the Aqua Dart operationally. We had previously tested the Aqua Dart on the Colorado River and in Subic Bay, Philippines, and felt we were ready for some combat test and evaluation."

Interrupting John, I said, "Tell me a little bit about the Aqua Dart [forerunner of the Jet Ski water craft of the 1980s and 1990s]. I've heard very little about it since Commander Condon's death."

John continued, "First, it was experimental and manufactured by Oceaneering. It was small, approximately four feet long and two feet wide. It was powered by a Mercury outboard motor of about twenty-five horsepower. The rear portion of the Aqua Dart was countersunk to make room for the operator/swimmer to lay down into and to support his chest. His waist and legs were left hanging outboard and off the stern. Just to the rear and outboard of the operator's armpits were two Aqua Dart fins that were designed to enhance the swimmer's control of the craft. His right hand controlled the engine speed while his legs and feet were used to steer left and right."

John looked at me, wanting some sign that I understood. When I nodded, he continued. "If he wanted to steer to the right, he would stick his right foot to starboard, thereby creating drag and causing the craft to move to his right. If he wanted to turn left he would stick out his left foot to port until he had attained the azimuth desired, then return his foot directly behind the craft. The main disadvantage at this point was that if the operator hit an unseen log or obstacle he would probably be castrated or worse and/or sheer the prop pin." John grinned and I chuckled. Going on, John said, "He was also very vulnerable to sniper fire. The Aqua Dart was further equipped with a fathometer and a camera that took a 350-degree picture. The swimmer operated the fathometer by pushing a button with his left thumb to get an instant reading of the stream's depth at that specific point. The camera was operated by using the right thumb. However, in theory, the Aqua Dart's primary advantage and mission was that it had a low profile and a good enough speed and range to recon uncharted rivers and harbors. It was also to gather point intelligence information to enhance aerial photographs of enemy positions and fortifications."

"Now you're getting down to where the rubber meets the road," I teased.

"Well, yes. That's why we were attached to the Mobile Riverine Force. They were very interested to see if the Aqua Dart and its operator could survive running the VC gauntlet during daylight hours and, if so, could we effectively and accurately gather timely intell info for them. In that light, Commander Condon came over to observe our first combat mission with the Aqua Dart and to familiarize himself with the Mobile Riverine Force's mission, tactics, and needs." John paused thoughtfully, drawing a long breath. Looking at me, he said, "On the eighteenth of January, '68, Commander Condon and PO2 Andy Anderson boarded a modified LCM-6 called a 'Zippo' boat. Myself and Gary Phelps boarded another modified LCM-6 called the Monitor boat. The Zippo was a type of supercharged flame-thrower which could shoot napalm out to approximately one hundred meters and could literally turn the VC inhabitants of riverbank bunkers into crispy critters. The Zippo had been equipped with a large tank filled with napalm that was about three or four feet aft of the bow ramp. Condon and Andy Anderson were sitting between the napalm tank and the bow ramp. We were proceeding up the stream separating Cai Lai and Cai Be districts of Dinh Tuong Province toward the Snoopy's Nose area, so named because the stream made an almost complete circle similar to the nose on Snoopy's noggin'."

"I remember the Snoopy's Nose area well," I interjected. "I went into the area a couple of times with the PRU in

'69. This area was controlled by units of the VC 309 Foxtrot Heavy Weapons Battalion who had heavy bunker complexes inland and alongside the stream banks."

Handing me his empty San Miguel beer bottle, John muttered, "Since you've interrupted my train of thought, hand me another beer." John grinned, took a long drag from the beer I handed him, then continued, "We received sniper fire continually after we entered the stream and during our movement toward Snoopy's Nose. Nothing serious, really. Suddenly, we heard a message over the radio that the Zippo boat's observer had been killed by an RPG-2 B-40 round." John took another big drink and finished his beer. Smacking his lips, he said, "It turns out that the B-40 round had hit the ramp, penetrating through it and eliminating Commander Condon's head. Anderson was sitting about two feet from the commander when his head totally disintegrated. Andy received schrapnel wounds in his leg and brains all over his face and neck."

Handing John another beer, I asked, "What happened to the Aqua Dart project?"

"It had too many tactical detractors. It could be used only during daylight hours for photographs and it was very susceptible to sniper fire, among others," John concluded.

When we finally turned in, it was after 0200 hours. At around 0300 hours, some young woman tapped on John's bedroom window, wanting to come inside. She sounded drunk. John, lying in bed, rolled over and simply ignored her.

When the sun came up later in the morning, I saw the woman lying in the driveway, sound asleep. John told me he had met her a few weeks earlier at a club and she had formed a habit of showing up at his place in the wee hours of the morning, which torqued John. He had told her several times in the past not to wake him during the night.

Disregarding the slumbering body in front of the house, John and I, clad in UDT swim trunks, walked across the lawn and down to the beachfront. We slipped on our face masks and fins and walked into the water until it was up to our waists. Then we shoved off the bottom and started swimming for deeper water.

We began free-diving and looking for shells. Instead of shells, we found two tiger or scorpion fish. Since I had been unable to hunt the dream tiger back at Cam Ranh, I thought we should hunt these two tiger fish. They made poor substitutes for the large, carnivorous mammal of the cat family, but at least the fish were very poisonous. And hell, they were available.

John and I were always looking for a thrill. Our eyes met for a moment, then John motioned for us to return to the surface.

"Tiger fish are becoming rare around here. Stay here and keep them located," John instructed. "I'll be back in a minute with a fishnet. I want to catch one of them to add to my aquarium back at the pad."

"Why, you communist Ethiopian warthog!" I replied. "Surely you don't think I'm going to remain out here alone, treading water a half mile from the beach in these shark-infested waters while herding a pair of aggressive tiger fish who appear to love white meat, just so you can add them to your aquarium."

"Yes, I certainly do," John said. "And furthermore, that's an order," John added with a grin.

As John started free-styling back to the beach, I yelled, "Your mother must've mated with a rattlesnake! And furthermore, I hope you develop a case of the piles!"

Spending a half hour swimming with two tiger fish amidst the coral formations turned out to be more fun than I had anticipated. I decided to probe their defensive reactions and pay special attention to their offensive tactics, if any. When I swam directly toward their enclave, they immediately separated and countered with flanking assaults. Abandon ship! I retreated quickly. In short order I was thoroughly familiar with the tiger fish's defensive reactions, or should I say offensive actions. My strategy would be simple.

John was back within thirty minutes towing a small fishnet with a short handle. "All right, Smitty, here's the plan. I'll sneak up behind them while you entice them from the front. While you're deceitfully maintaining their attention, I'll move in on their exposed rear and net them—as simple as that. Any questions?"

Grinning, I countered with my own feint. "And just how am I supposed to entice these aquatic predators without offering them some bait?"

"Surely you can think of something. An experienced SEAL like yourself must have a repertoire of feints and ruses hidden somewhere in the dark recesses of your mind," retorted John with a teammate's typical sarcasm.

"Well, whatever I come up with, I hope you're ready for the consequences—especially when you have such a short-handled net. When you're in position, I'll feign a frontal attack. If all goes well, you'll soon have the enemy wrapped up and under control."

As anticipated, the tigers made a right and left flank frontal assault. Initially I responded by offering them the tips of my fins, followed by giving the pair of aquatic tiger pricks the "backwash" treatment. As I kicked hard, the tiger fish were washed back toward John and within inches of his exposed face and chest. It was a good thing that he was a fine enough swimmer to have tried out for the '64 Olympics. He responded with incredible speed, no doubt motivated by total fear. He halfheartedly shoved the stubby-handled net toward the fish, but they maneuvered around it toward him. Departing his tactical position, John fled the scene. Sizing up the situation, I retrieved his fishnet and returned to the surface.

"You shithead!" John exclaimed. "What the hell do you think you were doing? You washed them back into me!"

Laughing, I explained, "Well, my strategy was based primarily upon the element of simplicity—when the enemy assaulted my vulnerable position, I first offered them my fins as a subterfuge, then I used my fins' backwash as a ruse to delay and discourage them until my escape was complete."

Feigning anger, John barked, "Give me my fishnet. I shall return or my name isn't John O-dusch. And, by the way, don't assist me in any manner. Stay completely away from me. Is that clear?"

"Aye aye, Your Lordship."

In short order, John did return with one tiger fish. We were both relieved—John had restored his honor and I had maintained my integrity. Calling it quits, we returned to John's house with the joyful anticipation of adding the deadly tiger fish to his 300-gallon saltwater aquarium.

On the way in, I noted that the woman was gone from the driveway. "Good riddance" was all John had to say about it. John again netted the fish, which had been transported from the bay in a five-gallon bucket filled with salt water. All went well until John placed the tiger into the tank and then tried to carefully disentangle the frisky beast from the small net.

"Damned if he didn't sting me!" exclaimed John. "He stuck me on the tip of my right ring finger. My finger is getting numb! If this numbness gets to my heart, I'm done for!"

A bit shaken, I asked, "What does it feel like? What are the symptoms?"

"It's an uncomfortable feeling similar to hitting one's funny bone on the point of somebody's head," John explained. "It's starting to move to my wrist. Shit! I'm going to die!"

"We had best catch a jeepney and head for a doctor, John," I recommended, feeling scared.

"By the time we find a good Philippino doctor, it would be too late, Smitty," John stated emphatically. Suddenly, he yelled with renewed optimism, "Get me a couple of San Miguel beers, fast! Let's sit down and see if they will work as an antidote."

I looked hard at John, and I couldn't believe that the dumb ass was smiling. "You got it!" I said, encouraged by his goofy grin. "And while I'm at it, I'll have a couple with you. Oh, by the way, do you have any strong line handy?"

"What the hell do you want with some line?" John demanded as he chugalugged a beer I tossed to him.

"Well, when you start having fits and convulsions and can no longer navigate, I'll tie you securely to your chair. That way I can continue to pour your favorite antidote down your gullet. How do you like my plan so far?"

"My antidote sounds fine; however, the second part of your plan shows a lack of patience and compassion. Bring me two more beers. Quickly!" John ordered. "It's definitely not time to wrap me up yet, and so far the tingling and numbness have only reached my elbow and haven't gone any further. Things are looking up. I feel more optimistic! I knew this beer would work! Now that I've survived this unfortunate incident, I'm going to kill that tiger fish and eat him for dinner," John commented with an air of finality. Incredibly, the poison didn't go beyond John's elbow and he had no aftereffects. Did the San Miguel work as an antidote? Only the Lord knows.

Several hours and many beers later, we went to a nearby Philippino café and ordered a hearty dinner of lumpia and pancet. The sunset was beautiful, the bay was calm, the food was good, and John had survived the sting of the deadly tiger fish.

Thinking of John's battle and close call with the tiger fish reminded me of what I had been sent over to do in Vietnam: fight. Fight for my country, my command, and my teammates. Win the war. Suddenly, I felt guilty that I wasn't back in the delta kicking ass and taking names.

I remembered all of the fighting and killing during my third tour of 'Nam with the PRU. I remembered the roar of the weapons, the sounds of pain and death, the smell of gunpowder and blood. Some of it was good and it was always exciting; some of it was detestable and occasionally depressing. Humanity is predatory by nature and men are hunters by instinct. I loved to hunt. It was in my blood. And I was now ready to head back to the bush, to hunt the biggest game in the world—man. Little did I know that, indeed, some challenging missions were coming up in my near future.

DEATH IN THE DELTA

Hotel, Commander J.J. Dam came forward and told me that Lt.Cdr. Sphinx commissioned him to find me.

CHAPTER TWENTY-TWO

I departed Cubi Point, Philippines, on July 3 at 0900 hours by C-130 and arrived at the 14th Aerial at Cam Ranh, Vietnam, at 1600 hours. I managed to bum a ride to the LDNN camp, where I found Ray Hollenbeck working on the adviser's jeep. Ostrander and John Fietsch were in Saigon, and Louis Boisvert had had to return to San Diego on emergency leave to attend his dad's funeral.

The next day I flew down to Tan Son Nhut and caught a motorbike to ComNavForV. Lieutenant Kuhn was in his office taking care of the neverending demands of military paperwork. He handed me my quarterly marks to sign. He had given me 4.0 marks across the board. I was very pleased and told him so. Lieutenant Kuhn had always taken good care of his men. He also told me I was up for a Navy Achievement Medal for my stint in Cambodia.

Later, I saw Lieutenant Commander Sphinx and asked him if he had written PO2 Scott an award for his service with us at Sea Float. He said that he hadn't and furthermore he didn't think that Scott deserved one. I told him that I disagreed and that if the two administrative yeomen assigned to SpecWar staff were getting bronze stars (without combat V) for end-of-tour awards and without ever leaving Saigon, surely Scott had earned at least a Navy Achievement Medal with combat V. Sphinx quickly stated that he didn't agree. I suggested to him that if he took care of his men, his men would take care of him. He turned around and left without comment.

As I was leaving to return to my room at the Metropol

Hotel, Commander O'Drain came over and notified me that I would be taking an LDNN platoon to Dong Tam and that I would receive further details the next morning. I told him that I was very pleased and I was ready to depart immediately. I was anxious to return to My Tho and visit with Sao Lam, Lieutenant Loc, and my PRU friends, and with John T., Ian S., and others at the Embassy House. In a way, it was like returning home.

On Tuesday, July 7, Chief Doc Riojas and I departed for Dong Tam to coordinate with the navy support facility concerning room and board for my LDNN platoon and myself. The CO, XO, and OPs officers were very cooperative and said, "We're glad to have you and the LDNNs come aboard." That's what I call hospitality. SEAL Team Two's Fifth Platoon was also staying at Dong Tam when they weren't at Nha Be. Lieutenant Ski and Lieutenant (jg) Tom Norris were Fifth Platoon's OIC and AOIC, respectively.

Departing Dong Tam, I headed for the PRU office in My Tho. Hung, the interpreter; Yao and Trin, the administrators; and Goldie, the office maid; and others were there. They quickly informed me that the Dinh Tuong PRUs were number one in IV Corps that month for killed and captured VCI. Hung also told me that Trung Uy Loc, the PRU team chief, had put the badmouth on Sao Lam (deputy team chief) to Dai Ta Le Minh Dao, the province chief. Apparently Colonel Dao and First Lieutenant Loc, both ARVNs, were jealous of Sao Lam's personal and unofficial control of the PRU. If Sao Lam didn't want to use his PRUs to assault an NVA/VC batallion complex in the northwestern area of Dinh Tuong Province, he simply ignored the proddings and threats of Trung Uy Loc and Colonel Dai. Sao Lam was secure, knowing that he had the covert backing of the national police chief for Dinh Tuong Province.

Sao Lam's being a member of the National Police's PSB and also the PRU's deputy team chief placed him in a position of overt administrative control and covert and/or clandestine operational control. Ideally, he was to obey the operational orders of Loc and the province chief and administrative orders as passed down from Chief Hue. What really ruffled the feathers of the province chief was that Chief Hue was operationally subordinate to the province chief by order of President Thieu. However, whoever had the administrative control of the police organization and its dossiers and agent nets, as did Sao Lam and Chief Hue, had manipulative control if he had the balls to stand up to Dai and Loc. It was a classic example of a superspook control and manipulation trichotomy—their administrative procedures through clandestine, overt, and covert manipulations effectively gave them unofficial operational control and plausible denial when anything went wrong. Fortunately for Sao Lam, and unfortunately for Loc and Dai, Loc had been shot in the head and killed several days earlier while assaulting an NVA/VC bunker complex in northwestern Cai Lai District. Sometimes the best way to convince a fellow was to let him have his own way.

Doc Riojas and I departed for Saigon and the VN navy base, where we headed for the LDNN headquarters to report to Tu Ta (Lieutenant Commander) Hiep, the CO of all LDNNs. I was to keep him informed as to all developing logistical support and operational information related to my LDNN platoon. Tu Ta was tall for a VN, about five feet nine inches in height, weighed about 160 pounds, and was very handsome. No doubt he had several wives and concubines. I discussed Dong Tam, files on each LDNN, etc., with him. He was extremely intelligent and spoke fluent French and better English than I. He had studied in France for several years. When we had finished, we discovered that it was raining cats and dogs and then remembered that our jeep had no side doors. Riojas and I decided to call it a day and head for our rooms at the Metropol Hotel.

A couple of days later I found my seabag at the Navy Post Office. I also managed to get some extra parts for my cut-down M-60. Then Captain Schaible, CO of SEAL Team One, arrived at SpecWar for a visit. He had started out as an enlisted boatswain's mate and was now my CO. He was greatly admired by all in the SpecWar community. He and

Al Huey had been classmates in UDT training class 2 in 1950. He was a good six feet in height, big-boned, and about 275 pounds on the hoof. His favorite drink was Johnny Walker Black on the rocks, and he gave a hard handshake with a penetrating stare as he crushed your hand. We all loved him and were a little bit scared of him after he decked a couple of guys that got obstinate at our weekly team beer-and-wine parties behind the team area.

At about 1300 hours, Lieutenant Kuhn, Joe Churchill, and I ate lunch at the Cheap Charlie Restaurant. The rest of the afternoon was spent chasing rabbits down endless trails trying to locate PRC-25s and other equipment for the LDNN platoons. I also took time to buy a black beret with the LDNN patch on it from a VN store, and I looked quite snappy in it, or so everyone said.

On July 20, Lieutenant Kuhn, Ostrander, and I went to see Tu Ta Hiep at the LDNN headquarters to inquire when the two LDNN platoons would be ready to depart for My Tho and Dong Tam. As usual, Lieutenant Kuhn could not tie Hiep down to a specific date. It was very frustrating for all of us. PO2 Ostrander was to take his platoon to My Tho and operate with Lieutenant Todd's Hotel Platoon in Kien Hoa Province while I was to go to Dong Tam and operate with Lieutenant Ski's Fifth Platoon in Dinh Tuong Province. Lieutenant Kuhn was getting short and we were all getting frustrated.

Finally, on July 23, 1970, PO1 Hardegrew and I got a Ford Falcon van, drove to the LDNN Headquarters, and picked up Tu Uy Son and the LDNN platoon plus gear, etc. We were headed for Dong Tam. It had only taken us twenty days! We arrived at Dong Tam by 0930 hours, set up racks and mosquito nets in our berthing space, and ate lunch. After lunch I notified the operations officer that myself and fourteen LDNNs had arrived and would be operating as soon as we could—pending good operational intelligence information.

Five Fifth Platoon guys were wounded in the morning on an op six klicks up Route 66, a canal that ran northeast of

Dong Tam and was noted for being big, bad Indian country. No one was hurt seriously. They hadn't gotten any decent intell in quite a while and had decided to go looking for trouble. The SEALs inadvertently found a heavily armed, large enemy unit that had much more firepower than they did. Surprisingly, the VC were able to outgun the SEALs, who were carrying three Stoners, two M-60s, several M-16/XM-148s, and an M-79 grenade launcher. Fortunately, the VC fired high, as usual. However, one of the VC was able to throw a grenade that wounded five SEALs. The SEALs were fortunate in that they were able to withdraw from contact and call for extraction. All's well that ends well.

At about 1700 hours, Jerry Waters, of Fifth Platoon, and I headed for My Tho to Juicy Fruit Row on the riverbank. The row consisted of a few small beer joints that were built on stilts over the edge of the river. The beer joints had catered to the U.S. Army's 9th Infantry Division before its return to CONUS in late 1969. Now that the 9th was gone, Juicy Fruit's only customers were a handful of U.S. Navy folks who occasionally strayed from their own bars at the Victory and Carter hotels, where the navy's support activity was located, and an occasional trooper from the Vietnamese 7th ARVN Infantry Division. Interestingly, the Victory Hotel formerly had been a French villa and monastery.

After a couple of beers, we headed for the National Police compound, where Sao Lam and a couple of platoons of PRU still lived. Jerry dropped me off and returned to Dong Tam. It had been almost ten months since I'd seen Sao Lam. It was really good to see the old fart. He immediately had a couple of cases of 33 Beer brought out. My good friend the "King Pig Killer" had recently been killed by a command-detonated claymore antipersonnel mine about five hundred meters up the creek from the National Police compound. He had had two wives. One was considered to be very good looking by the PRU. I never did find out who managed to acquire her.

Shortly, food was placed on the table and Sao Lam and

I began the long process of eating and drinking. Fortunately, I didn't have to do much chin-chinning. We talked and drank continuously until midnight, when Sao Lam had a couple of PRU set up the same cot in the same little room that I always slept in when I was there as their adviser in 1969.

As I lay on the cot in the darkened room, smelling old smells and eyeing old-but-familiar walls and shadows, I grinned slightly to myself. Seeing Sao Lam was a pleasure, and the memories we had shared at the dinner table had been pleasant ones.

I closed my eyes to sleep, fearing not at all that I might dream of past evils and many deaths, thereby submerging myself in a nightmare. Instead, I felt at peace and strangely released, confident that good dreams and good days lay ahead of me.

CHAPTER TWENTY-THREE

The next morning Sao Lam and I went to a local Chinese sidewalk restaurant and ate Chinese soup and drank strong French coffee as we had many times before in 1969. Chief Hue stopped by and drank some French coffee heavily laced with *sua* (thick cream) and raw sugar. Afterwards, I walked to the Embassy House to visit John T. and Ian "Sammy" S., Larry J. (Company folks), Major Wolfgang Hertwick, Captain Kozak (Phoenix advisers), and others. At the gate I met the Chinese Nungs who were the security guards of the Embassy House compound. It was good to shake their hands and see them all again.

I went into the old French villa and heard John T. in the head taking care of morning details. I decided to sneak up to the door and fake an assassination with a yell and my trigger finger. I eased up to the door, then jumped inside while pointing my finger, and screamed, "Bang, bang, you're dead!"

"Damn!" responded John. "You scared the piss out of me!" Recovering somewhat, he grinned and countered with, "Where's my Uzi? No broken-down Navy SEAL is going to come into my villa and scare the wits out of me without some form of reprisal!"

Sticking my right hand out, I said, "It's good to see you, John. What's this about an Uzi? Have you got one?"

"Yeah," John replied while he shook my hand. "Let me finish shaving and I'll show it to you in my room. Soon, we'll have to go to the rifle range by the Chieu Hoi center, and I'll let you try it out."

"Great! I'll bring my cut-down M-60 for you to test." It was just like old times. As one gun nut to another, John and I had spent many hours discussing all forms of weapons, firing and testing a variety of communist AK-47s and the newer AKM, playing with the old semiautomatic M-1D Garand sniper rifle, admiring the old Colt model 1911 .45-caliber semiautomatic pistol (not the newer M-1911-A1), shooting the Browning high-power M-1935 9-mm semiautomatic pistol for accuracy and handling compared to the S&W M-39 9-mm semiautomatic pistol, discussing the merits of the 7.62-mm NATO M-14E2 rifle with hand grip stock, etc.

Shortly afterward, I saw Ian S. He was the POIC (senior man) at the Embassy House. As we were shaking hands, he teased me by saying, "Are you ready for another try at beating me at arm wrestling, Smitty?"

"No, sir, I don't think so," I replied. "The last time I tried to beat you I wound up cracking one of my left ribs on the bar top over there as Randy Sheridan cheered me on. Remember?"

Changing the subject, Ian suggested that I stay and eat lunch with him and John. After lunch, John showed me the Israeli Uzi 9-mm submachine gun. "It easily fits into my attaché case and still leaves room for other things." John demonstrated.

After our initial excitement at seeing each other again, we finally settled down to business. I asked John for some good intell/info for my LDNN platoon. He said he'd do all he could for us and would also introduce me to the 525 folks at a later date. With that, John took me to the old 7th ARVN Infantry Division HQ, where Hotel Platoon of SEAL One was berthed. It was good to see Chief Kassa, PO2 Kaneakua, Lieutenant Todd, and others. They gave me a lift to Dong Tam with three SAS fellows named Smitty, Wayne, and Moore.

From there we all went to the Acey Deucey Club and began an evening of tales of derring-do followed by the neverending *chin-chin* toast to whatever tale or anecdote that was offered. There was never an angry word and the laughter never stopped. After the navy bar closed we headed for Fifth Platoon's barrack and continued the party until midnight, when we all hit the sack. We sure had a good time.

On the morning of July 25 I headed for My Tho to gather operational information and to fire a few weapons with John T. My first stop was at the PRU office, where I visited with Sao Lam and Hung, who had been my interpreter in 1969. Sao Lam began telling me about an upcoming mission in Tan Phu Dong, a village in Cai Lai District. Sao Lam, Hung, and I had all operated in that area three times last year. It was a hot area with large NVA/VC units hidden in the treelines. Our missions were always very successful against the VCI there because we had a great agent named Duc who had natural placement and access within the targeted area. Unfortunately, Duc had recently been killed by a command-detonated claymore while traveling by foot to his home village. He was the best agent that Sao Lam and his PRUs ever had.

After my visit with Sao Lam and Hung, I headed for the Embassy House to visit John for a spell. In short order, both of us were headed for the weapons range by the Chieu Hoi center with John's Belgian-made Uzi 9-mm submachine gun and my shortened and lightened M-60 7.62-mm NATO machine gun. John was really impressed with our modification of the M-60, and he especially enjoyed shooting it. I wasn't nearly as impressed as John with the Uzi because it didn't point as well as our S&W M-76 9-mm submachine gun. However, the S&W wouldn't fit into an attaché case without removing the barrel. With a little practice I began to shoot fairly accurately with it, though. Then, after our weapons familiarization and target practice, John gave me copies of the latest PSB intelligence information reports.

After lunch I visited with Major Muckelroy, the senior Phoenix adviser, who had relieved Major Hertwick earlier in the year. He gave me an update of the VCI and order of battle (OB) estimates and concentrations within the province and recommended that I work with the Sam Giang District DIOCC for the immediate future.

After returning to Dong Tam, Lieutenant Ski and I went to the ARVN 7th Infantry Division's tactical operations center (TOC), where we met Major Orlov, who was assigned there as an adviser. He said he would do all he could to reinforce our request for Huey slick and gunship assets and support for our ops. Gradually, everything began to fall into place. After returning to the SEAL/LDNN area I received a message that I was to report to Lieutenant Todd, SEAL Team One's Hotel Platoon OIC, the next morning at the old ARVN 7th HQ on Nguyen Hue Street in My Tho.

On the morning of July 30, I arose early and caught a ride to My Tho to meet Lieutenant Todd. I knew something was up. I first stopped by Hotel Platoon's berthing spaces and said howdy to Chief Ted Kassa, Doc "JJ the Razor" Jennings, Bob Davis, Pete Peterson, Butch Makul, Warpo Cellilo, Charlie Jones, Paul Geiss, Angie Angioi, James Day, Dodd Coutts, "T" Donovan, and Pete Berton. The BSU folks, who had saved many a SEAL's life, were berthed in adjoining rooms. Lieutenant (jg) Fred Stinson, QM1 Robert Easly, Bosco Clark, Howard Rupp, Del Rosario, Skip Loutsenhizer, Matt Matthews, Robert Custer, Tree Crabtree, and PT2 Bob Gardner from NavForV were frantically preparing the STABs and weapons for the upcoming op. Everyone was busy preparing his operational gear, etc., with an air of excitement, intensity, and a sense of urgency that motivated all SEALs and MSTs to prepare themselves mentally for a big operation. That type of atmosphere was very infectious, stimulating, and occasionally gutwrenching.

After taking care of the amenities, I went into Lieutenant Todd's makeshift office in a nearby room. He and Lieutenant (jg) Jon Rowe (AOIC) were intently studying a 1:25,000-scale map of the lower end of the Mekong Delta and the Thanh Phu Peninsula and its secret zone in particular and a 1:4,000-scale photo mosaic of the target. The secret zone was located at the tip of the peninsula between Ham Luong River to the east and Co Chien River to the west. The Thanh Phu Secret Zone was located approximately forty-five to fifty miles south of Saigon. When I was in UDT-12's Fourth Platoon during the fall of 1966, we were tasked to recon the tip of the peninsula. We completed an administrative hydrographic chart for an upcoming amphibious landing called Operation DECK HOUSE FIVE, which took place a few months later. The coastal area was made up of mangrove swamps and tidal flats that could be very difficult to patrol, especially at low tide.

"Good morning, sirs," I greeted. "What's up?"

Laying his grease pencil down, Todd started chuckling. "Hello, Smitty. Sit down. We've got a Bright Light on our hands and we're trying to make sense out of all the tactical requirements and units that have been thrust upon this mission by the army and the navy." Scratching his head, Todd continued, "I'm just thankful that I'm not the head honcho. We have unlimited resources—and there lies the problem. In order for NavForV to get army helo slick and attack aircraft and logistical support that is deemed necessary for the success of the op, they had to agree to include the army's Powder Valley Six demolition boys as part of the whole shebang. Supposedly, the general said we could have unlimited access to his helos and OV-10s if we would utilize the Powder Valley boys as the primary element to block the escape routes of the POW guard unit and U.S. and VN prisoners," he explained while shaking his head.

"Do we have any positive identification of the U.S. POWs?" I asked.

"More than we normally do," Lieutenant Todd answered. "According to the Bright Light report, a Vietnamese ARVN escapee reported that he'd seen three Americans held prisoner within a small bamboo pen. Apparently, he momentarily observed the Americans twice during his two-year stint at the POW camp, and the last sighting was six days ago. Our intelligence believes the U.S. POWs are army helicopter pilots."

"What's the enemy strength at the POW camp?" I asked.

Raising his right eyebrow with a gleam in his eye, Todd responded. "You'll love this! The camp is 'only' guarded by a special thirty-man guard unit and there's 'only' a thirty-man guerrilla unit in the immediate vicinity. What do you think?"

"Thank goodness! For a moment I thought we were in trouble. Let's hoist the flag and charge balls-to-the-wall!" I exclaimed.

"Rape, pillage, and burn!" Jon chuckled.

After we settled down, Lieutenant Todd continued.

"Our call signs and freqs are: Todd: Rocky Flier One; Ostrander: Rocky Flier Two; Smith: Rocky Flier Three; Powder Valley: Powder Valley Six; CnC ship: Dutch Master; Primary Freq: 37.80; Secondary Freq: 45.65."

Looking into my eyes, he said, "You haven't much time and neither does my platoon. You and your LDNN platoon are to wait at the Dong Tam helo pad until you're picked up by three army slicks at approximately 1600 hours this afternoon. You'll then be flown to Vinh Long, where your and Ostrander's LDNN platoons will spend the night. Captain Lucas will meet you on the Vinh Long helo pad and will brief you and Ostrander as to any changes to tactical responsibilities and any other up-to-date information." I nodded. Continuing, Lieutenant Todd said, "On the thirty-first at 0615 hours your LDNN platoon will insert at the designated target area near the POW camp as directed by the OSC [on-scene commander]. The LDNN platoon's primary mission is to reinforce my squad if needed and act as a blocking element while we're moving toward the POW camp."

Pointing at the Thanh Phu Secret Zone on the map, I asked, "When and where are you and your squad going to insert?"

Lieutenant Todd grinned, then explained while pointing to the map. "First, my squad will insert tonight by IBS here at coordinates XR752857 on the southeastern corner of the peninsula. Mr. Rowe and his squad will remain at sea as backup aboard an MSSC. My squad will patrol inland to a point near enough to the POW camp, located here on the mosaic at coordinates XR764865." Lieutenant Todd pointed at the spot. "We can set listening and observation posts until false dawn. At first dawn all fire support—ten slicks, OV-10s, boats—will move to the mouth of Rach Khau Bang and await further instructions. Once everyone is in place, I will give an advance signal to the OSC aboard the C & C ship that we're moving in toward the POW pen. Shortly afterwards, the OSC will direct your and Ostrander's helos to insert to my right flank. As usual, we'll more than likely have to play this part of the operation by ear after the shooting starts." Todd summarized his briefing by commenting, *"C'est la guerre!"*

"Roger that." I grinned. *"Dieu vous garde."* Thinking for a moment, I continued, "It all sounds good to me. Considering we'll be in isolation as of this afternoon, I assume that I have permission to brief Tu Uy Son and his LPO, Thuoc, as to the purpose of the mission after we reach Vinh Long and are briefed by Captain Lucas?"

Lieutenant Todd nodded while replying, "Yes, that will be fine. Any more questions?"

"No sir," I replied quickly. "I've got lots to do before 1600 hours. Y'all be careful, now, you hear. Don't worry about Ostrander and me, we'll be there through the thick and the thin."

With that I made hot tracks for Dong Tam. Time was awastin'. On the way back I started singing an old cowboy ballad Scotch Sutherland and I used to sing while we were washing cattle on the wash rack at the Bridwell Hereford HQ Ranch near Winthorst, Texas:

> Bacon in the pan,
> Coffee in the pot;
> Get up an' get it—
> Get it while it's hot.
>
> Wake up, Jacob!

Day's a-breakin',
Beans in the pot,
An' sourdough's a-bakin!

Carnation milk, best in the lan',
Comes to the table in a little red can.
No teats to pull, no hay to pitch,
Jes' punch a hole in the sonofabitch!

"Hallelujah! We're headed for the land of Caanan filled with heathens just waitin' to be shot," I thought in my excitement as I headed down the back road to Dong Tam.

After spending the night at Vinh Long, Ostrander, myself, Ken Peck, Tim Barren of SEAL Two's Fifth Platoon, PO1 Clinton (a photographer's mate from NavForV), twenty-eight LDNNs, and thirty-five army guys loaded seven helos and with three other slicks flew to Tra Vin to refuel. At 0600 hours we flew to the mouth of Rach Khau Bang (a secondary stream) and circled for thirty-five minutes before we were inserted near the POW camp. I didn't know about the situation on the ground, but the element of surprise was lost as soon as our ten helos appeared on the horizon, much less circled within a klick and a half of the target for thirty-five minutes. Also, the Coast Guard WPB, Swift boats, and MSSCs were located nearby at the mouth of the stream. Just the increase in nearby allied radio transmissions would alert the VC/NVA monitors that something was up. I felt that the mission had been compromised many hours ago. No doubt the U.S. POWs had already been moved to an alternate site sometime earlier.

After our insertion we set up perimeters and made flanking movements as directed by the on-scene commander. Ostrander's LDNNs behaved very badly by shooting a water buffalo and looting and burning VN hooches. Shortly afterwards, my LPO, Thuoc, opened up with his M-16 and shot another water buffalo. I became very angry and told Tu Uy Son that he must get control of his men or I would do it for him. I then turned to PO1 Thuoc and chewed on him enough that he settled down.

Unfortunately, Son totally failed to control his men—just as I had as a PRU adviser on two PRU missions. I had had many delegated responsibilities as an adviser but *no* authority (letter of the law) to discipline my counterparts. However, I could have and did draw upon my relational authority (spirit of the law) in situations like that as a last resort. Rarely, I did have to use anger to intimidate and manipulate, i.e., as a way to gain some form of control over the situation. It was during those times that I hated being an adviser.

Within a few minutes after my altercation with Ensigns Son and Thuoc, Lieutenant Todd and his squad rendezvoused with Ostrander and the LDNNs and slicked into two other locations, checking one out for guerrillas and the other for a cache. By noon the op was over. After the debriefing at Binh Thuy and our return to My Tho, Lieutenant Todd told me that the POW camp had been totally empty of people—no guards, no POWs. They did locate the POW retention pen, however. It was a ten-foot-square area that was secured by a bamboo fence with one side dug into a mound of earth that ended in a concave space for shelter. It was very well camouflaged with surrounding brush and trees. Todd was surprised that the local villagers were so near the POW camp during his squad's search of the area. The villagers appeared unafraid. He quickly questioned several of the locals as to the whereabouts of the U.S. POWs. Each one said, "They were moved from here three days ago." *C'est la vie!*

In a way, I didn't blame the army for wanting to participate in the op. Unfortunately, most Bright Light operations larger than a seven-man squad had failed to rescue U.S. POWs; only Vietnamese POWs were liberated. Another problem I took into account was the VC/NVA's ability to also collect intelligence information from HUMINT (human intelligence), SIGINT (signal intelligence), and ELINT (electronic intelligence). We were also aware that there were Soviet and Chinese advisers and two American turn-coats working with the VC and NVA within the delta.

One thing we knew for sure, our delta enemies were very capable and competent professionals. We had begun to realize that if we were ever to have a chance at liberating a U.S. POW, we'd have to coordinate and plan the mission covertly. Even then, the intelligence information would have to originate from an individual who had timely and firsthand knowledge of the target and, most important, had not compromised the information to any allied inter-rogators—U.S. or otherwise. Sadly, the chances of realistically rescuing a U.S. POW were reduced from slim to none because of interservice rivalry.

In October, Lieutenant Collins and X-Ray Platoon would relieve Lieutenant Todd and Hotel Platoon in Ben Tre, Kien Hoa Province, as part of DETACHMENT GOLF.

CHAPTER TWENTY-FOUR

Over the two weeks following the Bright Light mission, I spent a lot of time introducing Tu Uy Son to the Vietnamese military and civilian intelligence-collection community. We were always very careful to observe protocol and establish rapport. We did a lot of legwork, traveling back and forth to My Tho numerous times to meet with the U.S. advisers when possible and their counterparts with MSS, PSB, NPFF, PIC, the Chieu Hoi center, PIOCC, DIOCCs, PRU, sector and subsector S-2s, ARVN 7th Infantry Divisions G-2 and G-3, etc. Dick at 525, Captain Fowler at sector S-2, Chuck the NPFF adviser, and Med Justinia (retired Philippino army), the Chieu Hoi adviser. John, Sam, and Bob at the Embassy House were very helpful in pointing me in the right directions. Sao Lam (assistant PRU chief) took a liking to Tu Uy Son and introduced him to the new PRU team chief, Trung Uy Tranh Hoang Con. Slowly, Tu Uy and I were beginning to make some headway, but not without difficulty.

After a luncheon with Dick (525) on August 7, as he gave me a ride to the Embassy House, Dick made remarks about how dirty, unkempt, and unsquared-away the SEALs were. I disagreed with his assessment, but I understood the basis for the comments. The province senior adviser (PSA) of Kien Hoa Province was pissed because our (Ostrander's and mine) LDNNs killed the two water buffaloes and the chickens on the Bright Light op. Also, our SpecWar intelligence officer, who was sent to My Tho as an intelligence handler for the SEALs at Dong Tam, apparently offended much of the intelligence community in the area because of his methods. Additionally, in 1969 Lieutenant S's SEAL Two platoon had been careless in handling its agents. One of them turned out to be a double agent and was responsible for the setup on Thoi Son Island which resulted in the platoon's LDNNs' nearly getting killed in My Tho's provincial jailhouse. Within three days the SEAL Two platoon was run out of the country. These things initially made it difficult for me to cross-check any intelligence so that my LDNNs and I could go on an operation. All I wanted to do was to teach my LDNN platoon how to target VCI, use the established intell community, observe protocol, and establish rapport. In trying to accomplish my goals, however, I had to proceed slowly and cautiously due to the past.

On August 10, I went to NSWG in the morning. There I explained the problems I was having at My Tho and Dong Tam to Lieutenant Commander Clemente, the XO. He seemed to fully understand, but he hinted that regardless of the priority of targeting VCI, we would have to begin operations and kill enemy guerrillas whenever we didn't have VCI targets. He also made it clear that Tu Uy Son's platoon must produce results as soon as possible for political reasons. And worst of all, I was not to organize any combined PRU/LDDN operations. With that in mind, I was determined that SpecWar staff would get their way. However, they might not have many LDNNs left to play their numbers games after the next couple of ops, I thought.

I hitchhiked back to Dong Tam and arrived at around 1430 hours. Tu Uy Son wasn't there, so I hitched a ride to My Tho. I saw Lieutenant Todd and Ostrander. Ostrander told me that his platoon had captured or killed nine VC the previous night in Kien Hoa Province. His Chieu Hoi had been coming through with flying colors for him, leading the platoon on some pretty good ops.

After spending the night at the Embassy House, I went to the Chieu Hoi center and saw Med. He and I questioned two Hoi Chanhs who claimed they didn't know where any

VC or VCI lived or had ever lived. "Great intelligence gathering," I thought. I left disgusted.

I went to Dong Tam and advised Son that he should prepare his platoon to be on standby for an operation, as I was determined to make something happen and soon. Then I went back to My Tho and finished paperwork before calling it a day.

The next morning, Med and I drove to the Cho Gao subsector to see a Hoi Chanh. I also met an Australian named McEvoy who had some outstanding intelligence. The originator of the information was Team Three, Military Intelligence Detachment 493d (MID) Binh Phuoc, Long An Province.

Med and I got back to My Tho at about 1230, then I hitched a ride to Dong Tam and encouraged Tu Uy Son and his troops to be ready to mount out on short notice, as usual. I was told that Ray Hollenbeck had arrived with John Fietsch and they were in My Tho looking for me. I hitch-hiked back to My Tho and found the two on Juicy Fruit Row, looking really hard for me at the bottom of their beer glasses.

After discussing the latest news at the bar, John dropped Ray and me off at the Embassy House. We ate supper at the small navy mess, then walked to the PRU office. Trung Uy Con (the PRU chief) had finally gotten the intelligence report that I needed translated into English so I could request helos for that op.

Ray, Trung Uy, Tren, and I decided to meet Sao Lam at the police station. We did, then Sao Lam gathered some old friends and we went to his sister's home. There we ate chicken and drank beer to our hearts' content. At about 2100 hours, we finally returned to the Embassy House.

After breakfast the next morning, Ray and I walked to the PRU office and talked to the PRU intell cell leader. He was set to guide us on our op the next night. He said everything was a "go."

Ray and I then went to Dong Tam in time for lunch, after which we went to ARVN 7th TOC to see Major Orlov. I requested helos, aerial photos, and maps for a later mission, which the major assured me I would have. I was quite impressed with Orlov, as he seemed to be right on top of things and eager to help us. When Ray and I left his office, I was wishing there were more professionals like him.

Ray and I got a case of beer and went to the police compound in My Tho to visit with Sao Lam. Sao Lam never showed up, so Ray and I had a steam bath and called it a day. I was really tired by the time my head hit my pillow.

The next day we went to the PRU office and worked out the last details of the combined mission. Then we returned to Dong Tam and prepared our gear. I also briefed the LDNNs, lined up C rats for the op, and caught a little rest.

At 1600 hours, nine LDNNs, nine PRUs, Ray Hollenbeck, and myself departed My Tho via trucks to the Sam Giang subsector MACV compound. I notified Major Hardy (DSA) and Captain Moltane (DIOCC) that Ray and I and LDNNs were going to accompany the PRUs on this op and that our objective was to capture the 518 X-Ray company commander Ba Le of the 409F Heavy Weapons Battalion. The major said he couldn't believe we were going into such a hot, enemy-infested area. We just grinned at him.

At 1730 hours, we headed out for our destination on foot, simply because there were no roads between us and our enemy. Initially, our ruse was to move leisurely from the subsector village by heading away from our AO and toward an ARVN outpost. From there we would take several tangents before heading directly toward our target. There were occasional human sounds of normal conversations and activities coming from the randomly spaced rice-farm homes. Two little children were yelling and playing near their hootch and an old Vietnamese farmer was following his water buffalo while plowing in mud up to his axles. The afternoon was beautiful, but deceitfully quiet.

After reaching the outpost we took several tangents before heading directly toward our target (XS337434). We were careful from there on and used available cover when possible and maintained noise discipline at all times. At

1945 hours, we spotted several men with AK-47s approximately four hundred meters from our position walking across a series of rice paddies towards the targeted hootch that was supposed to be the company commander's office. They hadn't seen us so we decided to set up an OP (observation post) at XS340438, at the edge of a brushy tree line until dark thirty. Shortly before dusk, we saw several VC milling around near the hootch with weapons in their hands. Fortunately, it was to be a totally dark night—even the stars failed to shine brightly.

At approximately 2100 hours we patrolled to within two hundred or three hundred meters of the hootch (XS340435), where we quietly made final adjustments to our gear. Unfortunately, Trung Uy Con unilaterally decided to divide our small force into two groups. Worst of all, he was taking some of the LDNNs with him, leaving Tu Uy Son, Ray, and myself with the stay-behind group. Because Tu Uy failed to maintain command and control of his men, I stepped in and argued with Con.

"No way!" I whispered to him vehemently. "That's no good!"

"Why no good?" he spat out. Even in the scant starlight, I saw a miffed look on his face.

I stepped closer to him. Only a foot of air hung between our faces. "There is no tactical reason for dividing our men. Once the shooting starts it will probably be very difficult for you to link back up with us again. The night is very black," I said, staring into Con's eyes.

Con shook his head. "No problem," he said with a shrug. "I find you, no sweat."

"*Comb duc* [No good]," I said, filling up with frustration. "We have only one radio between us and I'm carrying it."

Our arguing was growing progressively louder and threatening to compromise the op. I could tell Con was not going to back down. He was adamant in holding fast to his ill-advised decision. He was also beginning to get very angry. Under the circumstances, I felt that it was time that I give in, and consented to divide the group. I looked at Ray

Hollenbeck and shrugged my shoulders. Ray just shook his head. I was sure wishing that Sao Lam was in charge. If Con wasn't careful he'd reap the same fruit as Trung Uy Loc—death.

Within a couple of minutes, Trung Uy Con took his combined group of four PRU and four LDNNs and headed for the hootch. The night was so black that Con's group faded from our view within ten meters. In the meantime, the rest of us (PRUs and LDNNs) quietly set up a skirmish line and waited for the ensuing action.

About an hour later, suddenly, all hell broke loose. Dozens of red tracers were coming from the vicinity of the hootch followed by green and red tracers (AK-47 and RPD machine gun fire) coming towards the hootch and us from 270 degrees of our position. In other words, we were almost surrounded. "Wonderful," I thought. Fortunately, the enemy fire was coming from three to four hundred meters away. Because it was pitch-black, the VC couldn't see us, so they were reconning by fire in hopes that we would reveal our position by returning fire. One of our men fired off a short burst of return fire, but I stopped him.

"No!" I barked, then with a hushed voice I said, "Don't return fire and expose our position." It would have been pure foolishness to start another firefight in the dark against a large number of enemy troops in a place known to be enemy infested. And then there was the small problem of not knowing for sure where in the hell Con and his men were at that moment, much less if he needed help and how many casualties he might have sustained. The words "I told you so" ran through my mind more than once over the ensuing hour of tortuous waiting for Con and his troops to return. There was only silence in the vicinity of the hootch.

In between the continual firing of the VC from three points of the compass and my coordinating with Major Hardy at subsector for standby 4.2-inch mortar H & I (harass and interdict) fire, we finally heard Con and his group screaming that they were coming toward our position and not to shoot.

A returning LDNN yelled to Tu Uy Son that Lam Van Doan was wounded as two PRUs carried him into our midst.

"We kill Ba Le—he company commander!" said a grinning Trung Uy Con. "We kill three bodyguards, too."

"You did very good, Trung Uy Con. How bad is Doan wounded and are there any other casualties?" I quickly asked.

"Doan wounded in wrist. You get medevac?" Son asked, then hesitated a moment while Trung Uy Con pointed at a woman they had brought with them while telling him about the woman and that she was the wife of the dead VC company commander.

I turned to one of the PRU and asked how badly the VC woman was wounded. He pulled the young woman's pajama top aside and showed me, with his red-lens flashlight, a bullet hole in her right breast and another hole where the bullet had exited out her back. The PRU then pointed to her left thigh, where she had been shot through the flesh, the bullet just missing her femoral artery. If Mrs. Ba Le survived the night and if she would respond to sound interrogation techniques, we should get some very good information from her for future operations, I thought.

However, the VC had other ideas. They were becoming more aggressive and accurate with their reconnaissance by fire and appeared to be moving to our right and left flanks to block our only escape route. I wasted little time in calling Major Hardy and requested 4.2-inch mortar fire with HE (high explosive) rounds on several VC positions. I also requested that a medevac be held on standby to extract two badly wounded VNs after we had reached a safer area where we would set up a defensive perimeter. "Thank goodness for our good ole army buddies!" I thought.

Once we got organized, we continued on, patrolling in grim silence, except for the LDNN's groans, toward a suitable landing zone for the medevac. Amazingly, the woman stayed on her feet and walked for over five hundred meters to the LZ. While the LDNN was carried behind me, the seriously injured woman continued on stoically beside me. She never complained, shed a tear, groaned, or made any sound. I couldn't believe her simple determination. She was a very courageous woman.

When our group reached a fairly large grassy area, Con had his PRU set perimeter security while I radioed subsector requesting the medevac evacuation of our two wounded. We waited for over an hour before we heard the *whump, whump, whump* of the medevac helo. I vectored it to our general location by radio, and Ray marked the LZ with two MK-13 day/night flares set fifty meters apart for visual contact. Finally, the Huey of mercy swooped in with its bright searchlights shining on us. We lost our night vision for thirty minutes or more, but it was worth it to get the LDNN and the woman extracted. We loaded the unconscious LDNN and the woman onto the helo, followed by several panic-stricken LDNNs, leaving the rest of us behind.

On the long patrol back to the MACV compound, I had to continually go to the back of the file and encourage the young LDNNs to keep up. "We are almost to subsector. We will be there soon," I encouraged. "You must not slow down! The VC will be coming after us soon." I'm afraid my PRU buddies weren't impressed with these LDNNs. I was very disappointed.

The wounded VN woman was taken to the Vietnamese hospital in My Tho. It was there that she either recovered from her wounds or she died. I don't know what happened to her, as I never saw her again, at least not physically. But I did see her again countless times in my mind's eye, remembering her as an authentic example of courage and heart. I took a piece of her grit on that dark, damp night and stuffed it into my own heart and soul. It helped to strengthen me later during a fifth tour of Vietnam.

After our group arrived at the MACV compound, Ray and I enjoyed three wonderful beers each with Major Hardy and Captain Moltane. They were both Special Forces officers and very experienced in this sometimes strange profession called counterinsurgency. There was a special camaraderie between us that night that only brothers in arms can understand. If it hadn't been for their support, Ray and I might not have been sitting with them enjoying a cold American beer. Ray and I returned to Dong Tam and hit the sack at about 0130 hours. The LDNNs had already returned and were sacked out in their bunks. I had already completed the LDNN spot report and LDNN personnel casualty report messages that were addressed to SpecWar in Saigon and had delivered them to the navy communications room for priority transmission. Well, I hoped SpecWar staff was satisfied—we finally got results: one LDNN wounded, four VC killed, one VC captured, I thought, grinning to myself as I crawled into my rack and snuggled my head deep into my pillow.

The next morning, August 15, I talked to Ensign Son about our getting ready for the afternoon's heliborne operation against the 309F Batallion's headquarters and communications company. I reminded him that we had helo slicks to insert us and many Cobra gunships and OV-10s for fire support and that the op would take only a couple of hours from start to finish.

Tu Uy Son looked down at his feet for a moment, then off into the distance and said, "We don't get any breakfast this morning and little sleep last night. Lam Van Doan is hurt bad. All LDNNs must go to Saigon to see Tu Ta Hiep. He say that everytime LDNN get hurt, we take off two weeks. Today we go to Saigon," Son stated emphatically.

I immediately went to the Naval Operations Center (NOC), where their communications equipment was located, and notified Major Hardy that my counterparts had turned chicken and were headed for Saigon despite my protest and pleas. In light of the situation, I said, I was forced to cancel that afternoon's helo op. The major understood and told me to rendezvous with Captain Moltane and Major Orlov at the ARVN 7th's HQ within an hour. Later, Major Orlov thoroughly debriefed me about the night op and was especially interested in the captured documents that the

PRU had retained. Immediately afterwards, Orlov recommended to his VN counterpart, Colonel An, that three companies be sent into the area where the 309F Battalion's headquarters and communications company were located.

Colonel An replied, "Maybe in three or four days."

In other words, Colonel An wasn't interested. "Some days chickens, some days feathers," I thought. There were days when I thought we were fighting on the wrong side of the fence.

Hollenbeck and I were now without a job and without counterparts. I called Lieutenant Kuhn at SpecWar and told him that there were only Hollenbeck and myself remaining at Dong Tam to carry on the war against the determined communist tyrants and their henchmen. However, as faithful subordinates, we would gladly remain at our location and continue on with absolute determination, and for the cause of freedom combine ops with some of my tired, true, and faithful Vietnamese comrades, better known as the PRU.

"That won't be necessary, Smitty. You and Ray have done all you can do. You've done a good job," Kuhn commented. "I'm glad you guys are maintaining a sense of humor." The lieutenant chuckled. "And don't worry about a thing. I'll take care of all of the details on this end. I want both of you to pack all of your gear and catch a ride to my office on Monday, the seventeenth. You'll be going home soon."

On Sunday, August 16, Sao Lam drove to Dong Tam and picked up Ray and me and took us back to My Tho to consume a few farewell beers and drinks at his home within the police compound. We spent a great afternoon and evening with Sao Lam and my other PRU friends laughing about old times, following that up by toasts and sealing it by the inevitable chin-chinning. It had been only eleven months earlier that Sao Lam and I had operated together as PRU counterpart and adviser respectively. Our combat experiences seemed to have taken place so very long ago.

"I made a toast to *Co Van* Smith, that he return to My

Tho again for remember sake to his PRU friends," Sao Lam stated with his glass of Japanese whiskey and water lifted high overhead.

"Chin-chin, chin-chin," my other PRU friends yelled at Ray as I lifted my glass of rum and Coke.

Before I downed its contents, I looked at Sao Lam and said, "If there is any way, I will return to My Tho again soon. I look forward to going on many more operations with you. I hope to spend many more good times, like the past and tonight, with you and all my other PRU friends. You are my special friend and brother, Sao Lam. I will never forget you."

Later, Ray and I were able to catch a ride with an ARVN two-and-a-half-ton truck back to Dong Tam. It was time to pack our bags and start the long process of returning to Saigon and eventually the States. The next morning, August 17, Ray and I rode a navy bus from Dong Tam to SpecWar in Saigon.

Finally, on August 24, I checked back into the SEAL Team One quarterdeck, where I reported in as ordered and for further assignment.

EPILOGUE

Two weeks after my return to SEAL Team One from annual leave, it was time for demolition, parachute jumping, and diving requalification with regular air, pure oxygen (called "the Emerson") and MK-VI mixed-gas scuba. After several weeks of working with explosives, night "ship attack" dives with the Emerson, deep dives with air and the MK-VI mixed-gas rig, and recreational dives for octopus, abalone, fish, and lobster off Point Loma, I was ready to settle down and get back to work. Little did I know just how much work I was about to get into.

"Smitty!" yelled Chief Barry Enoch (one of my UDT training instructors in 1965), as he came out of the training officers' office.

"What's happening, Chief?" I quickly asked as I was heading for the PT circle.

"You won't have time for PT and run this morning," Barry stated. "You, Knepper, and Czajkowski are going to Instructor School at NTC for two weeks starting Monday. You've also been assigned to SBI cadre. Ensign Jesse Tollison (a mustanger from SEAL Team Two) is the OIC and I'm the chief-in-charge. We'll have a cadre meeting at 0900 in the UDT briefing room, and don't forget to bring a pencil and pad."

From that day forward we were generally working sixteen to twenty hours a day and seven days a week until January 1971, when I was reassigned to November Platoon for my fifth tour in Vietnam.

When we (cadre) weren't in the desert or the Salton Sea

near Niland instructing, we were on the Strand writing and reproducing lesson plans, giving classroom and field instructions for newly created SEAL platoons. SBI training covered a long list of conventional and unconventional specialties: mission planning (warning orders and patrol leaders orders), advanced map and compass, airborne ops, underwater ship attacks, specialized weapons and ordnance, familiarization with the intelligence community in Vietnam, prisoner handling and interrogation, river and stream crossings, field communications, small unit tactics and formations, rappelling and the use of the McGuire rig for emergency extraction, emergency first aid, helo and boat insertion and extraction procedures, administrative inspections, last will and testaments for every man, weapons maintenance, range firing at Ream Field, live firing in the desert, etc. Our mission was to train and prepare every SEAL platoon professionally, mentally, and physically in the arts of direct-action riverine warfare within six weeks of their deployment to Vietnam. To insure that the SBI training was sufficient and effective, each platoon spent its last week demonstrating expertise in an FTX (final training exercise). SpecWar staff members were present to observe and grade the platoon's operational performance and to make recommendations and/or give attaboys to SEAL Team One and its SBI cadre.

All of the cadre instructors were totally dedicated to training each platoon to the best of their ability. There was always a sense of urgency, attention to detail, and follow-through while we were training teammates for unconventional warfare. I always felt a special burden to commit and focus all of my mental and physical energies toward the training of each platoon before its departure for Vietnam. The privilege of being a member of the cadre carried with it a rucksack full of responsibilities that became very burdensome at times. That meant that we were always motivated to go the extra mile to dig a punji pit larger and deeper, and then to dig more of them. We went to extra lengths to build realistic hootches and training areas similar to those found in Vietnam. We sacrificed time with our families so that every platoon departing for 'Nam was as well trained as we were capable of training them; most important, we wanted them to be successful in 'Nam and return home safely to their command, family, and teammates. However, on occasion, some of our best friends didn't return.

On December 21, 1970, while I was at Niland, we received word from the Strand (SEAL Team One) that my good friend Chief Frank Bomar (X-Ray Platoon's assistant officer in charge) and EM3 Ritter of second squad were killed in Kien Hoa province, Giong Trom district, where the small Rach Ba Tri canal entered the Ba Lai river while inserting from an MSSC (Medium SEAL Support Craft). During that operation RM3 Hetzell was shot in the neck, the round exiting from his back, and Ah's (the squad's Kit Carson Scout) right arm was shattered. The mission was to set a listening post for the night, but the SEALs inserted directly into a fortified VC ambush with six firing points. The VC waited until Frank's squad had inserted and the support craft departed before opening fire. Empty cartridge cases at each firing point revealed that Second Squad had received point blank 7.62X39mm RPD machine gun fire, 40mm M-79 grenade launcher HE rounds, and automatic rifle fire from four 7.62X39mm AK-47s. When LT Collin's First Squad and SEAL Two's Eighth Platoon arrived at the ambush site the following morning at first light, they saw that Frank Bomar had received two 40mm HE rounds in the abdomen and apparently died from shock and loss of blood because the 40mm projectiles hadn't traveled far enough to arm. EM3 Ritter had been shot in the heart and just above it. It was determined later that the operation had been compromised at Sector and Subsector TOCs where their multiple AOs had been previously approved. The VC knew when and where Frank's squad was going to insert. EM1 Lou DiCroce was later to reveal that one of their scouts (Tam) was a double agent and responsible for compromising many of their operations, including X-Ray's last operation of March 4, 1971.

On January 29 and 30, 1971, LT Collins with twelve SEALs, one Chieu Hoi, and two scouts went into the Binh Dai district in hopes of capturing a VC proselytizer. After insertion by MSSC, and during the patrol toward the targeted hootch, they were challenged by a well-armed VC unit. Both sides simultaneously initiated a maximum rate of fire upon each other resulting in one US KIA, two US WIA, one VN scout WIA, and three VC KIA. QMC Betz was shot in the right thigh and BM3 Trigg received shrapnel in his right foot. FN Birky was shot in the hip and eventually died of internal bleeding and shock during their return to the extraction point. The VN scout had to be carried out because of his severe wounds in both legs. LT Collins and his SEALs managed to carry their wounded to the Ba Lai river where they extracted by MSSC.

On February 28, 1971, YN3 Majors (patrol leader), CWO2 Jones (APL), EN1 Doyle, PT2 Walsh, SN Barnes, FN Barnes, SN McCarthy, Son (scout), and Pham (Chieu Hoi) were traveling by LSSC down the Ham Luong river in Mo Cay district for an early morning raid on a VC cache. During their journey the light SEAL support craft was attacked by a VC/NVA rocket team, resulting in five SEALs and two MST boat crewmembers WIA and two VNs WIA. The crippled boat managed to travel to the ARVN 10th Regiment Fire Support Base where three US WIAs were medevacked to Can Tho. In the meantime LT Collins and the remainder of X-Ray Platoon had received an emergency call at Ben Tre for assistance. They responded by MSSC and soon rendezvoused with the LSSC at the ARVN FSB. EN2 McClaren (MST) and SN Barnes lost their right legs. SN McCarthy had his right hip badly mangled and was also wounded in his right arm. Son, the scout, had his right calf blown apart, while YN3 Majors had both ear drums shattered and shrapnel wounds in his right leg. PT2 Walsh had both ear drums shattered, as did FN Barnes plus shrapnel wounds in his face, while QM1 Cronk (MST) also had one eardrum shattered. The Chieu Hoi died from massive leg wounds, shock, and loss of blood.

And finally, on March 4, 1971, LT Collins, CWO2 Jones, QMC Betz, EM1 DiCroce, HM2 Capalenor, RM2 Baker, YN3 Majors, YN3 Vader, BM3 Trigg, SF3 Shadnaw, ETR3 Barnes, SN McCarthy, FN Clayton, two VN scouts, and the MSSC crew were heading southeast toward the mouth of the Ba Lai river to a target in the Binh Dai district. At approximately 2000 hours a single RPG-2, B-40 round, hit the MSSC's canvas top rail and detonated next to LT Collins and Lou DiCroce's heads, killing Collins and seriously wounding DiCroce. Incredibly, all hands aboard were wounded resulting in seventeen WIAs and one KIA. Lou DiCroce was in coma for six days and eventually had to go through a long process of rehabilitation. The SEAL and MST casualty totals for that tour were: SEAL KIA: five; SEAL WIA: twenty-two; MST WIA: five; Chieu Hoi KIA: one; Chieu HOI/KCS WIA: six.

Every member of X-ray Platoon, including replacements, was wounded one or more times or killed. Afterward, there was never to be another X-Ray Platoon in SEAL Team One. Superstition? Who knows. It was a hard blow for all of us in Cadre. As one old timer commented, "Sometimes a feller jes' has to take his whippin', get back up, and keep on movin'."

After each platoon had finished its FTX on a Thursday morning, we all cleaned up, packed the gear aboard six-by-sixes for the trip back to the Strand, and made hot tracks for the Luck O' the Irish Cove—owned by Bill and Maxine—at Bombay Beach, on the north shore of the Salton Sea. That was the true final exercise for cadre and the platoon. Lord a'mercy, did we ever have fun! Bill and Maxine went all out to support our parties and arrange for a band. All types of vittles were available and a variety of refreshments was set up for the asking. It wasn't long before guys started throwing each other into the briny sea. The platoon personnel took great delight in tossing some of their instructors into the smelly muck.

During one of these get-togethers, Seaman Harrawood commandeered the microphone and began preaching the Word of God like an evangelist. He had obviously been well trained in a fundamentalist church or seminary. He reminded me of an old Southern Baptist preacher.

"Preacher" Harrawood began his sermon by screaming, " 'Repent ye: for the kingdom of heaven is at hand.' Repent and confess your sins before your holy and sovereign God, all you lost sinners! Your hearts are wicked and filled with inward corruption, bondage, and a vile and deceitful nature. Your hearts are deceitful above all things, and desperately wicked: who can know it. 'But after thy hardness and impenitent heart treasurest up unto thyself wrath against the day of wrath and revelation of the righteous judgment of God,' " Harrawood declared. "The only way to be forgiven for your sins past, present, and future, is through the blood of Christ Jesus, the Son of the Father, who took our place on the Cross and paid the penalty for our sins as required by God's holy law. 'For the law was given by Moses, but grace and truth came by Jesus Christ.' Jesus Christ crucified and risen! The only remedy for a lost man is found in Jesus. His atoning blood is the only refuge for a guilty man. His shed blood is the only cleansing agent to purge and wash a soul clean. His righteousness freely given to sinners is the only way to be made accepted with God. Only through the risen Christ is there victory over sin and the grave. He alone gives new life and new freedom. Only Jesus! Only Jesus! Only Jesus!" exclaimed Harrawood.

"Preach it, Harrawood! Preach it," yelled one of the guys.

Harrawood must have really been filled with the Holy Spirit that night. He continued, "God, in His love, will receive you sinners with open arms and will cast none of you away, but only those of you will be received who come on His terms. Answer God's calling by fleeing to Christ by prostrating yourselves at the foot of the Cross and plead for forgiveness and mercy, abandon your sins and ask Jesus to save you and deliver you from your sins! 'Come unto me, all you who are weary and heavy laden.' All Christ's sheep will hear God's voice," Harrawood declared emphatically. "God's Spirit will witness with your spirit that you are the child of God. From that time forward, you will be eternally secure in God's saving grace—no man or any other power can pluck you out of Jesus' hand. 'For my thoughts are not your thoughts, neither are your ways my ways, saith the Lord. So shall my word be that goeth forth out of my mouth: it shall not return unto me void, but it shall accomplish that which I please, and it shall prosper in the thing whereto I sent it,' " Preacher Harrawood concluded.

Those days were all done in great fun and many of us were closer than brothers. I've never worked harder than I did in those six months and I've never worked with a better bunch of guys, either. Chief Barry Enoch and Gunner Tollison were two of the most enjoyable teammates I'd ever had the privilege to serve with and under. They worked right alongside of their men, even to digging ditches for the new SEAL Butler building's sewage leech field near Siphon Ten. And they did it always with a smile on their faces. We were one big family with a continual dialogue between us—humorous country jokes and anecdotes, teasing sarcasm, and occasional witticisms. All of us were kind of like a barbed-wire fence—we had our good points. Morale was always the highest, simply because we had a true cause with a sense of urgency—we were serving our country and our loyalty was not only to our country but to our command, our families, and our teammates. A man couldn't ask for much more than that.

In January 1971, Knepper and I were reassigned to November Platoon. I was to be the leading petty officer, with Chief Layton Bassett as the platoon chief. Lieutenant Fletcher and Lieutenant (jg) Kleehammer were to be the platoon officers, and we were to deploy for Vietnam in April. As a platoon, we would have to start platoon training all over again. That meant Knepper and I would now be going through SBI with the platoon. It sure would be good to be carrying my old M-16 rifle #39 with an XM-148 grenade launcher on it again. Hoo-yah!

MASTER CHIEF,
the third and concluding
volume in Gary Smith's
Diary of a Navy SEAL,
will arrive in bookstores
September 1996

INTELLIGENCE COLLECTION AGENCIES

NOTE: Much of the following information is based upon my experiences as a PRU adviser in My Tho, Dinh Tuong Province, in 1969; an LDNN (Vietnamese SEAL) adviser in My Tho, Dinh Tuong Province, in 1970; and the LPO (leading petty officer) of SEAL Team One's November Platoon at Dong Tam, Dinh Tuong Province, in 1971. The original handout of "Intelligence Collection Agencies" was probably prepared by SEAL Team One's earliest PRU adviser, Bob Wagner, for his Special Operations training course for all potential SEAL PRU advisers in 1967. Bob was killed by a claymore mine while on a mission with his PRUs in July 1968. Until 1969, PRU training took place at Camp Billy Machen in the Cuyamaca Mountains of Southern California. The following information was later made available to all SEAL platoons deploying to Vietnam.

I'm especially thankful for all of the recommendations, advice, and support that I received as an LDNN adviser from U.S. Army majors Wake and Orlov (advisers to the ARVN 7th Infantry Division's G-2 and G-3), and Captain Dick Koons (OIC of 525, Dinh Tuong Province) in 1970. Also, I'm very thankful for the encouragement and guidance from Lieutenant G. K. Morrow (Naval Intelligence at NavForV in 1971) when I was a member of SEAL Team One's November Platoon as its intelligence petty officer.

Introduction: There are two basic rules that must be observed when establishing liaison with any U.S. or Vietnamese military or civilian intelligence collection agencies at sector and subsector: (1) observe protocol—in other words, follow the chain-of-command; (2) establish rapport—establish a cordial and friendly relationship *after* observing the chain-of-command. The Platoon Commander, Assistant Platoon Commander and the Platoon Intelligence Specialists should initially observe protocol by visiting the PSA (Province Senior Adviser), then the Province Chief, followed by all military and police intelligence agencies at sector and subsector as soon as possible after arriving in their new AO (Area of Operation). After the initial liaison is established, it's time for the platoon to: (1) organize, (2) prioritize, (3) motivate, (4) delegate, and (5) supervise. Specific personnel should be tasked to regularly visit each agency while other platoon members begin supporting the establishment of the platoon intelligence room, which should include the following: (1) card files [(a) OB, (b) VCI, (c) commo-liaison routes, and (d) prisoner]; (2) OB 1:50:000 scale map (of the AO) with overlays; (3) operational maps of 1:24,000, 1:50:000, 1:100,000, and 1:250,000 scales; (4) 1:4,000 split vertical aerial photographs to be pieced into mosaics for target analysis and plotted on an AO 1:50,000 map with overlays for Green Hornet and SLAR plots, etc.; (5) sector and subsector artillery fans; (6) SEAL agent files; etc. Work smarter, not harder. Don't head for the bush until you know your enemy.

1. NILO (Naval Intelligence Liaison Officer): The NILO will be a Lieutenant (jg) or Lieutenant whose office (if there is one) will be located in the Provincial capital within the MACV compound or at an allied Naval base. NILO is responsible for gathering pertinent intelligence/information on VCI (Viet Cong Infrastructure) and OB (order of battle) to support in-country UDT/SEAL platoons and other direct-action U.S. and Vietnamese Naval forces with timely intell/ info. He is familiar with the intelligence collection community and the Phoenix program and will have access to all available intell/info for the SEAL platoon. NILO has access to CICV (Combined Intelligence Center, Vietnam) funds for

intelligence purposes and limited access to aerial photos and/or mosaics. However, the GVN and U.S. military and civilian intelligence collection community support may vary somewhat depending upon the amount of corruption, collusion (GVN) with the VC/NVA, and their experiences with NavSpecWar personnel and NILO—in other words, you may be faced with hostility from your supposed allies. In these circumstances, the platoon commander will have to move very slowly and carefully, concentrating on developing a liaison established on trust. This is not the time to worry about the numbers game demanded by staff.

2. U.S. Army S-2: Located at sector (province) and subsector (district). The provincial adviser will live within the MACV compound. He may be a Captain or a Major. The S-2 at subsector (district) will also live within the MACV compound. He will usually be a First Lieutenant. Their targets will vary from VCI (Phoenix program) to OB. At subsector the S-2 will usually be tasked as the DIOCC (District Intelligence Operations Coordinating Center) adviser to his Vietnamese S-2 counterpart and the Phoenix/ Phung Hoang adviser. His sources of intell/info will be based upon interrogation reports from the MSS POW camp detainees, captured documents, Hoi Chanhs, informants, 525, and generally from the National Police, PSB, NPFF, PRUs, and interviews with Hoi Chanhs at the PIC's Chieu Hoi center, etc. He should have an "area studies" capability as well as aerial photos and some 1:4,000 scale mosaics of the province.

3. DIOCC: District Intelligence Operations Coordination Center is located at subsector and chaired by the District Chief, who is usually an ARVN Captain or Major. DIOCC is a smaller version of the PIOCC at sector and is run by the S-2, who is an ARVN Captain or First Lieutenant. The District Chief is advised by his own S-2, who runs the DIOCC. A U.S. Army Second or First Lieutenant (member of the District Advisory Team) advises and works with his Vietnamese S-2 counterpart. He resides within the MACV compound. The DIOCC collects intell/info from all available

sources and disseminates that information to the Province's Phung Hoang Committee and to direct-action units in accordance with the desires of the Province and District Chiefs, who usually maintain OPCON in one form or another. The DIOCC supervises all district level OB and counter-VCI operations. Ideally, all district military and National Police/PSB intell/info will have been received by the VN DIOCC, filed, and copies forwarded to the Phung Hoang Committee at sector for disposition. It is through the DIOCC that the U.S. Army DIOCC adviser has access to timely military and police sources of intell/info.

4. Phoenix/Phung Hoang Committee: located at sector and subsector through the PIOCC and DIOCC. The Province Chief (Lt. Col. or Col.) is the chairman of the Phung Hoang Committee and is advised by the Phoenix Coordinator, who is a U.S. Army Captain or Major. The adviser usually lives within the Embassy or OSA compound located in the provincial capital. The committee receives all OB and VCI intell/info from all civilian and military agencies at the provincial and district levels. They should have dossiers on all known VCI. They also have responsibility to keep the Provincial Blacklist of all VCI updated. However, not all VCI will be on the Blacklist. Some VCI are very powerful, with leverages and influences in high places. The basis of their control and manipulation is through blackmail and/or money. Occasionally a Province Chief and/or National Police Chief will fall into this category. The SEAL Platoon commander must insure that the targeted VCI *is* listed on the Blacklist.

There are two categories of VCI: (1) Illegal VCI political cadre: Their illegal status is based on at least two or three PSB/NP informant reports that they're actively working for the NLF/VC/PRP. They are overtly located with the VC military and political forces. They live with their wives in the hamlet at night and work in the VC bunkers at day. Only then is their name placed on the Phuong Hoang Blacklist and neutralized (turned-around, captured, or killed) by NPFF, NP, PRU, etc.; (2) Legal VCI political cadre: Their legal status is based on having acquired a government ID card by purchasing it through a corrupt National Police Chief and/or Province Chief within the province capital. If the NP/PSB refuse to gather evidence against a VCI, his name will not be placed on the Blacklist.

In 1969 a SEAL Team Two platoon's tour in My Tho was suddenly cut short when it unfortunately killed a legal VCI who happened to be a double agent working for the Company (CIA). Because of this incident the Embassy House in My Tho stopped giving intelligence information to any SEAL platoon in Dinh Tuong Province. Within three days of the incident the SEAL Two platoon was shipped out of 'Nam and on its way back to Virginia.

The committee (which comes under the operational and administrative influence, if not control of, the Province Chief) assigns Vietnamese military and/or paramilitary direct-action units, such as the PSB, PRU, NPFF, PFs, RFs to neutralize (defection-in-place/turn-around, capture, or kill) specific VCI and OB targets according to their repertoire and/or military and political leverage.

5. PIC (Province Interrogation Center): located at sector and is managed by the Vietnamese Police Special Branch (PSB). The Company sponsors and advises PIC. The U.S. civilian adviser resides at the Embassy or OSA house. PIC provides trained personnel for the interrogation of POWs, for gathering of intell/info, for operational and administrative purposes. All nonmilitary POWs are turned into the PIC for interrogation, exploitation, and disposition (military detainees are turned over to S-2 at sector or subsector). PIC maintain files of the organizational structure of the VCI by hamlet, village, district, and province within the echelons of the PRP and NLF and information considered "OB." PIC maintains personnel at the Chieu Hoi center for debriefing specific Hoi Chanhs only.

6. RD Cadre (Revolutionary Development): located at sector and subsector and is Company sponsored and advised by the Phoenix Coordinator, who is usually a U.S. Army Captain or Major. RD Cadre consists of VN teams of

about thirty men who move into VC contested and controlled hamlets and villages. Their primary objective is to develop the rural area and help set up hamlet security.

7. U.S. Army 525 Military Intelligence Group: intelligence specialist personnel with a civilian cover. Most of 525's personnel are located at sector with some covertly located within other province and district agencies. The OIC is usually a Captain. He advises the Vietnamese MSS, MI, and 101. He has access to and uses a polygraph testing specialist located in Saigon. 525 may have unilateral intell/info nets available for cross-checking special or sensitive intell/info. Ask if he has in-place agents within your AO (Area of Operation). If he doesn't, he may be willing to retask one of his agents who has natural placement and access and can obtain Essential Elements of Information (EEI). His bilateral nets are ideal for getting a covert BI (background investigation) of a potential SEAL agent (Chieu Hoi). In other words, "Is the potential agent already working for PSB or MSS or 525?" Other than NILO, 525 is your best friend within the Province, and he might be able to obtain guides for your operations.

8. Chieu Hoi Center: the Open Arms program is located at sector under the Ministry of Chieu Hoi in Saigon. The individual who defects to the GVN under the Chieu Hoi program is called a Hoi Chanh. Hoi Chanhs are usually former guerrillas with occasional low-level VCI and NVA. Chieu Hoi centers are usually advised by a third country national (Philippino) known as the Chieu Hoi adviser and operated by a Vietnamese Chieu Hoi Chief. Hoi Chanhs are encouraged to become guides, PRUs, or KCSs (Kit Carson Scouts). Visit them immediately after arriving within the province and don't forget to observe protocol and establish rapport. Assign one SEAL platoon member and interpreter to visit the center regularly to check for motivated Hoi Chanhs. Hoi Chanhs are an excellent source of intell/info and are potential guides for SEAL operations.

9. PSB (Police Special Branch): is located at sector and subsector and advised by AID (Agency for International

Development). They have full police powers of arrest and seizure. PSB manages PIC and is Company sponsored and advised. PSB specializes in "turning around" VCI to return to their hamlets and villages as informants. PSB also continually updates and maintains files on VCI and potentially powerful political organizations or religious sects, i.e., Cao Dais, Hoa Haos (Vietnamese and Cambodian Buddhists), Father Hoa and his (Chinese Catholics) Sea Swallow cadre in An Xuyen Province, etc.

The Sector PSB of Dinh Tuong Province is organized as follows:

1. PSB Chief Hue
   A. Plans Section
      1. My Tho Interrogation Section
      2. Provincial Interrogation Center
      3. Chieu Hoi Debriefing Section
      4. Operations Section
      5. Swan Section: female agents
      6. Internal Political Office
      7. Infiltration-Penetration Office
      8. VC Mang

The Subsector (District) PSB Chief within Dinh Tuong is organized as follows:

1. District PSB Chief
   A. Plans Section
   B. Interrogation Section
   C. Operations Section

10. NPFF (National Police Field Force): is located at sector and subsector and advised by a retired/active duty U.S. Army NCO or a U.S. civilian with police experience. Originally, NPFF was Company sponsored and advised. However, the Province Chief or the National Police Chief may have OPCON—depending on which one has the most lev-

erage on the other through blackmail, rank, or both. The Provincial NPFF are organized into companies with platoons assigned to each district/subsector. One of NPFF's primary responsibilities is to react upon VCI intell/info received from the PSB. Other responsibilities are to control riots throughout SVN, security missions, and any other task that the DGNP (Directorate General of the National Police) of the Ministry of Interior deems necessary. As a type of policemen they have the power and authority to arrest and seize as they see fit—in other words, you're "guilty until proven innocent," and the *people are the servants* of the government. Remember, you are operating within a police state with a National Police Force which comes under the Ministry of Interior.

11. PRU (Provincial Reconnaissance Unit): The PRU office and/or compound is located at sector. The adviser resides in the OSA/Embassy House. In some provinces the Province Chief has divided the PRU into platoons and stationed one within each subsector/district. After March of 1969, the PRU were placed under the administrative control of the National Police Chief and the operational control of the Province Chief. The PRU were financed by the Company with combat advisers consisting of Navy SEALS, Army Special Forces, Australian Army (SAS), Marine Corps enlisted men, and occasionally officers of all services until 30 September 1969. After September 1969, all PRU advisers were restricted to administratively advise the PRUs only—they were not to accompany the PRU into the field.

The PRU is an excellent source of intell/info. They have their own sources through family and friends. Combined operations with the PRU and PSB is highly recommended, when possible, for SEAL platoons for two reasons:

1. PSB will take care of complications relative to any inadvertent killing of legal VCI cadre, and
2. the PRU and PSB know the AO and the enemy better than anyone else within the province.

12. MSS (Military Security Service): located at sector. They are advised by 525. Their primary objective is counterintelligence within the GVN Armed Forces. They are tasked to detect VC/NVA sympathizers or those who have defected-in-place within the GVN armed forces. Many of the GVN sector and subsector TOCs (Tactical Operations Centers) are penetrated by VCI action agents. MSS has jurisdiction over all military personnel, civilians dealing with the war effort, and foreigners whose attitude and actions are not in the best interest of SVN.

GLOSSARY

APT (Armed Propaganda Teams): Armed VN Hoi Chanhs formed into propaganda teams who move into VC controlled/contested areas as one of the initial steps of pacification. They are CORDs sponsored and advised.

AIK Funds (Assistance in Kind): Funds that are available, usually through the province S-2 adviser, to pay rewards for captured weapons, VCI, intell/info, etc.

ARVN: Army of the Republic of Vietnam.

BRIGHT LIGHT: Code name for any U.S. operation designed to rescue U.S prisoners of war.

CIDG (Civilian Irregular Defense Group): Minority groups or tribes classified as civilians but organized along military lines as paramilitary forces. CIDGs are found in all provinces which border Cambodia and Laos. They are responsible for border interdiction and security and are U.S. Special Forces advised.

CIC (Corps Interrogation Center): The Military Region IV CIC is located in Can Tho. CIC processes, interrogates, and exploits high-level Hoi Chanhs and POWs.

CICV (Combined Intelligence Center, Vietnam): Located in Saigon. CICV has all intell/info and battle reports (nationwide) computerized. CICV will provide area studies to include enemy commo-liaison routes, terrain, enemy OB, landing zones, aerial photography, enemy base areas, etc. See your NILO officer for further information.

CHAPP (Chieu Hoi Armed Propaganda Platoons): Same as "Armed Propaganda Teams."

COMUSMACV (Commander U.S. Military Assis-

tance Command, Vietnam):** General Abrahms has relieved General Westmoreland.

CORDS (Civil Operations and Revolutionary Development Support): Created by MACV and responsible for coordination of all civilian and military pacification efforts.

CTZ (Corps Tactical Zone): U.S. and VN military subdivision of Vietnam into four military regions or CTZs I, II, III, IV.

DC (District Chief): Senior Vietnamese at the district level. He is usually an ARVN Captain (Dai Uy) and is responsible for all military and civil functions within his district. He reports directly to the Province Chief at sector. The DC is the U.S. Army DSA's (District Senior Adviser) counterpart.

DGNP (Directorate General of the National Police): He is responsible for all police organizations, i.e., National Police, PSB, NPFF, PRU, Maritime Police, etc. His boss is the Ministry of the Interior.

DPSA (Deputy Province Senior Adviser): He is second in command to the PSA (Province Senior Adviser). If the PSA is a U.S. Army Lt. Col. or Col. then the DPSA will usually be a Company civilian of equivalent GS rating. Company DPSAs are responsible for all nonmilitary programs (CORDS/USAID) at the province level.

DPCS (Deputy Province Chief, Security): He will be an ARVN Officer whose office is located at sector S-2.

DSA (District Senior Adviser): The DSA is the senior U.S. military adviser within the district/subsector. He will usually be an Army Captain or Major. The DSA reports directly to the PSA and advises the VN District Chief.

FWMAF (Free World Military Assistance Forces): The countries engaged in Vietnam are: Korea, Philippines, Australia, Thailand, and the U.S.

JPRC (Joint Personnel Recovery Center): MACV agency which coordinates and supervises all "Bright Light" operations and related intell/info reports. There is a U.S. representative in all provinces and all four military regions.

JUSPAO (Joint U.S. Psychological Assistance Pro-

gram): More commonly known as "Psyops." The JUSPAO representative's office will be located in the province capital's CORDS building.

LSSC (Light SEAL Support Craft): In 1968 the U.S. Navy SEALs in South Vietnam's Mekong Delta required a variety of specialized craft to support their diversified operations.

Grafton Boat Co. (Grafton, Ill.) developed a twenty-four-foot high-speed craft for the SEALs in Vietnam which featured high-performance gasoline engines mated to the Jacuzzi Water Jet Pumps. Other features of the new craft were low silhouette, multiple gun positions, radar, and ceramic armor plate.

The LSSC operated from shore bases and ships anchored in the rivers, typically operating alone under the cover of darkness while transporting a squad of SEALs to and from its patrol area. Operations included hit, run, attack; canal sweeps; and geographic/hydrographic data collection. Other types of operations were conducted with these silent craft, some of which are still classified by the government. Mobile Support Teams (MST) operated and maintained the craft in support of a variety of SEAL missions.

Specifications (1968)

- Manufactured by the Grafton Boat Co., Grafton, Ill.
- 25-foot welded aluminum hull with 9-foot beam
- 12,000 pound displacement (maximum)
- Twin Ford 427 CID Cobra engines with 12-inch Jacuzzi water pumps
- Aircraft foam-filled explosion-proof rubber fuel cells (210 gallon)
- Foam-filled hull (unsinkable)
- Ceramic armor-plated crew cockpit and engine areas
- Protection from .30-caliber armor piercing and .50-caliber bullets
- Raytheon 1900 series radar (7KW, 32-mile range)
- Dual VHF-FM radios (PRC-77 & VRC-46)
- Custom "silent" exhaust muffler system, with engine ex-

haust directed through three special chambers, then exhausted underwater

- Minimum water depth required at cruise—9 inches
- Boat crew: driver and co-driver with a SEAL squad of 5–7 men
- Painted black for night operations and camouflaged for day
- Low profile, highly maneuverable, with a top speed of 55–60 MPH
- Capable of turning around within its own twenty-four-foot length

Standard Weapons

A. Three M-60 machine guns, 7.62-mm NATO
B. One M2HB machine gun, .50-caliber
C. One MK-19 automatic grenade launcher, 40-mm
D. Optional: minigun (max. 6,000 rounds per minute) and 60-mm mortar

John K. Jadwinski, *Light SEAL Support Craft (LSSC) History* (Newport Beach, Calif.; Beryl Publications, 1987).

MI (Military Intelligence): The ARVN MI is located at province/sector. The U.S. Army's 525 Military Intelligence Group is their counterpart.

MIBARS (Military Intelligence Battalion Aerial Reconnaissance Support): In MR-4, the MIBAR office is located at the U.S. Army Can Tho Airfield, across the street from the PX. MIBAR is where 1:4,000 split vertical and hand-held aerial photo reconnaissance can be ordered. "Readouts"/photo interpretation of mosaics and individual photos may be requested from a complete filing system of all past photo runs. If time is critical, take along a bottle of Chivas Regal.

MILPHAT (Military Province Hospital Assistance Team): Consists of an Army, Navy, Air Force, or foreign medical advisory team with one doctor and several medics or corpsmen. Their responsibility is to assist and work with the GVN hospital staff. The hospital will be located in the province capital.

MOI (Ministry of Interior): A Vietnamese cabinet-level office responsible for many functions involving the internal administration of the Vietnamese government, one of which is the Police (DGNP), under which the PRU have been placed.

Mobile Strike Force (Mike Force): The MSF is a division of the CIDG and is usually advised and administered by Special Forces personnel. It is a highly mobile reaction force employed against specific targets. MSF may not remain within a province for more than a week, during which time it conducts raids, ambushes, combat patrols, and other mobile guerrilla operations.

NOC/TOC (Naval Operations Center/Tactical Operations Center): Located at all levels, i.e., Corps/Military Region, province, and district. NOC/TOC maintains a current status of all military and paramilitary operations being conducted or planned within its AO (Area of Operation). They coordinate all air and artillery strikes and continuously monitor all operational radio guard nets of subordinate commands and units.

OSA (Office of the Special Assistant to the Ambassador): OSA refers to the Company building/compound located in every province capital. In Kien Giang Province the Company compound is called "OSA House," whereas in Dinh Tuong Province the Company compound is called "Embassy House."

PC (Province Chief): The PC is usually an ARVN Lt. Col. or Col. and is the governor of the province. Each Province Chief is personally appointed by President Thieu. His U.S. counterpart is the PSA. The Province Chief has operational control of all military and civil functions within his province. He reports to the Ministry of Interior in Saigon.

POIC (Province Officer in Charge): The POIC is the senior Company officer within the province. His office and home are within the OSA/Embassy compound.

PSA (Province Senior Adviser): U.S. Lt. Col. or equivalent GS-rated civilian. The PSA advises the Vietnamese Province Chief. He is the senior member of all military and civic U.S. programs within the province.

PSDF (People's Self-defense Forces): PSDFs are GVN civilian militia and are recruited and organized within GVN-controlled villages and hamlets. Their responsibility is to protect their families and homes from the Communists.

PF (Popular Forces): PFs are GVN military forces recruited, organized, and deployed at the village and hamlet levels. They are responsible for the security of their own village and/or hamlet. A PF unit is comparable to a light infantry platoon.

RAGs (River Assault Groups): Vietnamese riverine Naval forces advised by the U.S. Navy.

RF (Regional Forces): RFs are military forces assigned to and under the operational control of the Province and/or District Chief. Their primary mission is to secure key installations and communications routes and act as reaction forces to assist village and hamlet forces under attack.

River Assault Flotilla One: Composed of the U.S. Navy's River Assault Squadrons Nine and Eleven. "The flotilla is composed of specially-designed assault boats. The workhorse is an armored troop carrier capable of carrying one platoon of combat-equipped infantrymen" (The U.S. Army 9th Infantry Division was located at Dong Tam, just north of My Tho, the provincial capital of Dinh Tuong Province; My Tho is located approximately thirty-five miles northeast of Saigon) "up the twisting rivers and streams to their objectives. Another boat, called the Monitor, after the Civil War ironclad, is designed to escort the troop carriers and provide firepower. A third boat is a Monitor-type vessel used as a command and communications boat. The fourth is the assault-support patrol boat, for minesweeping and base security, and for quick gunfire support during operations." (Source: *The Jackstaff News*, October 6, 1967; "Riverine Sailors Praise Instructors," by JO1 Jim French.)

TAOR (Tactical Area of Responsibility): Also referred to as AO (Area of Operation). The TAOR is assigned by NOC/TOC. It is a given area in which a unit is authorized to operate without interference from other friendly elements. All SEAL platoon commanders planning field operations must coordinate with and clear their TAORs with NOC/TOC—it is a mandatory prerequisite before all operations!

USAID (U.S. Agency for International Development): USAID distributes American economic assistance to most third world countries, including South Vietnam. The Agency provides money, material, and advisers for projects involving agriculture, education, construction, etc.

THE 5.56-MM STONER 63 WEAPON SYSTEM

Introduction: There has been much speculation over the years as to why the navy accepted the Stoner 63 Weapon System and the army and Marine Corps didn't. The following information from a variety of sources should give a good account for the decision by SEAL Teams One and Two to use the Stoner system as one of their primary AW weapons.

The Stoner 63A LMG has proven to be an extremely effective weapon in support of SEAL Special Warfare Missions. The firepower, reliability and lightweight portability of the Stoner 63A weapon ... has prompted SEAL Team detachments to develop and build firefight tactics around this weapon. This weapon has contributed greatly to many successful SEAL Special Warfare missions conducted during the investigation period and has increased significantly SEAL Team combat potential and effectiveness
—C.O., SEAL Team One, January 1969

The Stoner 63A light machine gun was evaluated by both SEAL Teams One and Two to determine its suitability, firepower capabilities, and reliability during 1,345 actual combat missions. The following is a summary of conclusions and recommendations:
The Stoner 63A LMG has proven by actual combat application to be significantly superior in firepower, reliability and lightweight portability as compared to the

M-60 machine gun. . . . It is strongly recommended that
. . . six (6) weapons per SEAL Platoon be procured . . ."
　　—BUDS training handout, January 1974, Lieutenant
Moser

The weight advantage of the 5.56mm round over
the 7.62mm round is clearly illustrated where seventeen rounds of 5.56mm ammunition is equal to only
eight rounds of 7.62mm ammunition. While 7.62mm
belted ammunition weighs 6.25 lbs. per 100, the
5.56mm belted ammunition weighs only 2.94 lbs.
Coupled with the 63A Stoner LMG, the ammunition ra-
tio over the 7.62mm weapon is 3:1.
　　—Stoner 63A Systems Pamphlet

A 5.56 bullet fired from a Stoner LMG will penetrate
standard U.S. body armor, but not a G.I. helmet at 600
yards. It will go through (5) 7/8-inch pine boards, but not
(8). It will not penetrate a sandbag at this range. Both
penetration and accuracy decrease rapidly beyond 600
yds. because the bullets do not weigh enough to hold
their velocity.
　　How important are these considerations? At 400 yds.
the 5.56 will penetrate any helmet presently in use
throughout the world and do just as serious an injury to
the wearer as a "Full Rifle Power" Cal. 30 bullet. There
is no practical way of protecting a soldier who moves
around with personal armor at ranges of 400 yds. and below.
　　—*Marine Corps Gazette*, March 1964